The
WORST YEARS
OF OUR LIVES

The
WORST YEARS
OF OUR LIVES

Irreverent Notes from a Decade of Greed

●••●••●••●••●••●••●

BARBARA EHRENREICH

pantheon books   new york

Permissions acknowledgments will be found on page 273.

Library of Congress Cataloging-in-Publication Data
Ehrenreich, Barbara.
The worst years of our lives: an outsider's view
of the eighties/
Barbara Ehrenreich.
p. cm.
ISBN 0-394-57847-3
1. United States—Politics and government—1981–
—Humor. I. Title.
E876.E34   1990   89-43257
973.927—dc20

Book Design by Anne Scatto
Manufactured in the United States of America
First Edition

Contents

●··●··●··●··●··●··●

The
WORST YEARS
OF OUR LIVES

Introduction: Family Values

•⋯•⋯•⋯•⋯•⋯•⋯•

SOMETIME IN THE EIGHTIES, Americans had a new set of
"traditional values" installed. It was part of what may someday
be known as the "Reagan renovation," that finely balanced mix
of cosmetic refinement and moral coarseness which brought
$200,000 china to the White House dinner table and mayhem to
the beleaguered peasantry of Central America. All of the new
traditions had venerable sources. In economics, we borrowed
from the Bourbons; in foreign policy, we drew on themes fash-
ioned by the nomad warriors of the Eurasian steppes. In spiritual
matters, we emulated the braying intolerance of our archenemies
and esteemed customers, the Shi'ite fundamentalists.

A case could be made, of course, for the genuine American
provenance of all these new "traditions." We've had our own
robber barons, military adventurers, and certainly more than our
share of enterprising evangelists promoting ignorance and paro-
chialism as a state of grace. From the vantage point of the conti-
nent's original residents, or, for example, the captive African
laborers who made America a great agricultural power, our "traditional values" have always been bigotry, greed, and belliger-
ence, buttressed by wanton appeals to a God of love.

The kindest—though from some angles most perverse—of
the era's new values was "family." I could have lived with "flag"

and "faith" as neotraditional values—not happily, but I could have managed—until "family" was press-ganged into joining them. Throughout the eighties, the winning political faction has been aggressively "profamily." They have invoked "the family" when they trample on the rights of those who hold actual families together, that is, women. They have used it to justify racial segregation and the formation of white-only, "Christian" schools. And they have brought it out, along with flag and faith, to silence any voices they found obscene, offensive, disturbing, or merely different.

Now, I come from a family—was raised in one, in fact—and one salubrious effect of right-wing righteousness has been to make me hew ever more firmly to the traditional values of my own progenitors. These were not people who could be accused of questionable politics or ethnicity. Nor were they members of the "liberal elite" so hated by our current conservative elite. They were blue-eyed, Scotch-Irish Democrats. They were small farmers, railroad workers, miners, shopkeepers, and migrant farm workers. In short, they fit the stereotype of "real" Americans; and their values, no matter how unpopular among today's opinion-shapers, are part of America's tradition, too. To my mind, of course, the finest part.

But let me introduce some of my family, beginning with my father, who was, along with my mother, the ultimate source of much of my radicalism, feminism, and, by the standards of the eighties, all-around bad attitude.

One of the first questions in a test of mental competency is "Who is the president of the United States?" Even deep into the indignities of Alzheimer's disease, my father always did well on that one. His blue eyes would widen incredulously, surprised at the neurologist's ignorance, then he would snort in majestic indignation, "Reagan, that dumb son of a bitch." It seemed to me a good deal—two people tested for the price of one.

Like so many of the Alzheimer's patients he came to know, my father enjoyed watching the president on television. Most programming left him impassive, but when the old codger came on, his little eyes twinkling piggishly above the disciplined sincerity of his lower face, my father would lean forward and commence a wickedly delighted cackle. I think he was prepared, more than the rest of us, to get the joke.

But the funniest thing was Ollie North. For an ailing man, my father did a fine parody. He would slap his hand over his heart, stare rigidly at attention, and pronounce, in his deepest bass rumble, "God Bless Am-ar-ica!" I'm sure he couldn't follow North's testimony—who can honestly say that they did?—but the main themes were clear enough in pantomime: the watery-eyed patriotism, the extravagant self-pity, the touching servility toward higher-ranking males. When I told my father that many people considered North a hero, a representative of the finest American traditions, he scowled and swatted at the air. Ollie North was the kind of man my father had warned me about, many years ago, when my father was the smartest man on earth.

My father had started out as a copper miner in Butte, Montana, a tiny mountain city famed for its bars, its brawls, and its distinctly unservile work force. In his view, which remained eagle-sharp even after a stint of higher education, there were only a few major categories of human beings. There were "phonies" and "decent" people, the latter group having hardly any well-known representatives outside of Franklin Delano Roosevelt and John L. Lewis, the militant and brilliantly eloquent leader of the miners' union. "Phonies," however, were rampant, and, for reasons I would not understand until later in life, could be found clustered especially thick in the vicinity of money or power.

Well before he taught me other useful things, like how to distinguish fool's gold, or iron pyrite, from the real thing, he gave me some tips on the detection of phonies. For one thing, they broadened the *e* in "America" to a reverent *ahh*. They were the first to leap from their seats at the playing of "The Star Spangled Banner," the most visibly moved participants in any prayer. They espoused clean living and admired war. They preached hard work and paid for it with nickels and dimes. They loved their country above all, but despised the low-paid and usually invisible men and women who built it, fed it, and kept it running.

Two other important categories figured in my father's scheme of things. There were dumb people and smart ones: a distinction which had nothing to do with class or formal education, the dumb being simply all those who were taken in by the phonies. In his view, dumbness was rampant, and seemed to increase in proportion to the distance from Butte, where at least a certain hard-boiled irreverence leavened the atmosphere. The best prophylactic was to study and learn all you could, however you could, and, as he adjured me over and over: always ask *why*.

Finally, there were the rich and the poor. While poverty was not seen as an automatic virtue—my parents struggled mightily to escape it—wealth always carried a presumption of malfeasance. I was instructed that, in the presence of the rich, it was wise to keep one's hand on one's wallet. "Well," my father fairly growled, "how do you think they got their money in the first place?"

It was my mother who translated these lessons into practical politics. A miner's daughter herself, she offered two overarching rules for comportment: never vote Republican and never cross a union picket line. The pinnacle of her activist career came in 1964, when she attended the Democratic Convention as an alternate delegate and joined the sit-in staged by civil rights leaders and the Mississsippi Freedom Democratic Party. This was not the action of a "guilt-ridden" white liberal. She classified racial prejudice along with superstition and other manifestations of backward thinking, like organized religion and overcooked vegetables. The worst thing she could find to say about a certain in-law was that he was a Republican and a churchgoer, though when I investigated these charges later in life, I was relieved to find them baseless.

My mother and father, it should be explained, were hardly rebels. The values they imparted to me had been "traditional" for at least a generation before my parents came along. According to my father, the first great steps out of mental passivity had been taken by his maternal grandparents, John Howes and Mamie O'Laughlin Howes, sometime late in the last century. You might think their rebellions small stuff, but they provided our family with its "myth of origins" and a certain standard to uphold.

I knew little about Mamie O'Laughlin except that she was raised as a Catholic and ended up in western Montana sometime in the 1880s. Her father, very likely, was one of those itinerant breadwinners who went west to prospect and settled for mining. At any rate, the story begins when her father lay dying, and Mamie dutifully sent to the next town for a priest. The message came back that the priest would come only if twenty-five dollars was sent in advance. This being the West at its wildest, he may have been justified in avoiding house calls. But not in the price, which was probably more cash than my great-grandmother had ever had at one time. It was on account of its greed that the church lost the souls of Mamie O'Laughlin and all of her descendents, right down to the present time. Furthermore, whether out of filial deference or natural intelligence, most of us have continued to avoid organized religion, secret societies, astrology, and New Age adventures in spiritualism.

As the story continues, Mamie O'Laughlin herself lay dying a few years later. She was only thirty-one, the mother of three small children, one of them an infant whose birth, apparently, led to a mortal attack of pneumonia. This time, a priest appeared unsummoned. Because she was too weak to hold the crucifix, he placed it on her chest and proceeded to administer the last rites. But Mamie was not dead yet. She pulled herself together at the last moment, flung the crucifix across the room, fell back, and died.

This was my great-grandmother. Her husband, John Howes, is a figure of folkloric proportions in my memory, well known in Butte many decades ago as a powerful miner and a lethal fighter. There are many stories about John Howes, all of which point to a profound inability to accept authority in any of its manifestations, earthly or divine. As a young miner, for example, he caught the eye of the mine owner for his skill at handling horses. The boss promoted him to an aboveground driving job, which was a great career leap for the time. Then the boss committed a foolish and arrogant error. He asked John to break in a team of horses for his wife's carriage. Most people would probably be flattered by such a request, but not in Butte, and certainly not John Howes. He declared that he was no man's servant, and quit on the spot.

Like his own wife, John Howes was an atheist or, as they more likely put it at the time, a freethinker. He, too, had been raised as a Catholic—on a farm in Ontario—and he, too, had had a dramatic, though somehow less glorious, falling out with the local clergy. According to legend, he once abused his position as an altar boy by urinating, covertly of course, in the holy water. This so enhanced his enjoyment of the Easter communion service that he could not resist letting a few friends in on the secret. Soon the priest found out and young John was defrocked as an altar boy and condemned to eternal damnation.

The full weight of this transgression hit a few years later, when he became engaged to a local woman. The priest refused to marry them and forbade the young woman to marry John anywhere, on pain of excommunication. There was nothing to do but head west for the Rockies, but not before settling his score with the church. According to legend, John's last act in Ontario was to drag the priest down from his pulpit and slug him, with his brother, presumably, holding the scandalized congregation at bay.

I have often wondered whether my great-grandfather was caught up in the radicalism of Butte in its heyday: whether he was an admirer of Joe Hill, Big Bill Haywood, or Mary "Mother" Jones, all of whom passed through Butte to agitate, and generally left with the Pinkertons on their tails. But the record is silent on this point. All I know is one last story about him, which was told often enough to have the ring of another "traditional value."

According to my father, John Howes worked on and off in the

mines after his children were grown, eventually saving enough
to buy a small plot of land and retire to farming. This was his
dream, anyway, and a powerful one it must have been for a man
who had spent so much of his life underground in the dark. So
he loaded up a horse-drawn cart with all his money and belongings and head downhill, toward Montana's eastern plains. But
along the way he came to an Indian woman walking with a baby
in her arms. He offered her a lift and ascertained, pretty easily,
that she was destitute. So he gave her his money, all of it, turned
the horse around, and went back to the mines.

Far be it from me to interpret this gesture for my great-grandfather, whom I knew only as a whiskery, sweat-smelling, but
straight-backed old man in his eighties. Perhaps he was enacting
his own uncompromising version of Christian virtue, even aton-
ing a little for his youthful offenses to the faithful. But at another
level I like to think that this was one more gesture of defiance of
the mine owners who doled out their own dollars so grudgingly
—a way of saying, perhaps, that whatever they had to offer, he
didn't really need all that much.

So these were the values, sanctified by tradition and family
loyalty, that I brought with me to adulthood. Through much of
my growing-up, I thought of them as some mutant strain of
Americanism, an idiosyncracy which seemed to grow rarer as we
clambered into the middle class. Only in the sixties did I begin
to learn that my family's militant skepticism and oddball rebel-
liousness were part of a much larger stream of American dissent.
I discovered feminism, the antiwar movement, the civil rights
movement. I learned that millions of Americans, before me and
around me, were "smart" enough, in my father's terms, to have
asked "Why?"—and, beyond that, the far more radical question,
"Why not?"

These are also the values I brought into the Reagan-Bush era,
when all the dangers I had been alerted to as a child were suddenly realized. The "phonies" came to power on the strength,
aptly enough, of a professional actor's finest performance. The

"dumb" were being led and abetted by low-life preachers and intellectuals with expensively squandered educations. And the rich, as my father predicted, used the occasion to dip deep into the wallets of the desperate and the distracted.

It's been hard times for a traditionalist of my persuasion. Long-standing moral values—usually claimed as "Judeo-Christian" but actually of much broader lineage—were summarily tossed, along with most familiar forms of logic. We were told, at one time or another, by the president or his henchpersons, that trees cause pollution, that welfare causes poverty, and that a bomber designed for mass destruction may be aptly named the *Peacemaker.* "Terrorism" replaced missing children to become our national bugaboo and—simultaneously—one of our most potent instruments of foreign policy. At home, the poor and the middle class where shaken down, and their loose change funneled blithely upwards to the already overfed.

Greed, the ancient lubricant of commerce, was declared a wholesome stimulant. Nancy Reagan observed the deep recession of '82 and '83 by redecorating the White House, and continued with this Marie Antoinette theme while advising the underprivileged, the alienated, and the addicted to "say no." Young people, mindful of their elders' Wall Street capers, abandoned the study of useful things for finance banking and other occupations derived, ultimately, from three-card monte. While the poor donned plastic outerware and cardboard coverings, the affluent ran nearly naked through the streets, working off power meals of goat cheese, walnut oil, and crème fraîche.

Religion, which even I had hoped would provide a calming influence and reminder of mortal folly, decided to join the fun. In an upsurge of piety, millions of Americans threw their souls and their savings into evangelical empires designed on the principle of pyramid scams. Even the sleazy downfall of our tele-messiahs—caught masturbating in the company of ten-dollar prostitutes or fornicating in their Christian theme parks—did not discourage the faithful. The unhappily pregnant were mobbed as "baby-killers"; sexual nonconformists—gay and lesbian—

were denounced as "child molesters"; atheists found themselves lumped with "Satanists," Communists, and consumers of human flesh.

Yet somehow, despite it all, a trickle of dissent continued. There were homeless people who refused to be shelved in mental hospitals for the crime of poverty, strikers who refused to join the celebration of unions in faraway countries and scabs at home, women who insisted that their lives be valued above those of accidental embryos, parents who packed up their babies and marched for peace, students who protested the ongoing inversion of normal, nursery-school-level values in the name of a more habitable world.

I am proud to add my voice to all these. For dissent is also a "traditional value," and in a republic founded by revolution, a more deeply native one than smug-faced conservatism can ever be. Feminism was practically invented here, and ought to be regarded as one of our proudest exports to the world. Likewise, it tickles my sense of patriotism that Third World insurgents have often borrowed the ideas of our own African-American movement. And in what ought to be a source of shame to some and pride to others, our history of labor struggle is one of the hardest-fought and bloodiest in the world.

No matter that patriotism is too often the refuge of scoundrels. Dissent, rebellion, and all-around hell-raising remain the true duty of patriots.

LURCHING
TOWARD
BABYLON

●··●··●··●··●··●··●··●

Spudding Out

•‥•‥•‥•‥•‥•‥•

SOMEONE HAS TO SPEAK FOR THEM, because they have, to a person, lost the power to speak for themselves. I am referring to that great mass of Americans who were once known as the "salt of the earth," then as "the silent majority," more recently as "the viewing public," and now, alas, as "couch potatoes." What drives them—or rather, leaves them sapped and spineless on their reclining chairs? What are they seeking—beyond such obvious goals as a tastefully colorized version of *The Maltese Falcon*?

My husband was the first in the family to "spud out," as the expression now goes. Soon everyone wanted one of those zip-up "Couch Potato Bags," to keep warm in during David Letterman. The youngest, and most thoroughly immobilized, member of the family relies on a remote that controls his TV, stereo, and VCR, and can also shut down the neighbor's pacemaker at fifteen yards.

But we never see the neighbors anymore, nor they us. This saddens me, because Americans used to be a great and restless people, fond of the outdoors in all of its manifestations, from Disney World to miniature golf. Some experts say there are virtues in mass agoraphobia, that it strengthens the family and reduces highway deaths. But I would point out that there are still a few things that cannot be done in the den, especially by someone zipped into a body bag. These include racquetball, voting, and meeting strange people in bars.

Most psychologists interpret the couch potato trend as a negative reaction to the outside world. Indeed, the list of reasons to stay safely tucked indoors lengthens yearly. First there was crime, then AIDS, then side-stream smoke. To this list should be added "fear of the infrastructure," for we all know someone who rashly stepped outside only to be buried in a pothole, hurled from a collapsing bridge, or struck by a falling airplane.

But it is not just the outside world that has let us down. Let's face it, despite a decade-long campaign by the "profamily" movement, the family has been a disappointment. The reason lies in an odd circular dynamic: we watch television to escape from our families because television shows us how dull our families really are.

Compare your own family to, for example, the Huxtables, the Keatons, or the peppy young people on *Thirtysomething*. In those families, even the three-year-olds are stand-up comics, and the most insipid remark is hailed with heartening outbursts of canned laughter. When television families aren't gathered around the kitchen table exchanging wisecracks, they are experiencing brief but moving dilemmas, which are handily solved by the youngest child or by some cute extraterrestrial houseguest. Emerging from *Family Ties* or *My Two Dads*, we are forced to acknowledge that our own families are made up of slow-witted, emotionally crippled people who would be lucky to qualify for seats in the studio audience of *Jeopardy!*

But gradually I have come to see that there is something besides fear of the outside and disgust with our families that drives us to spudhood—some positive attraction, some deep cathexis to television itself. For a long time it eluded me. When I watched television, mainly as a way of getting to know my husband and children, I found that my mind wandered to more interesting things, like whether to get up and make ice cubes.

Only after many months of viewing did I begin to understand the force that has transformed the American people into root vegetables. If you watch TV for a very long time, day in, day out, you will begin to notice something eerie and unnatural about the world portrayed therein. I don't mean that it is two-dimensional or lacks a well-developed critique of the capitalist consumer culture or something superficial like that. I mean something so deeply obvious that it's almost scary: when you watch television, you will see people doing many things—chasing fast cars, drinking lite beer, shooting each other at close range, etc. But you will never see people *watching television*. Well, maybe for a second, before the phone rings or a brand-new, multiracial adopted child walks into the house. But never *really watching*, hour after hour, the way *real* people do.

Way back in the beginning of the television era, this was not so strange, because real people actually did many of the things people do on TV, even if it was only bickering with their mothers-in-law about which toilet paper to buy. But modern people, i.e., couch potatoes, do nothing that is ever shown on television (because it is either dangerous or would involve getting up from the couch). And what they do do—watch television—is far too boring to be televised for more than a fraction of a second, not even by Andy Warhol, bless his boredom-proof little heart.

So why do we keep on watching? The answer, by now, should be perfectly obvious: we love television because television brings us a world in which television does not exist. In fact, deep in their hearts, this is what the spuds crave most: a rich, new, participatory life, in which family members look each other in the eye, in which people walk outside and banter with the neighbors, where there is adventure, possibility, danger, feeling, all in natural color, stereophonic sound, and three dimensions, without commercial interruptions, and starring . . . us.

"You mean some new kind of computerized interactive medium?" the children asked hopefully, pert as the progeny on a Tuesday night sitcom. But before I could expand on this concept —known to our ancestors as "real life"—they were back at the box, which may be, after all, the only place left to find it.

[1988]

Food Worship

●··●··●··●··●··●··●··●

ETHIOPIA REMINDS US that there are still people for whom food is primarily a means to biological survival. Here, to judge from the rapid conversion of real estate into takeout shops for gourmets and the sudden prominence of vegetables that begin with the letter *a*, food has come to mean much more: status, authority, entertainment, style, possibly religion. Among the upscale, trend-setting people who are held up for our admiration in commercials for credit cards and wine coolers, food appears to be more fascinating than either sex or trivia games. An evening on the town, which used to mean dinner and a show, now means a showy dinner, followed perhaps by a chaste gelato.

In fact, in anticipation of the time when food will have surpassed all other ingredients of high culture and when upward mobility will hinge on a mastery of puff pastry rather than a familiarity with computers or great books, I am thinking of substituting food emporiums for museums on my children's Sunday outings. Already, food has gained an equal footing with fashion and skin care in the men's magazines, driven diet books to the remainder shelves, and—as food history, food criticism, etc.—gained a foothold in academia. Those areas of artistic and intellectual endeavor that wish to survive may have to take up food themes or be content to make the same kind of accommodation to the restaurant that music has made to the piano bar.

As a longtime admirer of foods that outrank me in social status, I am not complaining. Thanks to the food fixation of the up-wardly mobile, pita bread and salad bars have sedimented down to Burger King, suggesting that cold poached salmon may not be far behind. And I will admit to having occasionally dined—on other people's expense accounts—at establishments so tony that the dishes are reportedly rinsed in Perrier and the beef has grad-uated from stress-free, organic grazing environments. So it is without envy or ingratitude that I have been wondering, why food? Why food of all the obsessions—sex, astrology, real estate, tropical bird breeding—available to those in the Gold Card bracket?

The first explanation I have come up with is a straightforward biological one. Upscale people are fixated with food simply be-cause they are now able to eat so much of it without getting fat, and the reason they don't get fat is that they maintain a profli-gate level of calorie expenditure. The very same people whose evenings begin with melted goat cheese and wind up, hours later, with raspberries cushioned on a lascivious crème à l'an-glaise get up at dawn to run, break for a midmorning aerobics class, and watch the evening news while racing on a stationary bicycle.

This explanation assumes that past generations of dieters—the mothers and grandmothers of today's big-time eaters—left a large proportion of our contemporaries genetically imprinted with a hunger of deep and savage proportions. After having been teased for so long with grapefruit halves and celery sticks, this vast hunger quite justifiably demands plates heaping with Tex-Mex, three-course lunches and between-meal pasta primavera pick-me-ups. Paradoxically, of course, the very occupations that pay well enough to finance gastronomic intake on such a scale—corporate law, international banking, cocaine retailing—involve almost zero energy expenditures in the course of a day's work.

Hence the wild aerobic flailings and desperate five-mile runs required to maintain a fast-track metabolism. Exercise is the yuppie version of bulimia.

Not to push this theory too far, you might say that exercise is to eating in the eighties as contraception was to sex in the sixties. The pill, IUDs, and eventually legalized abortion freed sex from its ancient biological consequences and helped usher in the sexual revolution. In the same way, jogging, jazzercise, and Jane Fonda's videotape have uncoupled gluttony from obesity and thus made possible what may someday be called the gastrointestinal revolution.

But hunger, revived hourly by workouts and runs, only explains why people eat, not what they eat. People who are merely hungry have been known to eat almost anything—bologna sandwiches, bowls of millet, unripe Brie. Something larger than hunger sends young account executives rushing out of their condos after dark to pick up an extra bottle of walnut oil or raspberry vinegar. And that can only be the drive to impress, intimidate, and inspire insecurity in one's dinner guests.

As a way of establishing one's own status or gauging another's, food has obvious advantages over our former cultural obsession, sex. A sexual encounter can only give you insight into your partner's personal warmth, generosity, capacity for whimsy, and so forth. But a bout of competitive eating, as it is now called, gives you fairly precise information about your dining partner's current and anticipated income, social class or origin, and probable taste in home furnishings. Does your date think sushi is still stylish? Then he has probably been passed over for a promotion and squeezed out when his apartment when co-op. If, on the other hand, he goes unhesitatingly for the baby bass en croute, he may have a Harvard MBA and a flair for currency speculation, just the kind of things that should, in the world of culinary high-rollers, make you want to eat with him more often.

The fact that physical exercise—at least when performed with no thought of wages or other compensation and preferably at some expense to the exerciser—is itself a high-status activity only heightens the necessity of conspicuous eating. Whereas a decade or so ago, the woman who ordered an abstemious chef's salad for lunch placed herself on a moral plane above her sister diners, today she would only be suspected of sloth. Clearly, one would have to be a dancercise dropout or a marathon reject to get by on less than two thousand calories at midday. In fact, when has anyone last seen chef's salad on a menu of any importance? Nor is it fashionable any longer to claim to require only coffee for breakfast: friends would suspect you of failing to jog to work and wonder where you even got the strength to grind the beans. Conversely, of course, anyone who makes a point of getting about town without running shoes risks being suspected of secret abstentions from béarnaise sauce and mousse. No one stays on the fast track these days without developing the metabolic capacity of the shrew, that tiny mammal that consumes three times its weight in food each day.

I hesitate to moralize about how this upscale metabolic speed-up might look to a resident of a sub-Saharan refugee camp, for I remember all too well how I responded, as a child, to any dinner-table reference to children so unfortunate that they would feel blessed to encounter my plate of fried Spam and potatoes. (So wrap it up and send it to India then.) Yet our parents' point sunk in: we all know that there is a connection between waste in one location and simultaneous starvation in another, between the gluttony of a few and the chronic hunger of the world's many. Perhaps if we could get our minds off the next meal and the caloric residue of the last one, we might figure out what to do about it.

[1985]

The Cult of Busyness

●··●··●··●··●··●··●

NOT TOO LONG AGO a former friend and soon-to-be acquaintance called me up to tell me how busy she was. A major
report, upon which her professional future depended, was due
in three days; her secretary was on strike; her housekeeper had
fallen into the hands of the Immigration Department; she had
two hours to prepare a dinner party for eight; and she was late
for her time-management class. Stress was taking its toll, she
told me: her children resented the fact that she sometimes got
their names mixed up, and she had taken to abusing white wine.

All this put me at a distinct disadvantage, since the only thing
I was doing at the time was holding the phone with one hand
and attempting to touch the opposite toe with the other hand, a
pastime that I had perfected during previous telephone mono-
logues. Not that I'm not busy too: as I listened to her, I was on
the alert for the moment the dryer would shut itself off and I
would have to rush to fold the clothes before they settled into a
mass of incorrigible wrinkles. But if I mentioned this little deadline of mine, she might think I wasn't busy enough to need a
housekeeper, so I just kept on patiently saying "Hmm" until
she got to her parting line: "Look, this isn't a good time for me
to talk, I've got to go now."

●   ●   ●

I don't know when the cult of conspicuous busyness began, but it has swept up almost all the upwardly mobile, professional women I know. Already, it is getting hard to recall the days when, for example "Let's have lunch" meant something other than "I've got more important things to do than talk to you right now." There was even a time when people used to get together without the excuse of needing something to eat—when, in fact, it was considered rude to talk with your mouth full. In the old days, hardly anybody had an appointment book, and when people wanted to know what the day held in store for them, they consulted a horoscope.

It's not only women, of course; for both sexes, busyness has become an important insignia of upper-middle-class status. Nobody, these days, admits to having a hobby, although two or more careers—say, neurosurgery and an art dealership—is not uncommon, and I am sure we will soon be hearing more about the tribulations of the four-paycheck couple. Even those who can manage only one occupation at a time would be embarrassed to be caught doing only one *thing* at a time. Those young men who jog with their headsets on are not, as you might innocently guess, rocking out, but are absorbing the principles of international finance law or a lecture on one-minute management. Even eating, I read recently, is giving way to "grazing"—the conscious ingestion of unidentified foods while drafting a legal brief, cajoling a client on the phone, and, in ambitious cases, doing calf-toning exercises under the desk.

But for women, there's more at stake than conforming to another upscale standard. If you want to attract men, for example, it no longer helps to be a bimbo with time on your hands. Upscale young men seem to go for the kind of woman who plays with a full deck of credit cards, who won't cry when she's knocked to the ground while trying to board the six o'clock Eastern shuttle, and whose schedule doesn't allow for a sexual encounter lasting more than twelve minutes. Then there is the economic reality: any woman who doesn't want to wind up a case

study in the feminization of poverty has to be successful at
something more demanding than fingernail maintenance or
come-hither looks. Hence all the bustle, my busy friends would
explain—they want to succeed.

But if success is the goal, it seems clear to me that the fast
track is headed the wrong way. Think of the people who are
genuinely successful—path-breaking scientists, best-selling
novelists, and designers of major new software. They are not, on
the whole, the kind of people who keep glancing shiftily at their
watches or making small lists entitled "To Do." On the contrary,
many of these people appear to be in a daze, like the distin-
guished professor I once had who, in the middle of a lecture on
electron spin, became so fascinated by the dispersion properties
of chalk dust that he could not go on. These truly successful
people are childlike, easily distractable, fey sorts, whose usual
demeanor resembles that of a recently fed hobo on a warm summer evening.

The secret of the truly successful, I believe, is that they
learned very early in life how *not* to be busy. They saw through
that adage, repeated to me so often in childhood, that anything
worth doing is worth doing well. The truth is, many things are
worth doing only in the most slovenly, halfhearted fashion possible, and many other things are not worth doing at all. Balancing
a checkbook, for example. For some reason, in our culture, this
dreary exercise is regarded as the supreme test of personal maturity, business acumen, and the ability to cope with math anxiety. Yet it is a form of busyness which is exceeded in futility
only by going to the additional trouble of computerizing one's
checking account—and that, in turn, is only slightly less silly
than taking the time to discuss, with anyone, what brand of
personal computer one owns, or is thinking of buying, or has
heard of others using.

If the truly successful manage never to be busy, it is also true
that many of the busiest people will never be successful. I know
this firsthand from my experience, many years ago, as a waitress.

Any executive who thinks the ultimate in busyness consists of having two important phone calls on hold and a major deadline in twenty minutes, should try facing six tablefuls of clients simultaneously demanding that you give them their checks, fresh coffee, a baby seat, and a warm, spontaneous smile. Even when she's not busy, a waitress has to look busy—refilling the salt shakers and polishing all the chrome in sight—but the only reward is the minimum wage and any change that gets left on the tables. Much the same is true of other high-stress jobs, like working as a telephone operator, or doing data entry on one of the new machines that monitors your speed as you work: "success" means surviving the shift.

Although busyness does not lead to success, I am willing to believe that success—especially when visited on the unprepared —can cause busyness. Anyone who has invented a better mousetrap, or the contemporary equivalent, can expect to be harassed by strangers demanding that you read their unpublished manuscripts or undergo the humiliation of public speaking, usually on remote Midwestern campuses. But if it is true that success leads to more busyness and less time for worthwhile activities—like talking (and listening) to friends, reading novels, or putting in some volunteer time for a good cause—then who needs it? It would be sad to have come so far—or at least to have run so hard —only to lose each other.

[1985]

Star Dreck

●···●···●···●···●···●···●

WHEN I WAS A KID, we knew very little about the stars, and much of what we did know was imprecise and speculative in nature. But such is the beauty of the human mind—forever reaching, forever grasping—that we now know far more than we can possibly absorb or usefully apply, and certainly far more than I ever expected to know in my own lifetime: not only what they eat for breakfast and what their favorite colors are, but their secret self-doubts and worries, their hair-management problems, and the names and locations of their unclaimed progeny.

As in all expanding fields, we are faced with what the scholars call an "information explosion," which is already taxing the resources of the available media. In the old days, there were only a few specialized journals, with titles like *Silver Screen* and *Swooning Starlets*. But today there are dozens of publications, such as *People* and *Us*, which make fast-breaking discoveries accessible even to the person of limited educational attainment. For the intellectual elite, we have such challenging sources as *Vanity Fair* and *Interview*, which provide the depth of analysis that is sadly lacking on *Entertainment Tonight*.

Of course there are still a few throwbacks who have failed to appreciate our expanding knowledge of the stars. They point out that most Americans are profoundly ignorant—prone to believe that Botswana is in Florida or that the *Yellow Pages* is a "great book." But retro-pedants like Allan Bloom never bother to quiz us on Burt and Loni's baby problem, or the tribulations of Cher's unfortunately monikered "Bagel Boy." They forget that, as far as the majority of the world's population is concerned, star trivia *is* Western civilization.

I don't want to boast, but I do try to keep abreast. Once, for example, I had the opportunity to shake the bejeweled hand of a very major star. But I didn't—not because I was shy; but because *I knew too much about her:* her former's husband's mega-vitamin problem, her hairdresser's recent breakdown, her ill-concealed rivalry with Joan Collins. There was simply nothing left to say.

Theory, as usual, lags behind the frenetic accumulation of new data, but already a few broad paradigmatic principles are beginning to emerge. There are three of them, just as there are three fundamental forces (not counting the fourth), three Stooges, and three Rambos. The first one is: all stars are related to each other.

It didn't used to be this way in the old days, when the average star was the abused daughter of an alcoholic Mississippian. But in the last two decades, the stars have undergone a sudden and astonishing genetic convergence: there's Jamie Lee Curtis (daughter of Janet Leigh and Tony), Carrie Fisher (daughter of Debbie Reynolds and Eddie), Michael Douglas (son of Kirk), Jeff Bridges (son of Lloyd), Charlie Sheen (son of Martin), Emilio Estevez (brother of Charlie), and so on. Frankly, no one knows what this means, although the search is on for the "star gene," which could then be transferred, by familiar bioengineering techniques, to piglets, mice, and intestinal bacteria.

The second principle, which is again the result of very recent research, is that *all stars work out*. Whether this is a response to the inevitable muscular weakening caused by inbreeding, or merely an attempt to fill in the empty hours between interviews for *Premiere*, no one knows, but it all began with Jane (daughter of Henry, sister of Peter).

The third and final principle, which we owe in part to the

dedicated researchers at *Star* and similar journals, is that all stars
—and especially those who do not work out—have had near-
fatal encounters with cocaine (Richard Dreyfuss), alcohol (Don
Johnson), food (Elizabeth Taylor), or the lack of it (Dolly
Parton). Here again, inbreeding may be at work, but the net
result is the unique life cycle of the star, which is not dissimilar
to the classic saga of the hero as charted by Joseph Campbell:
birth, abuse, the struggle against substances at Betty Ford—
followed by redemption and inspiring appearances in "Just Say
No" ads.

But as our knowledge increases, so does our frustration. Americans, after all, do not like knowing things (such as the location
of Botswana) that they cannot do anything about. So, I say, give
us some way of applying our ever-growing knowledge: let us *vote*
on the lives of the stars!

After all, we're better informed about the lives of the stars
than we are about such dreary matters as deficit management
and the balance of trade. In fact, we are probably in a better
position to make star decisions than the stars themselves. Consider that tragic misstep: Bruce's marriage to Julianne—which
led to the dullest album of his career and the temporary removal
of his earring. One hundred million American women were prepared to say, "No, don't do it. Wait for a Jersey Girl. Or, better
yet, wait for me to move to Jersey and become one!" But we
couldn't do a thing.

Imagine if we could have a referendum on Barbra and Don
(hold out, Barb, he's just a bimbo!). Or a plebiscite on Michael
Jackson's pigmentation (he'd be able to wear one of those "Black
by Popular Demand" T-shirts!). Imagine the debates, the mass
rallies and marches, the furious exchanges in the op-ed pages!

But of course the stars wouldn't accept that. They might
rebel. They'd go underground—get fat, go back to the substances of their youth, and hide out in unmarked mobile homes
in Culver City. I guess there are some things that humankind
just wasn't meant to tinker with—some things that will always
fill our souls with helpless awe, and show us how insignificant

and meaningless our own lives are in the grand scheme of things. And no matter how much we may learn about them, that is the function of the stars.

[1988]

Premature Pragmatism

•··•··•··•··•··•··•··•

THE SETTING WAS ONE of those bucolic Ivy League campuses where the tuition exceeds the average American annual
income and the favorite sport is white-water rafting—as far, in
other words, as one might hope to get from the banal economic
worries that plague the grown-up world. The subject, among the
roomful of young women who had come to meet with me, turned
to "life after college"—"if there is one" (nervous giggles). "My
dream was to go into psychiatric social work," offered a serious
young woman in overalls and a "Divest Now" button, "but I
don't think I could live on that, so I'm going into banking instead." When I protested that she should hold on to her ideals
and try to get by on the $30,000 or so a year psychiatric social
workers earn, she looked baffled, as if I were recommending an
internship with Mother Teresa.

"Ideals are all right when you're young," declared another
woman, a campus activist who certainly seemed to fit the age
group for which she found idealism appropriate, "but you do
have to think of earning a living." Well, yes, I thought to myself,
we older feminists have been saying for some time that the goal
of higher education for women is not the "MRS" degree, but
when did we ever say that it was *banking*?

Not that a little respect for the dollar isn't a fine thing in the
young, and a useful antidote, in my day anyway, for the effects

of too much Hesse or Kahlil Gibran. But no one in the room had gone so far as to suggest a career in almsgiving, washing lepers' feet, or doing literacy training among the Bushmen. "Idealism," to these undergraduates, was defined as an ordinary, respectable profession in the human services. "Realism" meant plunging almost straight from pubescence into the stone-hearted world of finance capitalism.

I call this mind-set, which you will find on almost any campus today, "premature pragmatism," and I am qualified to comment because I, too, was once a victim of it. I had gone to college with an intellectual agenda that included solving the mind-body problem, discovering the sources of human evil, and getting a tentative reading on the purpose of life. But within a few months I had dropped all that and become a chemistry major—partly because I had figured out that there are only meager rewards, in this world, for those who know the purpose of life and the source of all evil.

The result, twenty-odd years later, is more or less what you'd expect: I'm an ex-science major with no definite occupation (unless you count "writing," that universal cover for those who avoid wage slavery at all costs), and I am still obsessed by the Ultimate Questions, such as What It's All About and Whether the Universe Will Expand Forever. I could have turned out much worse; I could have stayed in chemistry and gone into something distinctly unidealistic like nerve gas or plastics, in which case I might have become rich and would almost certainly also have become an embittered alchoholic or a middle-aged dropout. The point is that premature pragmatism didn't work for me, and I doubt that it will work for any young person intending to set aside a "Divest Now" button for one reading "You Have a Friend at Chase Manhattan."

Yet premature pragmatism has become as popular on campuses as, in past eras, swallowing goldfish to impress one's friends or taking over the administration building to demand a better world. There has been a precipitous decline, just since the seventies, in the number of students majoring in mind-ex-

panding but only incidentally remunerative fields like history
and mathematics. Meanwhile, business—as an academic pursuit
—is booming: almost one-fourth of all college graduates were
business majors in 1983, compared to about one-seventh in 1973,
while the proportions who major in philosophy or literature have
vanished beyond the decimal point to less than 1 percent.

Even more alarming, to anyone whose own life has been
scarred by premature pragmatism, is the decline in "idealism"
as expressed by undergraduates and measured by pollsters. In
1968, 85 percent of college students said that they hoped their
education would help them "develop a philosophy of life," etc.,
etc. In 1985, only 44 percent adhered to such lofty goals, while
the majority expected that education would help them "earn a
lot of money." There has been, in other words, almost a 50
percent decline in idealism and a 100 percent increase in venality, or to put it less judgmentally, premature pragmatism.

I concede, though, that there are good reasons for the hard-
nosed pragmatism of today's college students. They face rougher
times, economically, than did my generation or the generation
before mine. As economists Frank Levy and Richard Michel
have recently shown, today's baby boomers (and especially the
younger ones) are far less likely than their own parents to be able
to buy a home, maintain a family on one income, or to watch
their standard of living improve as they grow older.

So the best comeback for the young woman in overalls would
have been for her to snap at me, "You think I should live on
thirty thousand dollars a year! Well, perhaps you hadn't noticed
that the National Association of Homebuilders now estimates
that it takes an income of thirty-seven thousand dollars a year to
be able to afford a modest, median-priced home. Or that if I
want to send my own eventual children to a college like this I
will need well over fifty thousand dollars a year. Or are you
suggesting I rely on a rich husband?" And she would have been
dead on the mark: in today's economy, idealism is a luxury that
most of us are likely to enjoy only at the price of simple comforts

like housing and education. The mood on campus isn't so much venality as it is *fear*.

But still, premature pragmatism isn't necessarily a winning strategy. In the first place, what looks like "realism" at age eighteen may become sheer folly by age thirty-eight. Occupations go in and out of corporate favor, so that chemistry, for example—which seemed to be a safe bet two decades ago—has become one of those disciplines that prepare people for a life in the retail end of the newspaper business. The same may eventually happen to today's campus favorites—like law, management, and finance. At least it seems to me that there must be an ecological limit to the number of paper pushers the earth can sustain, and that human civilization will collapse when the number of, say, tax lawyers exceeds the world's total population of farmers, weavers, fisherpersons, and pediatric nurses.

Furthermore, with any luck at all, one becomes a rather different person at age thirty-eight than one was at eighteen. The list of famous people who ended up in a different line of work than the one they first embarked on includes Clark Gable (former lumberjack), artist Henri Rousseau (postal clerk), Elvis Presley (truck driver), St. Augustine (playboy), Walt Disney (ambulance driver), and Che Guevara (physician). Heads of state are notoriously ill prepared for their mature careers; think of Adolph Hitler (landscape painter), Ho Chi Minh (seaman), and our own Ronald Reagan. Women's careers are if anything even more unpredictable, to judge from my own friends: Barbara (a biochemist turned novelist), Sara (French literature professor, now a book editor), cousin Barb (anthropology to medicine).

But the saddest thing about today's premature pragmatists is not that they will almost certainly be unprepared for their midlife career destinations, but that they will be unprepared for Life, in the grand sense, at all. The years between eighteen and twenty-two were not given to us to be frittered away in contemplation of future tax shelters and mortgage payments. In fact, it is almost a requirement of developmental biology that these years be spent in erotic reverie, metaphysical speculation, and schemes for universal peace and justice. Sometimes, of course, we lose sight of the heroic dreams of youth later on, as overdue bills and carburetor problems take their toll. But those who never dream at all start to lose much more—their wit, empathy, perspective, and, for lack of a more secular term, their immortal souls.

Then what about the fact that it takes nearly a six-figure income to achieve what used to be known as a "middle-class" lifestyle? What about my young Ivy League friend, forced to choose between a career in human service and what she believes, perhaps realistically, to be an adequate income? All I can say is that there is something grievously wrong with a culture that values Wall Street sharks above social workers, armament manufacturers above artists, or, for that matter, corporate lawyers above homemakers. Somehow, we're going to have to make the world a little more habitable for idealists, whether they are eighteen or thirty-eight. In fact, I suspect that more and more young people, forced to choose between their ideals and their economic security, will start opting instead for a career in social change. "The pay is lousy," as veteran writer-historian-social-change-activist Irving Howe likes to say, "but it's steady work."

[1986]

Good-bye to the Work Ethic

•··•··•··•··•··•··•··•

THE MEDIA have just buried the last yuppie, a pathetic creature who had not heard the news that the great pendulum of public consciousness has just swung from Greed to Compassion and from Tex-Mex to meatballs. Folks are already lining up outside the mausoleum bearing the many items he had hoped to take with him, including a quart bottle of raspberry vinegar and the Cliff Notes for *The Wealth of Nations*. I, too, have brought something to throw onto the funeral pyre—the very essence of yupdom, its creed and its meaning. Not the passion for money, not even the lust for tiny vegetables, but the *work ethic*.

Yes, I realize how important the work ethic is. I understand that it occupies the position, in the American constellation of values, once held by motherhood and Girl Scout cookies. But yuppies took it too far; they *abused* it.

In fact, one of the reasons they only lived for three years (1984–87) was that they *never* rested, never took the time to chew between bites or gaze soulfully past their computer screens. What's worse, the mere rumor that someone—anyone —was not holding up his or her end of the work ethic was enough to send them into tantrums. They blamed lazy workers for the Decline of Productivity. They blamed lazy welfare mothers for the Budget Deficit. Their idea of utopia (as once laid out in that journal of higher yup thought, the *New Republic*) was the "Work Ethic State": no free lunches, no handouts, and too bad for all the miscreants and losers who refuse to fight their way up to the poverty level by working eighty hours a week at Wendy's.

Personally, I have nothing against work, particularly when performed, quietly and unobtrusively, by someone else. I just don't happen to think it's an appropriate subject for an "ethic." As a general rule, when something gets elevated to apple-pie status in the hierarchy of American values, you have to suspect that its actual *monetary* value is skidding toward zero.

Take motherhood: nobody ever thought of putting it on a moral pedestal until some brash feminists pointed out, about a century ago, that the pay is lousy and the career ladder nonexistent. Same thing with work: would we be so reverent about the "work ethic" if it wasn't for the fact that the average working stiff's hourly pay is shrinking, year by year, toward the price of a local phone call?

In fact, let us set the record straight: the work ethic is not a "traditional value." It is a johnny-come-lately value, along with thin thighs and nonsmoking hotel rooms. In ancient times, work was considered a disgrace inflicted on those who had failed to amass a nest egg through imperial conquest or other forms of organized looting. Only serfs, slaves, and women worked. The yuppies of ancient Athens—which we all know was a perfect cornucopia of "traditional values"—passed their time rubbing their bodies with olive oil and discussing the Good, the True, and the Beautiful.

The work ethic came along a couple of millennia later, in the form of Puritanism—the idea that the amount of self-denial you endured in this life was a good measure of the amount of fun awaiting you in the next. But the work ethic only got off the ground with the Industrial Revolution and the arrival of the factory system. This was—let us be honest about it—simply a scheme for extending the benefits of the slave system into the age of emancipation.

Under the new system (aka capitalism in this part of the world), huge numbers of people had to be convinced to work extra hard, at pitifully low wages, so that the employing class would not have to work at all. Overnight, with the help of a great number of preachers and other well-rested propagandists, work was upgraded from an indignity to an "ethic."

But there was a catch: the aptly named *working class* came to resent the resting class. There followed riots, revolutions, graffiti. Quickly, the word went out from the robber barons to the swelling middle class of lawyers, financial consultants, plant managers, and other forerunners of the yuppie: Look busy! Don't go home until the proles have punched out! Make 'em think *we're* doing the work and that they're lucky to be able to hang around and help out!

The lawyers, managers, etc., were only too happy to comply, for as the perennially clever John Kenneth Galbraith once pointed out, they themselves comprised a "new leisure class" within industrial society. Of course, they "work," but only under the most pleasant air-conditioned, centrally heated, and fully carpeted conditions, and then only in a sitting position. It was in their own interest to convince the working class that what looks like lounging requires intense but invisible effort.

The yuppies, when they came along, had to look more righteously busy than anyone, for the simple reason that they did nothing at all. Workwise, that is. They did not sow, neither did they reap, but rather sat around pushing money through their modems in games known as "corporate takeover" and "international currency speculation." Hence their rage at anyone who actually works—the "unproductive" American worker, or the woman attempting to raise a family on welfare benefits set below the average yuppie's monthly health spa fee.

So let us replace their cruel and empty slogan—"Go for it!" —with the cry that lies deep in every true worker's heart: "Gimme a break!" What this nation needs is not the work ethic, but a *job* ethic: If it needs doing—highways repaired, babies

changed, fields plowed—let's get it done. Otherwise, take five.
Listen to some New Wave music, have a serious conversation
with a three-year-old, write a poem, look at the sky. Let the
yuppies Rest in Peace; the rest of us deserve a break.

[1988]

FRAUD AND
LOATHING

●··●··●··●··●··●··●··●

The Unbearable Being
of Whiteness

●··●··●··●··●··●··●··●

THIS COLUMN IS ADDRESSED to my fellow white people and contains material that we would prefer to keep among ourselves. God knows we have suffered enough already from the unique problems that have confronted white people over the centuries: the burden of bringing Christianity to heathens so benighted that they usually preferred death. The agony of sunburn. But now we face what may be the biggest problem of all. You know what I mean, brothers and sisters, *low self-esteem*.

It started with the Asian menace. Many years ago "Made in Japan" applied chiefly to windup toys and samurai movies. No one thought twice about sending their children off to school with the sons and daughters of laundrymen and chop suey chefs. But now, alas, the average white person cannot comprehend the inner workings of the simplest product from the Orient, much less read the owner's manual.

In the realm of business, our most brilliant blue-eyed MBAs admit they are as children compared to the shoguns of Mitsubishi and Toshiba. As for education, well, the local high school is offering a full scholarship to the first Caucasian to make valedictorian. And what white parents have not—when pressed to the limit by their brutish, ignorant, dope fiend children—screamed, "Goddamn it, Stacey, [or Sean], why can't you act more like an Asian-American?"

Yes, I know the conventional explanation: white people lack convincing role models. Consider President Reagan, whose own son grew up believing—hoping?—that his true parents were the black help. Or consider the vice president, George Bush, a man so bedeviled by bladder problems that he managed, for the last eight years, to be in the men's room whenever an important illegal decision was made. Or consider how long it took, following the defeat of Robert Bork, for the conservatives to find a white man who was clean-shaven, drug-free, and had also passed his bar exam.

Then there were the nonblack Democratic candidates, who might be considered the very flower of white manhood. For months, none of them could think of anything to say. Political discourse fell to the level of white street talk, as in "Have a nice day."

Then, stealthily, one by one, they began to model themselves after Jesse Jackson. Even the patrician Al Gore, surely one of the whitest men ever to seek public office, donned a windbreaker and declared himself the champion of the working people. Richard Gephardt borrowed Jackson's rhyme about how corporations "merge" with each other and "purge" the workers. Soon he was telling moving stories about his youth as a poor black boy in the South, and how he had inexplicably turned white, clear up to and including his eyebrows.

Confronted with the obvious superiority of the black candidate, many white voters became perplexed and withdrawn. We had liked to think of blacks as simple folk with large thighs and small brains—a race of Head Start dropouts, suitable for sweeping floors and assisting blond cops on TV. In fact, there is clear evidence of black intellectual superiority: in 1984, 92 percent of blacks voted to retire Ronald Reagan, compared to only 36 percent of whites.

Or compare the two most prominent men of television, Bill Cosby and Morton Downey, Jr. Millions of white Americans have grown up with no other father figure than "Cos." Market researchers have determined that we would buy any product he endorses, even if it were a skin-lightener. No one, on the other hand, would buy anything from Downey, unless it was something advertised anonymously in the classified section of *Soldier of Fortune.*

Perhaps it is true, as many white people have secretly and shamefully concluded, that these facts can only be explained by resorting to genetic theories of IQ. But I still like to think there are environmental explanations. A generation ago, for example, hordes of white people fled the challenging, interracial atmosphere of the cities and settled in the whites-only suburbs. Little did we know that a life-style devoted to lawn maintenance and shrub pruning would, in no time at all, engender the thick-witted peasant mentality now so common among our people.

At the same time, the white elite walled themselves up in places like Harvard to preserve white culture in its purest form. Still others, the brightest of our race, retired to Los Alamos to figure out how to bring the whole thing to a prompt conclusion. Unfortunately, our extreme isolation from people of alternative races meant there was never anyone around to point out the self-destructive tendencies inherent in white behavior, which is still known collectively as "Western civilization."

Let's face it, we became ingrown, clannish, and retarded. Cut off from the mainstream of humanity, we came to believe that pink is "flesh-color," that mayonnaise is a nutrient, and that Barry Manilow is a musician. Little did we know that all over the world, people were amusing each other with tales beginning, "Did you hear the one about the Caucasian who . . ."

I know. It hurts. Low self-esteem is a terrible thing. Some white men, driven mad by the feeling that people are laughing at them, have taken to running around the streets and beating on random persons of color or threatening to vote Republican.

Believe me, that kind of acting out won't help. If white people are ever to stand tall, we're going to have to leave our cramped little ghetto and stride out into the world again. Of

course, there'll be the inevitable embarrassments at first: the fear
of saying the wrong thing, of making mathematical errors, of
forgetting the geography of the southern hemisphere. But gather
up little Sean and Stacey and tell them, "We can do it! If we
study and try very hard, even we can *be somebody!*"

[1988]

Language Barrier

THOSE ENGLISH-ONLY TYPES have finally gone too far. It all started with the commendable impulse to keep public-health doctors from communicating with immigrants in a language they can understand. At least this was the original modest intent of the Suffolk County, New York, English-only bill. And since even us real Americans can't always grasp the complex vocabulary of medical science (you know, "deductible," "unreimbursable procedure," "coinsurance," and so forth), why should a bunch of foreigners have the advantage?

But then the English-only people got carried away. First they took away the *au pairs*, *divas*, and *masseurs*. Then they moved in on the states and California street names. La Cienega Boulevard became Swamp Street. Colorado became Colored (until, of course, an emergency referendum renamed it Greater Denver). Next it was the turn of the legal profession, which—without its *amicuses* and *de jures*—was left speechless for upwards of twenty minutes. After that, a hush fell over the literati, deprived as they were of the delicate *frissons*, *scandales*, and *folies* with which they had for so long maintained their *esprit*. I didn't utter a word of protest, I blush to admit, not even when quiche turned into egg pie.

I used to be gung ho for English-only myself, on the grounds that my ancestors had spoken English-only for at least twenty generations, and not much of it at that—idle chitchat being considered a sign of insecurity or ill intent. The less sophisticated of my forebears avoided foreigners at all costs, for the very good reason that, in their circles, speaking in tongues was commonly a prelude to snake handling. The more tolerant among us regarded foreign languages as a kind of speech impediment that could be overcome by willpower. When confronted by one of the afflicted, we would speak very s-l-o-w-l-y and loudly, repeating ourselves until the poor soul caught on, or—as was more often the case—ran off in search of more quick-witted company.

Of course, people are drawn to English-only for all kinds of good reasons. Some of them, for example, have been to Paris, where they strayed from the Holiday Inn and were spat upon by waiters for ordering "un-coffee" or "croy-sints." Others of them are driven by the fear, mounting to panic in the border states, that the United States will experience the same fate as Canada. And we all know what happened to Canada, which was once a semitropical paradise—famed for its tempestuous rhythms and piquant cuisine—until the tragic imposition of bilingualism rendered it large, cold, and boring.

Then there is the fear, common to all English-only speakers, that the chief purpose of foreign languages is to make fun of us. Otherwise, you know, why not just come out and *say* it? No FUMAR, for example. I used to see it all over the place, and who knows what that means—CHILL OUT, GRINGO FOOL, maybe? Or that inscrutable message inscribed in so many airplane restrooms: POR FAVOR NO TIRAR EL PAPEL DENTRO DEL INODORO. What is that supposed to mean? DO YOURSELF A FAVOR AND SOAK YOUR UGLY ANGLO HEAD IN THE TOILET? And if that isn't what it means, why do I see so many foreigners—no doubt bilingualists—winking and smirking as if they knew something we didn't?

But the real motive is patriotism. Look, we can't keep out foreign *people,* without whom we'd have to bus our own dishes, clean our own houses, and manage our own factories. And we can't keep out foreign *things*, without which there'd be no color TVs, calculators, or Nintendo. So we can at least draw the line at *words;* and words are important because they are so often the unwitting carriers of *ideas.* Think of the foreign ideas that have leaked in over the last two hundred years and the trouble that could have been saved by stopping them dead at the border: communism, Catholicism, calculus, and cubism—not to mention Freudianism, existentialism, fascism, and french fries.

For there can be no more ancient and traditional American value than ignorance. English-only speakers brought it with them to this country three centuries ago, and they quickly imposed it on the Africans—who were not allowed to learn to read and write—and on the Native Americans, who were simply not allowed. Today, our presidents and vice presidents proudly stand ready to prove in a court of law that they don't know anything and have forgotten what they did know. In fact, the original anti-immigrant movement of the nineteenth century, the forerunner of English-only, called itself, appropriately, the "'Know-Nothings." They believed, as many patriots still do, that the mind of America should remain a—how do you put it in English?—*blank slate?*

But the movement has finally gone too far. It was a professor at Dartmouth, I believe, who first pointed out that English itself is a mongrel language—a corruption of the pure Saxon spoken by my ancestors before the disastrous events of 1066. Then a team of linguists at the Heritage Foundation issued the first "Saxon-only" manifesto, listing the many social problems that could be eliminated immediately by expunging all traces of foreign (i.e., Romance-language) influence: homosexuality, pornography, pederasty, feminism, and democracy—and that's just for starters!

There are advantages, I mean, good things about this Saxon-only thing. Like it's nice I can carry the *Oxford Unabridged Dictionary* in my hip pocket now. And I don't need a lot of big words to *express*—I mean, say, what I gotta say. And we're all Americans now, no "bi" or "multi" nothing. But there's something about this language—you know, *talking*—thing that makes me feel sort of, well—how do you say it in Saxon? *Dumb,* you know what I'm trying to say? Real dumb.

[1989]

Give Me That New-Time Religion

●··●··●··●··●··●··●··●

IT'S A DRAG, getting everyone dressed and out of the house by ten on Sunday morning, but I feel I have to do it for the children's sake. Last week's sermon on Voltaire was a real sleeping pill, if you know what I mean, but we always wind up by standing and holding hands while we chant the periodic table, and that's kind of moving, if you're in the mood for it. I'm talking about Secular Humanist church, of course, which the courts are finally beginning to recognize as a genuine religion, just like Transcendental Meditation, Differential Calculus, or any of the others.

There's still a lot of misunderstanding about us, and there are people who think we're some kind of sect that is totally out of touch with the modern Fundamentalist world. I admit that we have a kind of closed little world of our own, what with Secular Humanist Bingo and Secular Humanist Pancake Breakfasts and the annual Secular Humanist Benefit Car Wash. And I feel the narrowness of it sometimes when I look at the reading material in my own home—which is pretty much restricted to the *New York Times*, the *Encyclopedia Americana*, Stephen King, and things like that, which are what you'd expect to find in a Secular Humanist household.

I guess I'm used to it, though, because I was raised in a real strong Secular Humanist family—the kind of folks who'd ground you for a week just for thinking of dating a Unitarian, or worse. Not that they were hard-liners, though. We had over seventy Bibles lying around the house where anyone could browse through them—Gideons my dad had removed from the motel rooms he'd stayed in. And I remember how he gloried in every Gideon he lifted, thinking of all the traveling salesmen whose minds he'd probably saved from dry rot.

Looking back, I guess you could say I never really had a choice, what with my parents always preaching "Think for yourself! Think for yourself!" no matter what the subject was. To this day, I have my moments of doubt, when I rush over to the pastor's office and go, "I just can't think for myself anymore! Give me an Objective Morality laid down by a Higher Power!" Then, if he's in a bad mood, he sends me home to watch three segments of the PTL Club, two Jimmy Swaggarts, and a half hour of prime-time CBN, and pretty soon I feel my faith coming back in a powerful rush, almost like being born again right there in the family room.

What gets me is all the mean things people say about Secular Humanism, without even taking the time to read some of our basic scriptures, such as the Bill of Rights or *Omni* magazine. Like the rumor that we lure little Christian children into the church basement and force them to undergo "values clarification." Or that we're trying to get Rousseau's *Émile* inserted into the third-grade reading list. Or that we're raising money to send missionaries to do sex education door-to-door in Orange County. And I've heard some awful things involving scale models of Australopithecus, but never mind about that.

They even like to claim that we infiltrate the other religions and do things to discredit them. For example, I've heard it said that it was a Secular Humanist electronics engineer who put that flashing 800 number under Jerry Falwell's chest so he'd look like one of those sleazy characters who sell Four Tops albums on TV at 2 A.M. This was not our idea, although whoever writes Falwell's scripts must really have it in for Christianity.

I know Catholics, for example, who are convinced there is a

Secular Humanist plant in the Vatican whose job is to keep the pope's mind in the gutter, thinking about nothing but sex and semen and condoms and so forth. And there are plenty of Christians who believe it must have been one of us who set up poor Jim Bakker with that Pentacostalist cutie-pie from Long Island —not to mention persuading his devoted wife, Tammy Faye, to say yes to drugs. But believe me, we're just not that devious. We didn't even give Tammy Faye the idea of starting her own line of Christian cosmetics—clever as that was, from an atheistic vantage point.

The real reason the other religions resent Secular Humanism so much is that we can be pretty evangelical about it. But if you've heard the Good News, why not spread it? For example, you might as well know that it was us who got the Copernican model of the solar system into the school textbooks. I know the other side says it's just a "theory" that the earth goes around the sun and not vice versa. But we don't hold with Old Testament astronomy; you can see the trouble it's gotten NASA into already.

Also, it was one of our people who wrote "The Three Little Pigs," that classic allegory of free thought and individual decision making, which simultaneously illustrates Newton's Third Law, the perfidy of the real-estate industry, and the need for a global approach to the housing crisis.

Finally, for the record, it was a Secular Humanist who got the plural of the word "religion" into Webster's dictionary back in 1923. As you probably know, there was a whole grass roots movement of Fundamentalists to keep out "atheism," "relativism," and a bunch of innocuous little words like "option" and "if," but nothing got their dander up like the plural of "religion." Because, of course, if each religion is God's one-and-only revealed truth, and if there's more than one religion, then it follows that each and every one of them is total hogwash. Or that God was only kidding, a conclusion that is also entirely consistent with Secular Humanist theological thinking.

Now I can guess what you're thinking. You're thinking, "How

is it that Secular Humanism, which is the absence of religion, can be a religion, too?" Don't think we haven't asked ourselves that question! But our pastor just winks and says this must be one of those things—like the Immaculate Conception—that is just beyond human comprehension. Besides, if nonreligion is a religion, too, isn't *everybody* tax-exempt?

[1987]

The Great Syringe Tide

•··•··•··•··•··•··•··•

I USED TO GET *so* depressed about the environment. Like last summer, when we just had to get to the beach because of the greenhouse effect, but you couldn't go into the water because of all the syringes and bloody IV tubing washing up in the surf, and you couldn't sunbathe either because the ozone layer wasn't up to par that day. So there was nothing to do but dig up crack vials from the sand and pelt the seagulls with them. But even that's not much fun anymore because the seagulls haven't been very peppy since the last oil spill, even the ones that still have two legs and a functional wing.

But I feel much better since I joined my Environmental Grief Counseling Group, which is a wonderful New Age approach to gaining the personal serenity you need in a world of melting ice caps, shrinking rain forests, and toxic lakes.

The first thing we learned is that the environment is all just a matter of *attitude*. In fact, you can think of your attitude as your "inner environment," which can be as fresh and green and perky as you like, even when the Great Lakes turn to solid waste and the Himalayas are placed on smog alert.

It's not just touchy-feely either in Environmental Grief Counseling; everyone's encouraged to *do something* so long as it's something really manageable where you know you can make a difference. That's why we've all gotten involved in the anti-smoking movement these days.

Maybe acid rain has turned the Black Forest a moldy gray and mabye there aren't any fish larger than anchovies left in the Atlantic, but we've just about cleaned up those dense clouds of side-stream smoke that used to hang over every city and hamlet in America. And if anyone should be so gauche as to light up in our presence, we just keep zapping 'em with our water guns until the cops can get 'em cuffed and hauled away.

Of course, there's always some twisted character in the group who likes to point out that if we'd spent half as much energy on the capital-E Environment as we did on cigarette smoke, maybe we wouldn't have to make our ice cubes out of Evian water today. Suppose, she says, we'd gone after the *polluters* with our water pistols, or lobbied for Styrofoam-free sections of McDonald's. Or passed a law making the plutonium manufac-turers, Union Carbide executives, and other ecocriminals sit all cramped up in the back of the airplane with the cigarette smok-ers. Maybe we'd be windsurfing right now instead of sitting around in Grief Counseling passing the Kleenex box.

But this is just negativism, our group leader tells us, which is the mental equivalent of toxic waste. Look what we've accom-plished in just the last few weeks by thinking *positively:* at the beach, underneath the sign that says NO BEER, NO RADIOS, NO PETS, NO PROFANITY, NO SWIMMING, NO SUNBATHING, AND NO BARE FEET, we've had a new sign posted saying, just as clear as can be: AND THANK YOU FOR NOT SMOKING!

Thinking positively means taking responsibility for creating your *own* environment. Let's face it, some of us can't handle colors like sky blue and forest green anyway. We look a whole lot better in a pink and chrome situation, which is how I've done up my house, along with a new air-filtering system and lead window shades. I feel it expresses the real *me* a lot better than any random collection of trees and clouds and rocks *ever* could.

But the most liberating thing I've learned in Environmental Grief Counseling is when to let go, say good-bye, and stand on your own two feet. I mean, human beings have been clinging to the environment for aeons now, creeping around on the rocks, eating the berries, filling their tires with the air.

This is *dependency,* and dependency is a form of *addiction.* What the human race needs is a heavy-duty twelve-step program to wake us up to the fact that the environment is just a crutch— a great big security blanket that we can finally set aside.

In fact, the dependency goes both ways. Think of all those sequoias huddling in state parks, not to mention all the endangered species begging for a soft berth in a zoo. And what about the rain forests gorging themselves on our carbon dioxide? Or the lab animals enjoying the nice, clean, high-tech decor at the National Institutes of Health—all at the taxpayers' expense?

We wouldn't put up with that kind of mooching from people, so why do we have to take it from pandas? Maybe it's time we said, "Sayonara, fellas, you go your way, we'll go ours!"

Some of us still get all weepy when we think about the Gaia Hypothesis, the idea that the earth is a big furry goddess-creature who resembles everybody's mom in that she knows what's best for us. But if you look at the historical record—Krakatoa, Mt. Vesuvius, Hurricane Charley, poison ivy, and so forth down the ages—you have to ask yourself: Whose side is she on, anyway? And even if you love your mom, does that mean you have to *live* with her forever?

I'll admit I still get a tiny bit depressed when I try to think about it from her point of view. Imagine spending 4 billion years stocking the oceans with seafood, filling the ground with fossil fuels, and drilling the bees in honey production—only to produce a race of bed-wetters!

Maybe we're not 100 percent ready to set aside the environment and strike out on our own as a species. Maybe we should do something while there's still time, something *really* militant; like, maybe we should make buttons saying, "Thank you for not dumping, defecating, or defoliating. Thanks *awfully!*"

[1988]

Our Neighborhood Porn Committee

●···●···●···●···●···●

EVER SINCE THE ATTORNEY GENERAL declared open season on smut, I've had my work cut out for me. I'm referring, of course, to the Meese commission's report on pornography, which urges groups of private citizens to go out and fight the vile stuff with every means at hand—spray paint, acetylene torches, garlic, and crucifixes. In the finest spirit of grass-roots democracy, the commission is leaving it up to us to decide what to slash and burn and what to leave on the library shelves. Not that we are completely without guidance in this matter, for Commissioner Frederick Schauer ("golden Schauer" to those wild and crazy boys at *Penthouse*) quotes approvingly a deceased judge's definition of hard-core porn: "I know it when I see it."

Well, so do I, thanks to the report's thoughtful assertions that pornography is something that "hurts women" and, in particular, "bears a causal relationship to the incidence of various nonviolent forms of discrimination against or subordination of women in our society." My little group of citizens—recruited from the PTA, Parents Without Partners, and the YWCA aerobics class—decided to go straight to the heart of the matter: all written, scrawled, and otherwise-depicted manifestations of sexism, whether found on daytime TV, in the great classics of Western civilization, or in the published opinions of Donald ("women can't understand arms control") Regan.

I can understand why the commission decided to restrict its own inquiry to the sexier varieties of sexism, commonly known as pornography. How often, after all, does a group composed largely of white male Republicans (you will pardon the redundancy) get to spend months poring over material that would normally only be available in dark little shops on the seamy, low-rent side of town, and to do so entirely at public expense?

But with all due respect, I believe they erred by so limiting themselves. Violence against women, to take the most unpleasant form of "subordination," predates the commercial porn industry by several millennia. Those Romans who perpetrated the rape of the Sabines, for example, did not work themselves up for the deed by screening *Debbie Does Dallas*, and the monkish types who burned a million or so witches in the Middle Ages had almost certainly not come across *Boobs and Buns* or related periodicals.

I thought my citizens' group should start its search for materials damaging to women with the Bible, on the simple theory that anything read by so many people must have something to do with all the wickedness in the world. "Gather around," I said to my fellow citizens. "If those brave souls on the Meese commission could wade through the likes of *Fellatio Frolics* and *Fun with Whips and Chains*, we can certainly get through Genesis."

It was rough going, let me tell you, what with the incest (Lot and his daughters), mass circumcisions, adultery, and various spillings of seed. But duty triumphed over modesty, and we were soon rewarded with examples of sexism so crude and so nasty that they would make *The Story of O* look like suffragist propaganda. There was the part about Eve and her daughters being condemned to bring forth their offspring in sorrow, and numerous hints that the bringing forth of offspring is in fact the only thing women have any business doing. There were injunctions against public speaking by women, and approving descriptions of a patriarchal dynasty extending, without the least

concern for affirmative action, for countless generations from
Isaac on. And then there were the truly kinky passages on the
necessity of "submitting" to one's husband—an obvious invitation to domestic mayhem.

We wasted no time in calling the newly installed Meese commission hot line to report we had discovered material—widely
advertised as "family" reading—that would bring a blush to the
cheek of dear Dr. Ruth and worry lines to the smooth brow of
Gloria Steinem. "Well, yes," said the commissioner who picked
up the phone, "but could this material be used as a masturbatory
aid? Is it designed to induce sexual arousal in all but the most
priggish Presbyterian? Because it's the arousal, you know, that
reinforces the sexism, transforming normal, everyday male chauvinism into raging misogyny."

We argued that we had seen a number of TV preachers in
states of arousal induced by this book, and that, furthermore,
religious ecstasy might be far more effective at reinforcing sexism than any mere tickle of genital response. But we reluctantly
agreed to stop our backyard Bible burnings and to try to focus on
material that is more violent, up-to-date, and preferably, with
better visuals.

A week later we called the hot line to report we'd seen *Cobra*,
Raw Deal, three episodes of *Miami Vice*, and a presidential address on the importance of Star Wars, and felt we now had material that was not only damaging to women but disrespectful of
human life in all forms, male and female, born and unborn. "But
is it dirty?" asked a weary commissioner. "You know, *sexy?*" And
we had to admit that neither the sight of Arnold Schwarzenegger
without a shirt nor the president in pancake makeup had ever
aroused in us any feeling other than mild intestinal upset.

Now I think we're finally getting the hang of it. The problem,
as identified by the Meese commission, isn't violence, sexism,
or even sexual violence. The problem is sex, particularly those
varieties of sex that might in any way involve women. So in the
last few weeks, our citizens' antismut group has short-circuited

six vibrators, burned three hundred of those lurid little inserts found in Tampax boxes, and shredded half the local supply of *Our Bodies, Ourselves*. It's a tough job, believe me, but as Ed Meese keeps telling us, someone's got to do it.

[1986]

Drug Frenzy

●‥●‥●‥●‥●‥●‥●

IF THERE IS ANYTHING more mind-altering—more destructive to reason and common sense than drugs—it must be drug frenzy. Early signs include memory loss, an inability to process simple facts, an unnatural braying of the voice, and a belligerent narrowing of the eyes. Almost everyone is susceptible: liberals and conservatives, presidential candidates and PTA moms, the up-and-coming and the down-and-out. In fact, even *drug users*—a category that, scientifically speaking, embraces wine-sippers and chocolate addicts—are not immune.

Drug frenzy is not, as many people like to think, just a quick and harmless high. It is an obsession, overshadowing all other concerns, and capable of leaving a society drained, impotent, and brain-damaged. The candidates have made drugs a top issue in the presidential campaign—second only to the pledge of allegiance. It easily overwhelms poverty, homelessness, and the federal debt. The worst thing you can say about a candidate is not that he's a fool or a faker, but that he isn't "tough enough on drugs." In foreign policy, drugs have replaced communism as the scourge of the earth, and when we can't depose a Third World strongman, we indict him for dealing.

Our civil liberties may be the most serious casualty of the frenzy: boats and cars are being confiscated for containing as little as a tenth of a gram of marijuana. The Supreme Court has ruled that the police have a right to search your garbage—and they're not after the five-cent deposits on your soda-pop cans.

There seems to be no stopping drug frenzy once it takes hold of a nation. What starts with an innocuous HUGS, NOT DRUGS bumper sticker soon leads to wild talk of shooting dealers and making urine tests a condition for employment—anywhere. The Reagan administration would like to change a 110-year-old law prohibiting military involvement in domestic matters in order to unleash the armed forces in the "war" on drugs. There's talk of issuing "drug-war bonds," and worse talk about incarcerating drug offenders in "prison tents" to be set up in the Nevada desert. In drug frenzy, as in drug addiction, the threshold for satisfaction just keeps rising.

Now I have as much reason to worry about drugs as anyone. I am the mother of teenagers. I am also, it pains me to admit in print, the daughter of drug-abusers. But the drugs that worry me the most, the drugs that menaced my own childhood, are not the drugs that our current drug warriors are going after. Because the most dangerous drugs in America are *legal* drugs.

Consider the facts: Tobacco, which the surgeon general recently categorized as an addictive drug, kills over 300,000 people a year. Alcohol, which is advertised on television and sold in supermarkets, is responsible for as many as 200,000 deaths annually, including those caused by drunk drivers. But the use of all illegal drugs combined—cocaine, heroin, marijuana, angel dust, LSD, etc.—accounted for only 3,403 deaths in 1987. That's 3,403 deaths too many, but it's less than 1 percent of the death toll from the perfectly legal, socially respectable drugs that Americans—including drug warriors—indulge in every day.

Alcohol is the drug that undid my parents. When my own children reached the age of exploration, I said all the usual things —like "No." I further told them that reality, if carefully attended to, is more exotic than its chemically induced variations. But I also said that, if they still felt they had to get involved with a drug, I'd rather it was pot than Bud.

If that sounds like strange advice, consider the facts: Unlike

alcohol, cocaine, and heroin, marijuana is not addictive. Twenty
million Americans—from hard hats to hippies—use it regularly.
In considering whether to legalize it for medicinal purposes, a
federal appeals court judge found that "marijuana, in its natural
form, is one of the safest therapeutically active substances
known to man." And unlike alcohol use, a frequent factor in
crimes like child abuse, marijuana does not predispose its users
to violence.

Not that marijuana is harmless. Although marijuana is not
chemically addictive, some people do become sufficiently dependent on it to seek help. According to the National Institute
of Drug Abuse, however, there are no deaths that can be un-
equivocally attributed to marijuana use. Five thousand "mari-
juana-related" hospital emergencies were reported in 1987, but
80 percent of these were known to involve another drug—most
commonly alcohol. Nor is there any clear evidence that marijuana "leads to" harder drugs, unless you count alcohol and the
occasional truly dire drugs, such as PCP, that have been known
to contaminate marijuana bought from street dealers. Taken
alone, and in moderation, it is still the safest "high" on the
market.

But one of the first symptoms of drug frenzy is an inability to
make useful distinctions of any kind. The drug that set off the
"war," the drug that is enslaving ghetto youth and enlisting
them into gunslinging gangs, is cocaine, specifically crack. But
who remembers crack? We're after "drugs"! In an alarming example of drug-frenzied thinking, a recent *Time* magazine drug
cover story lumped cocaine, heroin, and marijuana together as
the evil drugs in question. Nineteen years ago, before drug-
frenzy-induced brain damage set in, *Time* was still able to make
distinctions, as this quote from the January 5, 1970, issue shows:
". . . the widespread use of marijuana, sometimes by their own
children, is leading many Middle Americans toward a bit more
sophistication, an ability to distinguish between the use of pot
and harder drugs."

So what turned all these sober Middle Americans into drug-frenzied hawks? Historians point out that Americans have long been prone to episodes of "moral panic." One year it's communism; the next it's missing children—or terrorism, or AIDS, or cyanide-laced cold pills.

Usually, the targeted issue conceals a deeper anxiety. For example, as historian Barbara Epstein has argued, the late nineteenth-and-early-twentieth-century temperance crusade—which was every bit as maniacal as today's war on drugs—was only incidentally about alcohol. The real issue was women's extreme vulnerability within the "traditional marriage." Husbands leave, husbands get violent, husbands drink. But you couldn't very well run a mass crusade to abolish *husbands* or—in the nineteenth century—to renegotiate the entire institution of marriage. The demon rum became what the psychohistorians call a "condensed symbol" of male irresponsibility and female vulnerability—focusing the sense of outrage that might otherwise have gone into the search for radical, feminist alternatives.

Drugs also play a powerful symbolic role in our culture. Generically speaking, we imagine drugs as a kind of pact with the devil: What you get is ecstasy or something pretty similar. But the price you pay is eternal thralldom, dependency, loss of self. Only a few drugs—"hard" ones—actually fit our imaginings. But in mundane, drugless, ordinary life, we're offered a deal like this every other minute: buy this—sports car, condo, cologne, or whatever—and you'll be happy, suave, sexy . . . forever!

We are talking about the biggest pusher of all—the thoroughly legal and entirely capitalist consumer culture. No street-corner crack dealer ever had a better line than the one Madison Avenue delivers at every commercial break: Buy now! Quick thrills! You deserve it! And, of course, we love it—all those *things*, all those *promises*! If we could only have a little *more*! But, deep down, we also mortally resent it, this incessant, hard-sell seduction. The sports car does not bring fulfillment; the cologne does not bring love. And still the payments are due . . . .

Drug frenzy, we might as well acknowledge, is displaced rage at the consumer culture to which we are all so eagerly, morbidly addicted. Consider this recent statement in *Time* magazine by Harvard psychiatrist Robert Coles, who is otherwise a pretty thoughtful guy. We can't legalize drugs, he said (including, presumably, marijuana), because to do so would constitute a "moral surrender," sending what *Time* called "a message of unrestricted hedonism." What a quaint concern! We are already getting "a message of unrestricted hedonism" every time we turn on the TV, glance at a billboard, or cruise a mall. But we can't very well challenge *that* message, or *its* sender, even as mounting debt— personal and social—gives that message a mean and mocking undertone.

So we feed our legal addictions and vent our helplessness in a fury at drugs. We buy our next chance at "ecstasy" on credit and despise those poor depraved fools who steal for heroin or kill for crack. The word for this is "projection," and it's the oldest, most comforting form of self-delusion going.

The only hopeful sign I can see is the emerging debate on drug legalization. The advocates of legalization, who include such straitlaced types as the New York County Lawyers' Association's Committee on Law Reform, argue that drug *prohibition* has become far more dangerous than drug abuse. Prohibition causes about 7,000 deaths a year (through drug-related crime, AIDS, and poisoned drugs) and an $80-billion-a-year economic loss. And prohibition drives up the price of drugs, making dealing an attractive career for the unemployed as well as the criminally inclined.

There are problems with wholesale legalization: crack, for example, is so highly addictive and debilitating that it probably shouldn't be available. But I agree with the *New York Times* that we should consider legalizing marijuana. We could then tax the estimated $50 billion spent annually on it and use the revenue to treat people who want to get off the hard drugs, including alcohol and tobacco.

But we're not even going to be able to have a sane debate about legalization until we come down off the drug frenzy. The only cure is a sturdy dose of truth, honesty, and self-knowledge

—and those things do not, ancient countercultural lore to the contrary, come from drugs. Since there's no drug for drug frenzy, we're all just going to have to sit down, cold sober, to face the hard questions: who's hurting, what's hurting them, and what, in all kindness and decency, we can do about it.

[1988]

Someone You Know?

●··●··●···●··●··●···●··●

"ANNE" ACTS LIKE a fugitive from justice. She agreed to talk to me only on condition that I not use her real name or any other detail—physical or geographical—that might identify her. Still, she was nervous, moving from the sofa to a straight chair and back, fussing with the magazines on the coffee table, refilling our mugs with tea. When the doorbell rang halfway through our talk, she snatched up the book she had brought out to show me and put it away in another room before going to the door. The book was the *AIDS Information Resources Directory* and Anne has been "underground," in her own personal way, since she found out, just a few months ago, that her son had tested positive for the AIDS virus.

Until the moment when AIDS entered her life, Anne was not the kind of person who had to jump when the doorbell rang. She was a community activist in her suburban town, branching outward, over the years, from PTA to environmental and feminist issues. "Warm and funny" were the words a mutual friend used to describe Anne—the old Anne, that is. Her husband is a respected local businessman. Her son is still famous among the science teachers at the high school where he graduated, with highest honors, only a half-dozen years ago.

But now, in the worst crisis of her life, Anne is watching her social world shrink in around her. Parties and potluck dinners are out. "I'm just not the old ha-ha person I was before," Anne explains. When her husband, Jim, is home, it's his job to answer the phone. Anne herself is long past small talk. "When I can't talk about *this*, well, there's nothing much to say," and it is axiomatic, in Anne's world, that you can't talk about "this."

I had thought we were, collectively, at a somewhat higher point of consciousness. Movie stars talk about AIDS, so does the surgeon general and, I presume, the average high school soccer coach-turned-sex-educator. Looking for the upbeat, I had gotten the impression that America was mobilizing around AIDS— marching on Washington, making quilts, organizing new services, searching its soul. I hadn't really noticed how *few* people were doing the mobilizing. So I wasn't prepared to find the people at the heart of the crisis—those with the virus or the disease and those who love them—so totally alone.

"Why all the secrecy?" I asked, wondering if Anne wasn't being more paranoid than the cultural mores of 1989 require. First, she explained, there are the "practical" problems: Her son doesn't live in the same town, but if word of his condition were somehow to leak out to his employer, he would probably lose his job. If he lost his job, he would lose his health insurance, and the medical bills—for checkups and for an alarming fungal infection—are already running into hundreds of dollars a month.

Then, if word got out, he would probably lose his apartment —his last claim on an independent life and a future of his own. And "future" is not out of place in this context. It is a concept that still applies—or ought to—to people who are HIV-positive, people with AIDS-related complex, and even people with AIDS.

After the "practical" reasons, Anne comes to "stigma," though the distinction here is a fine one. Anne's town is not Greenwich Village or San Francisco. Even the local AIDS hot line does not give out *locations* of services or events without screening people over the phone. Nothing has happened yet, but Anne tells me of a family in a nearby town whose garage door was spray-painted "AIDS" in oversize letters after neighbors figured out why the ailing son was living at home again.

Jim's business could suffer. "There are a lot of families in the
suburbs now," Anne says, "whose sons are dying of 'leuke-
mia.' "

Anne has her own reasons, too, for withdrawing. "I can't be
around anyone who ever made a homophobic remark in my presence, I just can't." This eliminates most family members and
the two women who were Anne's closest friends for years. "And
I'm not about to tell anyone," she tells me in a hard voice,
"whose first response is going to be, 'Oh, but I didn't even know
he was gay!' "

Then there are the people who just drift away on their own.
A couple that Anne describes as once being "wonderful and
generous" called to find out where Jim and Anne had been keeping themselves these days. Jim told them, breaking down in
tears for what was probably the first time in his adult life. That
was all these "wonderful" people needed to hear. They didn't
call for five weeks, and when they did call, it was to borrow a
punch bowl—not a word about the tragedy that was closing in
around their friends. "It's too heavy," Anne frowns. "No one
wants to deal with it."

Slowly, Anne and Jim have been reaching out for support.
"This is not something that can stay within a marriage," Anne
says, and it's hard to imagine any relationship being large enough
for so much pain. "If I'm upset, Jim gets impatient, but if he's
upset—and he'll shut himself in the bedroom sometimes for
hours—I go, 'Oh, no, why don't I just kill myself now?' but of
course you have to be strong, even if it's the biggest act you ever
put on."

But the support Anne has been able to find is coming almost
entirely from people who have already learned to live in the
shadow of AIDS. PFLAG (Parents and Friends of Lesbians and
Gays) led them to a therapist who happens to be a lesbian and
doesn't mind talking about AIDS. The local hot line led them to
a weekly meeting for HIV-positive people and their loved ones.
A newsletter also helped Anne track down two programs specifi-

cally for *mothers*—MAP (Mothers of AIDS Patients) in Los Angeles and one at AIDS Family Service of New York. These groups are too far away to attend, but they've provided Anne with new, long-distance friends—other mothers "who don't mind dropping everything to talk for a while."

There's a problem with Anne's new support network, though. It's "all AIDS," as she says, and AIDS is not a monolithic condition. Some of the parents Anne is thrown in with are grieving for their dead. Some have sons who, like Anne's, are not sick at all, only HIV-positive, and who may have years to live. But the world of AIDS support is not yet large enough to make distinctions. Anne has already left one support group because she "wasn't ready" to be around mothers who are caring for dying sons (or, more rarely, daughters). In the narrow world she has entered, the entire crisis—from the first positive test, through illness, dying, and bereavement—tends to be condensed into a single, overwhelmingly crushing trauma.

Anne is deeply grateful to her support network and has even begun to volunteer on the hot line, but she would also like to rejoin the "mainstream." She wishes she would get phone calls now and then from people whose lives aren't already marked by AIDS—people who just care about her, and about her husband and son. "It wouldn't take much," she says, "to make me feel *connected* again." But prejudice has pushed her—along with millions of others, gay and straight, already afflicted and just "at risk"—into a shrinking world of secrecy and dread.

I left Anne's feeling vague shame for people like myself, the "mainstream" majority whose lives have so far not been touched directly by AIDS. Americans, I've always liked to think, are stand-up folks when it comes to helping out. Earthquake victims, crippled children, a baby trapped in a well—even a trapped *whale*—inspire our contributions and tearful sympathy. But not AIDS victims and their families. As Susan Sontag argues in her book *AIDS and Its Metaphors*, we don't tend to see AIDS as a disease like any other, we see it as a "metaphor"—a moral allegory of sin and punishment. Anne is living this metaphor: isolated from the community she belonged to, as if she had done something horribly, unforgivably wrong.

Maybe we *should* be thinking of AIDS as a metaphor. Maybe we should be thinking of it, however, not as a judgment but as a test. Except that the people who are being tested are not people like Anne or her husband or son. They are the rest of us, people who have been fortunate enough to be able to see AIDS as "someone else's problem." This is a test of our fundamental morality, of our ability to reach out—in the most simple and banal ways—to those who hurt. And what I learned from Anne is that, so far, this is a test that we have failed.

[1989]

DEMOCRACY
IN DECAY

●···●··●···●··●···●··●···●

Automating Politics

•··•··•··•··•··•··•··•

I WAS RAISED the old-fashioned way, with a stern set of moral principles: Never lie, cheat, steal, or knowingly spread a venereal disease. Never speed up to hit a pedestrian or, of course, stop to kick a pedestrian who has already been hit. From which it followed, of course, that one would never, ever—on pain of deletion from dozens of Christmas card lists across the country—vote Republican.

But that was in the old days before the political process had been fully automated. Back then, the parties actually had *members*, and the members went to *club meetings*, and argued and factionalized and held spaghetti dinners and canvased their wards and otherwise engaged in what was called "politics"— before that word was downgraded to shorthand for lying, cheating, and the rest of it.

Some oldsters say the first step to automation was the automatic voting booth, which eliminated the handcrafted X and gave the voter the sensation—not of stepping into the political process—but *out*, as it were, to take a leak. Then came computerized polling, which eliminated the canvasing and spaghetti dinners. Then came the televised campaign commercial, which eliminated the issues and, hence, the arguments.

But the final step was taken only recently, probably in the late seventies, when some young political software genius noticed that it was possible to hook up the various pieces of electronic hardware—the voting machines, the polling computers, the television sets—up to each other in one vast closed circuit extending from Iowa and New Hampshire right through Washington, D.C. In other words, it was possible at long last to *take the voters out of the loop*.

The Republicans were the first to apply the new technology, because—possessed of assets on the scale of the federal deficit —they had never needed people anyway. But the Democrats added an ingenious touch of their own. Not content to electronically eliminate the membership, the party Insiders sought to robotize their conventions with the introduction of "Superdelegates." These life-size, male-looking, fully-programmed delegoids are manufactured in a huge shed outside Memphis where —party Insiders assure us—they are assembled by union labor using very few parts from Taiwan.

But why, you may wonder, would a party—especially the party of the "average guy" and the "common folk"—want to shed its members and constituencies? For two good reasons, the Insiders will tell you: First, because people introduce a dangerous element of uncertainty into the electoral process—no matter how thoroughly they have been polled by the pollsters or coached by the commercials. Secondly, the presence of people tempts candidates to make reckless promises, such as catastrophic dental insurance and reduced highway tolls. And if there is one thing no up-to-date, high-tech candidate wants to be accused of, it is "pandering"—to anyone, including the voters.

Most people took the hint and began to register as Independents, if they registered at all. There was still the problem of shaking the last few clingy die-hards, and the solution to this was the 1984 Democratic campaign. Nineteen eighty-four, as any Insider could tell you, was designed as a form of aversion therapy for any lingering party loyalists.

Yes, there was a woman on the ticket, but this was a ruse designed to flush out the millions of female party members who did not realize that they had become an unwholesome "special interest" dragging down the party. When they called by the thousands, volunteering their services to the campaign, they were greeted by a recorded message saying, "You have reached the Democratic party. Thank you for your interest in the democratic process. . . ."

Most of the remaining Democratic constituencies were easily repelled by Walter Mondale's campaign, which only proved Harry Truman's old adage: "When the voters have a choice between a Republican and a Republican, they'll choose the Republican every time." Throughout the eighties, party Insiders kept the voters at bay with the catchwords "growth," "strength," and "family," which everyone recognized as the kind of vocabulary a pediatrician might employ in discussing a four-year-old.

Everything might have proceeded smoothly to full mechanization if the Jackson campaign had not thrown an enormous monkey wrench into the process. As he swept through the primaries, gaining strength from state to state, party Insiders began to speak of him in terms of "dilemma," "quandary," and finally "crisis." The problem was not that he was "unelectable" (at least this had never been viewed as a drawback in twenty years of Democratic candidacies). Nor was it, as some Insiders claimed, that Jackson was "the extreme left" (for the record, Jackson is a liberal; *I* am the "extreme left").

The problem was *people*. Enraptured by Jackson's bold talk of empowerment and justice, millions of them, of all genders and hues, came pushing and shoving their way back into the political process, trampling important pieces of political machinery underfoot.

Naturally, the Insider reaction will be to dispatch these Luddites as quickly as possible back to the state of comatose apathy normally inhabited by the voting public. But there is an alternative. We could make politics *labor-intensive* once again; reactivate the clubs, the canvasing, the arguments, the spaghetti dinners. We could let people *back into the loop*.

"But we can't do that," groaned a faceless Insider I was able to reach by advanced electronic methods of communication, "because then we'll *owe* them something!" Exactly so; the price of labor-intensive politics will be *people*-oriented programs; national health care, housing subsidies, child care, high-wage jobs, better schools. . . . Not to mention a little room on the Inside.

Of course, there's always the argument that it's more cost-effective for the party to owe nothing to anyone except the few rich folks who currently subsidize the computers and the commercials. But rich folks already have a party, and a grand old one at that. It's the rest of us who need one.

[1988]

The Liberals'
Disappearing Act

●··●··●··●··●··●··●··●

THE DEMOCRATIC PARTY, which was once thought to be an essential ingredient of the two-party system, has gone underground. This is, of course, a time-honored way of responding to political adversity, and the Democrats arranged their disappearance with the thoroughness of a Communist party cell preparing for the Nazi occupation.

First there was a long silence, after which party chairman Paul Kirk announced a meditative retreat in search of "new ideas," which optimists interpreted as a code for "while male voters." But it soon emerged that no voters at all were being sought. Loyal rank-and-file members—the women, minorities, union members, environmentalists, gays, consumers, etc., known in eighties political jargon as "special interests"—were asked to burn their voter registration cards and withdraw discreetly into private life.

As if to set an example, leading figures like Ted Kennedy and Geraldine Ferraro surfaced briefly to announce that they would no longer be available to run for high office and would be acquiring unlisted phone numbers. In New York, longtime liberal favorite Carol Bellamy, no doubt acting under party orders, actually assumed a new identity as an investment banker. This left the donkey as the only high-profile Democrat in public life, until the party announced that it would be put out to pasture until a

more appropriate mascot could be found, possibly one of the
nocturnal-feeding mammals.

To be perfectly nonpartisan about all this, I should say that
the existence of the Republican party has also been in doubt for
some years now. There are no known Republican volunteers or,
in most places, local headquarters. There may not even be any
flesh-and-blood Republican elected officials—only that genial
holographic projection that we know as President Reagan and a
row of congressional P.O. boxes manned by Richard Viguerie.
But then, the Republicans hardly need a party and the cumber-
some cadre of low-level officials that go with one; they have a
bankroll as large as the Pentagon's budget, dozens of fatted
PACs, and the well-advertised support of the Christian deity.

It is not the Democratic party that I will miss, so much as the
liberals who once gave it its distinctive character. Since the word
itself has almost dropped from our political vocabulary, I should
explain that "liberal" was not always used in a loose way to cover
everyone from sex eduators to socialists. In fact, traditional liberals had nothing against capitalism or what we now call "free
enterprise." They believed it was a fine idea—except for a few
rough edges (poverty, unemployment, discrimination, for example) that could be smoothed out by judicious government action.
Thus Hubert Humphrey was a liberal; Malcolm X was not—a
distinction that is, of course, meaningless from the vantage point
of the Moral Majority or the Christian Broadcasting Network.

Some of the most outstanding liberals (the elder Kennedy
brothers, Martin Luther King, Jr.) died highly unnatural deaths;
others (Walter Mondale) have appeared to be suffering from
wasting diseases. Most of the erstwhile liberals, however, have
no such excuse: they slunk off on their own into the mists of
political obfuscation and reaction. First to go was the small circle
of once-liberal New York intellectuals who renamed themselves
"neoconservatives," which the reader will recognize as Latinate
for New Right. Next to defect was a group of younger men who
might have called themselves neoconservatives if they had lived

in New York and been friends with Norman Podhoretz, but instead were stuck with the more compromising term "neo-liberal." With "neo" used up and "new" already getting a bit worn, the latest refugees from liberalism have been commissioning polls to test "moderate," "populist," and "progressive"— and although it hasn't been mentioned yet, someone is bound to come up with "tory."

Why so many well-known liberals have chosen to change their names (literally, in the case of Gary Hart, né Hartpence) and go underground is not entirely clear. There have been no pogroms, no lynch mobs besetting liberals on the street. In fact, the label of liberalism is hardly a sentence to public ignominy: otherwise Bruce Springsteen would still be rehabilitating used Cadillacs in Asbury Park and Jane Fonda, for all we know, would be just another overweight housewife.

Nor can it be said that liberalism has been defeated in the realm of ideas. The traditional liberal goals—such as national health insurance, adequate income supports for the poor, publicly supported child care, and so forth—all of which are now known as "old ideas," are simply the decent, obvious ideas that most civilized nations have already put into practice. But for the right, the only truly new ideas it has come up with in the last twenty years are (1) supply-side economics, which is a way of redistributing the wealth upward toward those who already have more than they know what to do with, and (2) creationism, which is a parallel idea for redistributing ignorance out from its fundamentalist strongholds to those who know more than they need to.

Apparently, liberalism just went out of style—at least among the influential upper middle class—more or less like wide ties, gold chains, and broccoli quiche. The right had something to do with this, of course. One of its most venerable themes is that real men don't get all hot and bothered by issues like poverty, inequality, or the nuclear threat; only women and wimps vote liberal. More recently, rightists have added the charge that liberalism is "elitist," which is tantamount to arguing that programs like Medicare and Social Security are an aristocratic plot while corporate welfarism is the will of the masses.

But if there is one thing an elite hates—especially a low-level, insecure elite—it is to be detected and labeled: witness the swift backlash against the perfectly accurate and sociologically brilliant notion of "yuppies." Tell a certain class of man that he must be a liberal if he likes Chablis, or that he must be a sissy if he's inclined toward arms control, and he'll soon be spouting Reaganisms over his beer.

The sad result of the liberals' disappearance is that there has been no organized, principled, mainstream opposition to the real elite—the corporate elite that is so ably represented by the Republican right. True, there have been scattered skirmishes over the price of the Pentagon's ashtrays and the administration's moves to free the superrich from the burden of taxation. And there has been just enough congressional resistance to keep Reagan from scrapping Social Security, rescinding the food stamp program, or leasing the Vietnam Veterans Memorial to a theme park. But there has been no consistent and audible dissent from the overall direction the right is taking us: no voice to utter the old liberal truism that government belongs to the people—not to the highest bidder—and exists to make things better for them.

Ironically, while our political leaders have been abandoning liberalism for the various neo-isms, the general public has been becoming *more* liberal than it was before the age of Reagan. They may have voted for a Republican president, but in poll after poll they favor cuts in military spending and increases in domestic social spending—and to a greater extent than they did in 1980. And my source on this, incidentally, is not some wishful-thinking left-wing professor, but one of the charter members of the neoconservative clique, Seymour Martin Lipset. Asked the right questions ("Mondale or Reagan?" not being one of them), the public is liberal, but unfortunately there are very few public figures left to translate their liberal sentiments into public policy—or even to echo them in public debate.

But politicians are nothing if not opportunists, and for that reason alone liberalism should soon be back in style, probably rediscovered first by the neoconservatives, who will no doubt call themselves something fancy like "paleo-Democrats." The more prescient thinkers of the New Right will not be far behind; at least the Heritage Foundation—sobered by its own poll results showing startling levels of public support for Aid to Families with Dependent Children—is currently rethinking the merits of the welfare state. The neoliberals will insist they never lost the faith and announce that public spending for the public good is the new idea they've been waiting for all along. Finally, Paul Kirk and his band of partisans will emerge, pale and dazed, from their survivalist holdout in the Carlsbad Caverns and offer to lead the liberal renaissance.

I can't wait for the liberals to make a comeback, and not because I am one of them. When the liberals went underground, it was left to the rejects of the Democratic party—the feminists, peace activists, rainbow coalitionists, socialists, union militants —to hold up the liberal banner. We were left to defend social programs, like welfare and Medicaid, that were never halfway adequate in the first place, and to argue—a little wearily—for the mild reforms that might make life marginally more secure for the average person. What else was there to do in such a desolate political landscape, with no one—except perhaps George Bush and a few neoliberals—occupying the long expanse between us, on the left, and the likes of Jimmy Swaggart on the far, far right? But if the Democrats find the courage to get back to their business—working for the slow and piecemeal reform of our far-from-perfect society—maybe we'll be able to get back to ours. And that is, as it has always been, to insist that slow and piecemeal reform is just not good enough.

[1986]

The Unfastened Head of State

●··●··●··●··●··●··●

SOMEDAY OUR GRANDCHILDREN will look up at us and say, "Where were you, Grandma, and what were you doing when you first realized that President Reagan was, er, not playing with a full deck?" One of my neighbors says she was vacuuming when it dawned on her that a man who believes that a thousand TOW missiles could easily be carried on board an airliner and stored in the overhead baggage rack might be, as they put it in junior high, *unfastened*.

I myself was in the kitchen, chuckling fondly at one of the president's witticisms, when the truth dawned on me. Discounting worries about his age—at the time only a verdant seventy-four—he had quipped that he was not really as old as people thought, because they had "switched babies in the hospital." "Ha, ha, switched him with an *old* baby," I thought, and then felt myself freeze in horror as the concept hit me with full force. Just how old do babies get, anyway?

The editors of *Newsweek* were, as far as I can reconstruct, gathered in the executive conference room cooking up a cover story on missing sexually abused infant crack addicts when they stumbled on the truth. A frantic copy editor broke in, waving the president's latest statement on Iranscam ("I've taken all these steps to find out the facts and to fix what went wrong . . . and I really mean—all of these indications that maybe I know more than I'm talking about. . ."), which was about to be type-set under the headline "Reagan Clears Air, Scandal Subsides."

"The president used a transitive verb," gasped the copy editor, "but there's no direct object in sight." "Possibly some odd California usage," suggested a senior editor, "a variant of 'like I mean, *really*.' " But, too late, a queasy silence had settled over the room. "Maybe the rumor's true," whispered the science editor, "about that last-ditch effort to transplant Casey's brain—or was it just the tumor?—to the commander-in-chief. . . ."

By sometime in early 1987, every last member of the electorate had figured out that the president was not all there, out to lunch, or—as we have learned to put it delicately—*cognitively impaired*. Already, there is talk of bypassing impeachment and going straight for a medical discharge—or simply hoping that the next surgeon to tackle the polyps *is* a Republican, under party orders.

But is this any way to treat the cognitively impaired? We do not, after all, toss around epithets like *crip* anymore when we could say *disabled*, or *disabled* when we really mean *differently abled*. Surely the more sensitive among us know better than to grease the floor in front of an old person coming by on a walker, or to direct one of the visually impaired into the path of a deregulated Mack truck.

So it is hard to believe that, in this enlightened age, a man can be treated like a day-old rutabaga for an impairment that is certainly no worse than the one poor Caligula developed, back in the old days, from the toxic levels of lead in the local vintages. In fact, why shouldn't one of the cognitively impaired be president?

Oh, I can imagine the pious objections. First, of course, there is the matter of "details," a White House "detail" being any fact of less sweeping world historic importance than the absolute perfidy of the Soviet Union—for example, the location of Yemen or the names of the cabinet members. Well, I would remind you that the last president to have any command of details, Jimmy Carter, once reported that he had been attacked by a killer rabbit

—while canoeing!—and no one suggested a psychiatric fur-
lough.

Then there is the objection that many chiefs of state, whom
the president must meet in the course of his work, are not "differently abled" at all. We strain to imagine what went on, for
example, in the mysterious encounter in Reykjavík. But what
would be wrong with having heads of state relate to a cognitively
impaired president on *his own* terms? In fact, wouldn't it do more
for the cause of peace if they abandoned those boring, technical
discussions of missile payloads and just got down on the floor
together for an afternoon of simple board games and movie
trivia?

So let's set aside our archaic prejudices toward the differently
abled. Let Reagan be Reagan and let Nancy assume powers of
attorney. Some of the current staff will have to go, of course.
They should be replaced by professionals, as everyone has been
saying all along—neurologists, registered nurses, psychiatric social workers, who will henceforth accompany the president
everywhere in a little white-robed cluster.

Not that it will always be smooth sailing, relating to a cognitively impaired president. At times, we will all feel irritated,
impatient, even outraged. But we can learn much about the day-
to-day management of the cognitively impaired from the ladies
and gentlemen of the press. Look at how patiently and support-
ively they have handled years of non sequiturs, run-on sen-
tences, lies, half-truths, and fantasies—as if nothing at all were
wrong!

Finally, think what we may have been spared by the president's impairment. He took office with the intention of, among
other things, abolishing domestic spending, paving over the national park system, and implementing Armageddon in our own
lifetime. Mercifully, he forgot much of this program, or else
confused it with Nancy's plan to renovate Camp David. And
whom do we have to thank for our temporary deliverance from
the right-wing agenda for America? Not the Democrats, who

spent most of the last six years cowering and weaseling in their warrens, but the sagging synapses of the presidential forebrain.

All in all, it will be a sad day when the president is forced to step down to make room for someone "normal"—which is bound to mean, in this line of business—one of the merely morally impaired.

[1987]

The Bathtub Tapes

●··●··●··●··●··●··●

WHEN HER HUSBAND was governor of California, Nancy
Reagan got into the habit of taking long baths, during which she
would hold "imaginary conversations" with anyone who had
ventured to say a mean thing about "Ronnie." These one-sided
conversations, presumably staged out loud, must have been
deeply satisfying. As Mrs. Reagan tell us, in a humorous tone,
"With nobody to answer back, I always came out the winner."
My Turn is the distilled bathwater of Mrs. Reagan's life. It is
for the most part sweetish, with a tart edge of rebuke, but dis-
appointingly free of dirt or particulate matter of any kind. We
learn, for example, that the Reagans eat eggs only once a week,
that Gorbachev had never had a soufflé until Mrs. Reagan served
him one, that Ronnie once taught his daughter Maureen to sing
"La Marseillaise," and that the Johnsons' china set, which has
the state flowers around the edge, was "more suitable for a lun-
cheon than a formal state dinner."
But of that great mystery of the eighties—when President
Reagan's mind unwrapped and who or what filled in for it—we
learn nothing except that Ronnie is often "remote" and, of
course, hard of hearing. Even on that secondary mystery of our
time—how the White House scheduling came to be entrusted
to a San Francisco astrologer (who, it should be noted, neglected
to warn us of the recent quake)—we learn nothing new except

that Mrs. Reagan now regards her superstition as a "habit." This is the Betty Ford defense, and comes as a mild surprise from the world's foremost advocate of saying no.

Most of the milestones of the Reagan years go unnoted here, or appear only as backdrops to some larger crisis of interior decoration. We hear nothing, for example, of the recession of 1982 and '83, of the savage cutbacks in social spending, of the wars in Central America, of the bombing of the Marines in Beirut, or the raid on Tripoli. Grenada is favored with a mention, but only because Ronnie announced the "rescue operation" to congressional leaders in the Yellow Oval Room:

> When we first moved in I found it cold . . . but over time, and with the addition of two sofas from storage, two or three coffee tables, porcelain figures, and other *objets*, the room seemed more inviting and became a favorite of mine.

No, the purpose of *My Turn* is not to inform or amuse, not even to absolve Mrs. Reagan of her reputation as a senescent bimbo with a lust for home furnishings. Instead, we are invited to appreciate how much she has suffered from hundreds of insults and slights, illnesses and assaults, over her years in public life. A few episodes of joy are recorded—inaugurations, an evening on a yacht with Queen Elizabeth II—but it is the pain that is meant to surprise and enlist us. The purpose is to make us pity her. And in this weary enterprise, she teaches by example.

She tells us at the outset that her eight years in the White House were "the most difficult years of my life." Her mother died; she underwent a mastectomy; Ronnie developed a cancerous polyp; Ronnie was shot—this last creating for Mrs. Reagan a trauma of equal magnitude: "His was mainly to the body; mine was to my spirit." These genuine trials are so magnified by the cruelty of the press and traitorous others—the Reagans' daughter Patti Davis, for example, or Don Regan —that at times we seem to be inching our way through a vale of tears. There must have been moments of surcease with Jerry Zipkin and the rest of Mrs. Reagan's airhead crowd, but none of these is recorded.

In the spirit of the bathtub soliloquies, the reader is forced to review numerous instances of calumny and disrespect. Each of these follows the same pattern, until a certain numbing rhythm sets in. First there is a statement of Mrs. Reagan's good and utterly reasonable intentions. The governor's mansion in Sacramento had to be replaced with a brand-new mansion because the old one was a fire hazard, and unsafe for little Ron. The White House, which could not be replaced, had to be expensively renovated because it was "shabby," plus "we actually found half-eaten sandwiches and empty beer cans in some of the drawers." And so on.

Next there is a summary of the vicious things said about the utterly reasonable intentions, often with the offending quotes masochistically reproduced. At this point, Mrs. Reagan is sustained by Clare Boothe Luce's comment, "No good deed goes unpunished," though other aphorisms, involving overly hot kitchens, spring immediately to mind. Certainly there is nothing in this book, or in other accounts of Mrs. Reagan's career, to suggest that she was dragged, limp and resisting, from Los Angeles to Sacramento, and from Sacramento to Washington.

Finally, there is the vindication, in which other voices are called upon to defend Mrs. Reagan's effort, or at least her intentions. Often these turn out to be the voices of Democrats, who serve no other role in *My Turn* except to round out the ritual of Ronnie's elections. Thus Tip O'Neill is cited enthusing over the White House renovation. Barbara Mikulski is recruited to endorse Mrs. Reagan's campaign against Don Regan. Margaret Truman weighs in on the side of the new china. My guess is that, in Mrs. Reagan's world, Democrats can serve as disinterested authorities simply because they are so peripheral to the crucial intrigues, not to mention frumpily dressed. Or perhaps she has simply intuited—post-Iranscam, post-HUD, post-Meese, Deaver, etc.—that credibility increases as one travels outward from the centers of Republican power.

But it is hard, even for a reader who has psyched herself into a mood of bipartisan sisterhood, to feel the sympathy Mrs. Reagan so obviously craves, in part because she herself has so little to offer. Envy, for example, is a major theme in *My Turn*, either attributed to others or expressed by Mrs. Reagan. She hypothesizes that some of the press's unkindness derives from female envy of her figure: "Some women aren't all that crazy about a woman who wears a size four." She suggests that Barry Goldwater refused to endorse Ronnie's presidential bid in 1976 only because he came "to resent Ronnie's leadership of the conservative movement." She herself was jealous of the superior box Betty Ford was assigned at the 1976 convention: "Maureen [Reagan] was convinced that this was done deliberately, to give the Fords an advantage." And when she observes that "although the White House is a state home, its scale is nothing like that of Buckingham Palace or Windsor Castle," I began to see how lightly we had gotten off in the matter of renovations.

Mrs. Reagan's pique is least becoming when directed within her family, at the errant daughter, Patti. It might be thought that young Ron, with his ballet career and *Playboy* assignments, would be a dubious asset with the fundamentalist crowd, but he comes off as an ideal son. Patti, however, can do nothing right. She became a radical in the sixties; she wrote an autobiographical novel in which Mrs. Reagan was portrayed as a cold and distracted mother; she was insufficiently nurturing after the mastectomy; she was even, it is revealed here, a bad baby:

> When we put her down at night, she would scream for hours —at least it *seemed* like hours. . . . There were also problems with eating. Sometimes after she had been fed she would lean over in her high chair and *throw* up. That was *lots* of fun, as you can imagine.

Except for the newly revealed capacity for self-pity, the picture that emerges in *My Turn* is not too different from the many unflattering portraits we have already seen: of a vain woman, forever checking out the female competition (Betty Ford, Geraldine Ferraro, Raisa Gorbachev), addicted to *objets*, and, of course, ferociously protective of her affable, out-to-lunch husband. Early in the book, she asserts that she does have "interests," but one waits in vain to find out what they are. Her best-advertised interest, the antidrug campaign, appears as from the clear blue sky, inspired by no moment of reflection or alarm. We are told only that it "stemmed from the values that Mother had embodied," but even this stunningly redundant explanation is lifted from someone else, her friend Mike Wallace.

So it is easy to forget, in the shallows of *My Turn*, that Mrs. Reagan has already *had* her turn, that she is not just your everyday aggrieved executive wife, struggling to keep up with her husband's career moves, "nesting" (to use one of her favorite words) in a series of barely habitable dwellings. As Ronnie slipped into personal reverie or the prodromal phase of Alzheimer's, she was making her stealthy advance on the presidency. She managed his schedule (with astral assistance, of course); she drove out the hateful Regan; she filled in for the cue cards that otherwise prefigured all presidential utterances. Recall her famous stage whisper to a drifting Ronnie, when a question was raised about arms control: "We're doing everything we can." Not "*Tell them* we're doing everything we can"; just the line itself, suggesting that an element of ventriloquism had entered into this fond relationship.

Behind the dizzying camouflage of borrowed gowns and extorted china, Mrs. Reagan carried on brilliantly. To be sure, she was hobbled by her inability to attend Cabinet meetings and by the fractiousness of Ronnie's various employees, but the fact that her husband was not impeached—or more mercifully disqualified on medical grounds—attests to her remarkable performance as a substitute president. On the more positive side, it was she who converted Ronnie from his boyish "Evil Empire" views, she who nudged him into meeting with Gorbachev, and she (it is revealed here) who thought to seat the two men by a cozy fire.

My Turn also reveals in detail, and perhaps for the first time, the tremendous suffering Mrs. Reagan endured for the cause of world peace. Not on account of Gorbachev, who comes off here as a creampuff, but in the hands of the formidable Raisa, who is presented as a rude, erratically dressed pedant of fluctuating hair color ("It became less red over the years"). Raisa's sins included neglecting to offer condolences for the mastectomy or for Mrs. Reagan's mother's death—which was inexcusable, since "the Soviets know everything." Almost as bad, she was prone to giving boring "lectures" on the Soviet Union. Fortunately, there were other witnesses to this appalling behavior, so that Mrs. Reagan can say, in the general spirit of the book, "I was glad that other people could see what I had been going through."

Why she was willing to pay such a high price for peace we may never know. Certainly she was no more a pacifist than the man whom even Goldwater rejected, in 1976, as too dangerously reactionary. Maybe she divined, in her Bloomingdale-Lauren circle of friends, that Ronnie's flamboyant Armageddon talk was a little déclassé. Or maybe, in some bathtub session, she settled on peace as the perfect retort to all those critics, including Patti, who thought of Ronnie as a "warmonger."

But she did it. And, having done it, it's too bad she can't give herself more credit. Mrs. Reagan, however, is very much a prefeminist (even the issue of her age is, once again, coyly skirted); and old-fashioned gals exert power only through male vehicles. Nothing hurt her more, in all the years of hurts, than Don Regan's charge that she was a "dragon lady," and William Safire's echo that she was "power-hungry." *My Turn*, with all its whining, stands as one long rebuttal to such nasty charges: proof that underneath the Marie Antoinette packaging was someone who never even quite made it as a mother—just a tearful, vulnerable, little girl. Her book may represent the Reagans' last campaign: an effort to prove that Ronnie really *was* president after all.

Since it's my turn for a moment, I would suggest that Mrs. Reagan wipe that unbecoming pout off her face, forget the barbs of the ignorant and the envious, and try to look back on her reign with quiet pride. She did good. Maybe she even saved the world. And since I said it, and I'm a Democrat—worse, an actual leftist—it must be true.

[1989]

My Reply to George

●···●··●··●··●··●··●

DEAR GEORGE,

Thank you for your nice note! No, of course there are no hard feelings. In fact, you really won me over with your promise to "take an interest in government." That's not the kind of thing we expect from a president, but in my book, it's a real plus! And don't worry for a moment: I wouldn't even *think* of impeachment —not even if you sold arms to one of those L.A. drug gangs, or fornicated with a foreign dictator on the White House lawn! That's the really neat thing about Dan Quayle, as you must have realized from the first moment you looked into those lovely blue eyes: *impeachment insurance.*

It's true we don't have a lot in common. You're . . . well, I won't say the word, but as Barbara might put it, with her incredible finishing-school tact: it rhymes with "bitch." You have Kennebunkport; I summer in the backyard. You're a member of Skull and Bones; I was never interested in piracy. And so forth. But this doesn't mean we can't *work* together, like two little points of light, for a world that is gentler and kinder toward all those afflicted with tennis elbow, sailboat shins, or the grievous responsibility of managing multiple trust funds.

You asked me to explain the gender gap, and frankly that isn't easy, since the other guy was pro-rape, and not only that, his wife is thin. But thanks to a recent scientific breakthrough, we may finally have a clue. You see, when women's estrogen levels are high, their spatial perception goes down. Then it was really hard for them to see how much taller you were than the other guy. When the estrogen levels get so high that they're really *toxic*, no woman could see the difference between you and Ronald Reagan, even with you standing three feet away and a couple of millimeters to the left.

But not to worry, George, all this will change with menopause, which is—as the prochoice members of the Supreme Court approach their dotage—the ardent goal of every healthy, red-blooded young woman in America. Frankly, I adore your catchy slogan, "Adoption, not Abortion," although no one has been able to figure out, even with expert counseling, how to use adoption as a method of birth control, or at what time of month it is most effective. I've been thinking of adopting a little foreign baby: possibly—if the Greek-American theme doesn't bother you too much—little Athina Onassis. Until then, George, try to see the gender gap in a positive light, for what it really is—a mandate for menopause!

And George, don't just focus on women. Other kinds of people voted against you too: flag-burners, professional rapists, Nazis who are still slavishly indebted to the ACLU for defending their right to march through Jewish neighborhoods, not to mention the powerful and growing pro-crack backlash. And don't forget black men, who voted for the other guy at a rate of nine to one, despite everything you and Ron have done during the past eight years to relieve them of the terrible embarrassment of being *singled out* for special treatment, like affirmative action.

But let's let bygones be bygones and get right down to the issues thing: I think it's *neat* the way you've kept your plans for the economy a *secret* during all those months of campaigning and the last few weeks of writing personal notes to each and every member of the electorate. And, like millions of Americans, I was absolutely intrigued by your recent statement on the deficit.

Remember how you put it? "I am from all these people as to what—not only what the situation is but what we do about it."

Atta *boy*, George! I love a man who can stand up to those "English-only" freaks and say exactly what's on his mind. We all realize that a deficit—in the financial, rather than mental, sense—is a concept alien to your social class. We obviously can't tax the rich as Jesse Jackson suggested (may he find a nice parish somewhere and settle *down*!) because it would be unfair to penalize them for a problem they can't even begin to comprehend.

So I like the little plan you leaked to me—of putting the burden on the people who really *pig out*, on a daily basis, at the federal trough. If every penitentiary inmate would simply volunteer to skip one meal a week, or desserts on alternate Sundays, then you're absolutely right: there would be enough money left over in the federal budget to buy the contras the nuclear weapons they so desperately need if Nicaragua is ever to be free again.

And, yes George, I'd be happy to help Barbara out on her literacy campaign. It's a disgrace how many Americans remained baffled and clueless when you told them "Read my lips," but this problem can be solved with a little coaching. I also promise to ask my friends to stop it with those Quayle jokes. It's disgusting how much prejudice there is against the rich and stupid, when obviously this is a congenital condition that no one can do anything about. I mean, would you abort a baby just because prenatal tests showed it was rich and stupid? Besides, as we all know from your stunning résumé, George, no one has ever held it against you.

And don't hesitate to write as often as you feel the urge. I may be moving a considerable distance away—I may, in fact, be moving four or five time zones away. But there'll always be a forwarding address for you, George.

[1989]

Put on a Happy Face

●··●··●··●··●··●··●··●

NOW THAT THE SOVIET DISSIDENTS have been roused from
their Thorazine stupors and sent back to their jobs in the samiz-
dat industry, it may be safe for me to reveal an ugly secret about
our own fair country. My attorney (actually a law-school dropout
now driving a school bus) advises that I keep this to myself
unless I want to see my future literary career restricted to the
writing of bad checks. But you, the reading public, deserve to
know the truth: *Everything you read in the American media, possibly
including this column, has been censored.*

Let me give you an example, a true story of capitalist censorship in action. (Only the details have been altered to protect
whatever remnants of a career may remain to me.) It had taken
the obligatory three-Perrier lunch to convince one of New York's
leading magazine editors to let me write a story on the feminization of poverty. He had demurred through the cold pressed-duck
salad, digressed during the medallions of baby veal, and scowled
through the Death-by-Chocolate course. Finally, over the decaf
expressos, he sighed, "OK, do your thing on poverty, but be
sure to make it upscale."

From this I learned Rule 1 of capitalist censorship: You can
write about any social problem—sweatshops, starvation, child
labor—so long as it is a problem experienced primarily by the
rich.

Here is another example, from back in the days when I was naive enough to believe that the "marketplace of ideas" had room enough for everyone. I was trying to persuade an immensely powerful, dressed-for-success editor to assign a story on the plight of Third World women refugees. "Sorry," she said with a charming wave of dismissal, "Third World women have never done anything for me."

I'm sure she didn't mean to deny that they had, in all probability, stitched the French seams in her cashmere suit, swept her office in the middle of the night, and chopped the broccoli for her salad-bar lunch. She just meant that they didn't *sell*. And from this I learned Rule 2: You can write about any number of persons of color so long as they are Whitney Houston or Philip Michael Thomas.

A related rule is that you must learn not to stray from your assigned sociodemographic stereotype. As a woman, I am generally asked to write on "women's topics," such as cooking, divorce, how to succeed in business, diet fads, and the return of the bustle. These are all fine topics and give great scope to my talents, but when I ask, in faltering tones, for an assignment on the arms race or the trade deficit, I am likely to be told that *anyone* (Bill, Gerry, Bob) could cover that, whereas my "voice" is *essential* for the aerobic toothbrushing story. This is not, strictly speaking, "censorship"—just a division of labor in which white men cover politics, foreign policy, and the economy, and the rest of us cover what's left over, such as the bustle.

I pieced together a fourth rule from the dozens of manuscripts returned to me over the years with comments such as "too angry," "too depressing," and "where's the bright side?" This rule was first enunciated, back in the fifties, by the prolific Herbert Gold, who had learned through bitter experience that the American media want only "happy stories about happy people with happy problems." In other words, you can write about anything—death squads, AIDS, or the prospect for a Pat Robertson victory in '88—so long as you make it "upbeat."

Now no one in publishing ever comes right out with the truth

—namely that most magazines are beholden to advertisers who are interested only in reaching the yuppie overclass, and then only with articles that will not disturb the stupor induced by six straight pages of Calvin Klein ads. Instead, they say things like, "Darling, I'd do anything to run this, but you *know* it's never going to get past Katharine Graham [or whoever]," meaning, "*I've* mastered the art of self-censorship; why haven't you?"

But the most common excuse for censorship is *you,* dear reader. Most editors despise you and regret that, for purposes of attracting advertisers, they are required to make their magazines available to the general public. I have been told, "*I* get it, of course, but our readers, they *read with their lips.*" Or: "Of course, *we* care about world hunger, but our readers' eyes just *glaze over* the second we wander from thinner thighs."

The result is that most of our major women's magazines now have the intellectual texture of bread pudding. Ditto, I would add, for most of what you'll find in *GQ, Vanity Fair,* or *M;* and on a diet like this, the American reading public will soon be reduced to the state of slobbering, retarded narcissism that is so congenial to American advertising.

The really seasoned writer will, of course, find a bright side even to censorship. "It shows that the printed word still matters," gushes one writer friend of mine, holding up a manuscript with as many deletions as her FBI file. It sharpens the writer's craft, argues Soviet émigré writer Joseph Brodsky, on the theory that the wild circumlocutions required to get around a censor are the genesis of great prose. True enough, I am proud of my lists of innocuous synonyms for words like "capitalism," "class," or "clitoris." But I don't see Brodsky heading back to the USSR to polish up his subordinate clauses.

I can imagine the editors I have "worked with"—as the literary expression for having lunch together goes—reading this and snarling, "That wretched ingrate, let her go to Russia and try out the tractor-production beat at *Pravda!*" Indeed, in low moments, I have thought of defecting to that land where the censorship is straightforward and aboveboard, and no one confuses bread pudding with "freedom of speech." It would not be so bad once I mastered the local rules governing the sayable and the printable. And in the case of conflict—why, at least the Thorazine is on the state.

[1987]

The Moral Bypass

•··•··•··•··•··•··•

THE MOST NUMBING PHRASE in the American vocabulary must be "local government," followed by "federal government," and then, perhaps, by "electoral politics." Even "Sears catalogue" carries livelier possibilities, in everyday usage, than those terms that refer to our collective enterprise as citizens; and, if I still have your attention, I would include among those words and phrases that inspire talk show hosts to change the subject and neighbors to retreat to their own backyards: "social policy," "federal programs," and, of course, "politics" itself. Not all nationalities are so repelled by their own communal affairs. Europeans and those Latin Americans who are free to speak without disappearing into permanent silence still consider public issues to be an acceptable subject for café chitchat. Even Russian émigrés complain about the American aversion to political discussion. We who officially value freedom of speech above life itself seem to have nothing to talk about but the weather.

Why are public matters so bereft of content—or, let us say, mere interest—for most Americans? That is not, in itself, a strictly political question; the decline of citizenship cannot be plotted along a straightforward left-right axis. It is not only liberals who are misfits today; so is the odd person who follows policy closely and eagerly for some purpose other than divining his or her own tax liability. As dozens of commentators have observed, American culture has been privatized, atomized, and perhaps irreversibly idiotized by the combination of television and Epcot-style education. The consumer culture, which we enjoy in our "private" lives, is sensuous and thrilling, while the public sphere, represented by the Internal Revenue Service and the occasional ghastly presidential intrusion on our regularly scheduled programming, lies before us as a desert.

Habits of the Heart is the latest and perhaps the kindest attempt to assess the American character and figure out whether we might still amount to something. In the grand tradition of David Riesman—and the less grand tradition of any number of neoconservative nags—Robert Bellah, Richard Madsen, William Sullivan, Ann Swidler, and Steven Tipton find that we have, for the most part, lost the way but that the stuff of redemption lies all around us, if we are only willing to give it a try. They have talked to hundreds of Americans about work, love, success, religion, and civic affairs; and when I say they are kind, it is because they seem to have listened with such patience and with none of the arrogance their subjects might easily have provoked. Most of these people get fatuous and silly when they try to talk about "values" and "commitments"; no transcendent purpose lights up their lives, and history as a human project eludes them utterly. But others of them are fine people (a number of local political activists are profiled), and all of them would like to find some meaning to life beyond the next promotion or home improvement. Out of such humble aspirations, the authors believe, we may fashion a more engaging notion of citizenship and perhaps turn back the rising tide of barbarism.

Like others before them, and I think primarily of Christopher Lasch, Bellah and his colleagues find Americans crippled by the very individualism that is supposed to be our proudest trait. Once it was the "utilitarian individualism" of capitalism's rugged early years; now it is the softer "expressive individualism" of the consumer society. Riesman charted this character transformation three decades ago, but Bellah et al. add a fine dissection of the therapeutic mentality, which has become our dominant ideology. In it, each self is seen as pursuing its own trajectory, accompanied by its own little planetary system of values, seeking to negotiate the best possible deal from the various "relationships" that come along. Since all values appear to be idiosyncratic satellites of the self, and since we have no way to understand the "self" as a product of all the other selves—present and in historical memory—we have no way of engaging each other in moral discourse, much less in a routine political argument. As a result, life is not only a lonely business but, as the authors point out, an ascetic one. To be these pleasure-seeking, inaccessible selves, we must learn to repress and deny the *amour sociale* that calls us to one another and to what is most human in us all.

But I have perhaps stated their case a little floridly, for *Habits of the Heart* is not only a kind book but an awfully *nice* book, with no undertones of mad optimism or wild grief. I realized it would be that way at the first of many hundreds of invocations of de Tocqueville, whose name, in settings like this, is a reliable banner signifying great blandness to come. Indeed, Bellah and his crew have no ear at all for the nuttiness that lies just one cortical layer under all this therapeutic, self-optimizing rationality. In my experience, if I may introduce an empirical quibble, most Americans may talk about "impacting this" and "impacting that," or "following Plan A or Plan B," as the people quoted here do, but give them a few hours and a sympathetic face to look at and they'll be telling you about the Bermuda Triangle, or a personal appearance by Jesus or a deceased relative, or what they were doing three hundred years ago in another incarnation. When social life lacks a transcendent dimension, people start cultivating secret visions and hustling the occult. But, for that matter, isn't it also patently mad to describe the great and wrenching turning points of one's life in the language of one-minute management, as a choice between Plan A and Plan B?

If the authors haven't detected any nuttiness, neither have they found much pain in the heart of America. Part of this may be a result of the selection process; many of their informants are either therapists or graduates of the therapeutic experience and have presumably mastered the art of upbeat, positivistic self-presentation. Then, too, all the informants are white and middle-class, even wealthy in some cases. But even given these restrictions, where are the drunks, the secret abusers of wives and children, the divorcées sliding toward destitution, the veterans who wake up screaming in the night, the racists and Rambo fans? Pain and madness show up only rarely and only in the margins of *Habits of the Heart.*

If the problems discovered by Bellah and his colleagues are moderate and containable, so, too, are the solutions. We need social movements, they tell us, because movements can anchor our fretful selves in the community of purpose we so deeply crave. That is true, and the political activists who are interviewed come across as admirable people, whether one's criteria come from twentieth-century psychology or eighteenth-century republicanism. But there is a problem in looking to social movements to ease our souls: people can find community and purpose in a movement to exclude black children from the local schools just as surely as they can in a more just and generous cause. In fact, if the problem is to save the troubled, fragmented souls of the middle class, why not turn at once to that ready-made institution of salvation, transcendent purpose, and community—organized religion? Indeed, this is what Bellah et al. recommend, telling us in the hushed tones that secular scholars reserve for the sacred and mysterious that "it would seem that a vital and enduring religious individualism"—which is, apparently, a good kind of individualism—"can only survive in a renewed relationship with established religious bodies."

Well, this is Daniel Bell all over again, who went to the mountaintop in *The Cultural Contradictions of Capitalism,* surveyed the wreckage of our hedonistic, consumerist civilization, and prescribed religion as the glue that would bring us together and put some starch in our backbones. Perhaps there is some index social scientists use that lists under "Cohesion, Social" such entries as "tradition" or, if that doesn't work, "religion." But powerful, communitarian religious feeling can no more be willed into existence and applied to social problems than "tradition" can. (As an atheist, I think I understand that as well as anyone.) Neither, for that matter, can social movements be conjured up to heal the spiritually lost and the psychotherapeutically misguided. Religious passion, like political passion, has an elemental quality that must forvever elude the cautious reformer and would-be social engineer.

I could go on, in a dogmatic vein, about the evils of organized religion, particularly some of the fundamentalist varieties that the authors cast a mild, uncritical eye on in their search for community. True, you will find community in the likes of Jerry Falwell's Lynchburg congregation; you will also find meanness, bigotry, sexism, and sleaze. But quite apart from the question of the social value of religion, I think it is unbearably patronizing for social scientists, who are about the most paradigmatically secular folks around, to recommend religion for everyone else. If modernism hasn't worked out all that well, then let us all march into postmodernism—whatever that is exactly—together. It's not fair for a few prescient scholars, coiled over their word processors, to send the rest of us scurrying back to traditions like Original Sin, premarital (female) virginity, and the willful ignorance of biology, physics, and cosmology.

It seems to me that the book's prescription reflects something very like the therapeutic mentality its authors decry. If the problem is our character, our hearts, the fragile and jury-rigged "selves" we propel through life, then there are indeed all kinds of possible solutions, including religion, civic activism, or perhaps a new and superior kind of therapy. What will actually work? Presumably, we'll have to see what makes us feel better, more "authentic," "whole," etc. In other words, we'll be traveling the same solipsistic closed circuit so well described in *Habits of the Heart*—casting about for some values to define ourselves with and testing them by seeing if they "feel right," with no external reference point, no actual "others" to suffuse the universe with moral gravity.

But the problem is not just the emptiness of middle-class

American life, even for the emptiest among us. The problem includes all the pain and dread that has been pressed back into the margins and final, wistful pages of *Habits of the Heart:* the hunger of the world's majority, the draining misery of most people's daily labor, torture and repression, the threat of nuclear annihilation. If we who are currently comfortable and affluent need a moral reference point, we will not find it in the mirror tricks of therapy *or* religion, but in other people's pain.

At the risk of sounding sectarian, I would say there is one other way in which *Habits of the Heart* fails to rise above the depoliticized culture it describes so well. One of the most important messages of the book is that we have lost the vocabulary for collective moral discourse. Even the activists interviewed, like Campaign for Economic Democracy organizer Wayne Bauer, stumble when they try to explain what they're working for and how it all adds up. Now, there *is* one word and that would help here, at least as another reference point, and that is "socialism" —or, more properly, *"democratic* socialism." I do not mean to suggest that "socialism," dangled in front of the alienated middle class or stamped in large letters in the final paragraphs of books like this, would wake us from our daze. The word has become too alien, some would say too sullied by historical experience, to address the yearning in our hearts. But it is still the only word we have that attempts to bridge the gap between our private notions of decency and morality and the public sphere of the political economy. And it is still the only vision we have— the only modernist vision, that is—of a world in which individual desire might be reconciled with collective need. To neglect the socialist tradition and possibility as much as Bellah and his colleagues do is to contribute to the impoverishment of the political imagination they have so ably documented.

Still, *Habits of the Heart* has an urgent message for the left. If what we are up against is not "false consciousness" but the civic *un*consciousness of the therapeutic mentality, then we will not get far with a dessicated, technocratic approach to politics. "Economic alternatives" and the like, no matter how humane, will not rouse people to a stirring new vision of public life. We need a politics that speaks more directly to the heart and to the repressed need for social connectedness that lies buried there, bruised and stunted. Some will conclude that we can revivify politics by grafting religion onto it, but that, I believe, would be to concede that "politics" really is too dreary to stand on its own. The alternative is to rediscover socialism itself as an evangelical, visionary cause, and the only one ultimately capable of reclaiming the lost language of human solidarity.

[1985]

THE MAN EXCESS

●··●··●··●··●··●··●··●

Tales of the Man Shortage

●··●··●··●··●··●··●

YOU CAN'T SAY ANYTHING NASTY about men these days.
There just aren't enough of them around to defend themselves.
At least that's my friend Dawn's theory, and all I had said was
"Hmmph, men!" A very mild statement, I thought, considering
that we were talking about the sex that invented nuclear warheads and that makes those peculiar guttural sounds in the bathroom every morning. But Dawn looked at me as if I were
proposing to barbecue the last three members of some endangered species. "Hush!" she said. "Don't you know there's a man
shortage?"

It's not that I didn't know about the man shortage. Who could
miss it? I'd been alerted to it some time ago by the magazines at
the supermarket checkout stand, the Phil Donahue show, and a
mysterious note from an ex-boyfriend whom I had dismissed
years ago with the words, "I wouldn't care if you were the last
man alive!" ("Maybe I will be," said the note. "Too bad you
missed your chance.")

In fact, never has any demographic fact been so well publi-
cized, one might even say advertised. After all, men aren't the
only part of the population in limited supply, but have you ever
seen a headline about the shortage of Palestinian pacifists, or
Iranian atheists, or Ethiopian millionaires? Of course not, but let
one male baby boomer of marriageable age fall dead in his jogging

shoes and news teams rush to the site, ready to warn us about the latest decline in the man supply. The hype began two or three years ago, I calculate, probably at the very same moment that Diane Keaton dropped Woody Allen and it began to look, for the first time in recent history, like women actually had a choice.

My first reaction was to demand a recount. Everywhere I look there seems to be a shocking man excess. Take the U.S. Senate, with ninety-eight men and two women—a man excess of ninety-six. Or if you can't take the U.S. Senate as presently constituted, try taking the 6 P.M. Eastern shuttle out of Washington, where you'll risk being trampled by two hundred massed males in three-piece suits stampeding for the aisle seats.

Once you start looking for it, you'll see the man excess everywhere—for example, on the op-ed page of your daily newspaper, which probably features "Joseph," "Garry," "George," and a host of other like-named fellows. Or there's the tenured faculty at Harvard: 853 men and 45 women, for a man excess of 808. It's even possible to be alone in a room with one's husband, lover, or boss, and discover that, as far as you're concerned, there's a local man excess of exactly one.

Not so long ago, feminists were dedicated to eliminating the man excess. Some, who at the time were considered to be moderates, proposed that women simply crowd them out of the Senate, the Eastern shuttle, the Century Club, and the rest of their warrens and hiding places. Others, like the briefly famed Valerie Solanas, a member of Andy Warhol's crowd and author of the SCUM (Society for Cutting Up Men) Manifesto, suggested a program of freelance euthanasia. In this atmosphere, I was terribly embarrassed when my second child turned out to be a boy, but I was able to calm my more radical friends by promising to raise him as a girl.

Incidentally, for those of you who might be alarmed by that statement, I did raise him as a girl, meaning I raised him exactly the same way I raised my daughter. He's turning out very nicely, thank you, so don't come along in ten or fifteen years and try to blame *me* for the man shortage.

Dawn was not impressed by my theory of the man excess. She had just read a scientific study showing that her chances, at age thirty-one, of finding a man to marry were about the same as the probability of being struck dead in midtown Manhattan by a 747 piloted by a Croatian terrorist. At age thirty-two, according to this same prestigous study, everything would be the same except it would be a one-eyed Croatian terrorist. And so on to age thirty-five, at which point, the scientists solemnly predicted, she would be thankful to be struck dead by anything.

Not one to mope, Dawn moved into action. First, she took a "Reticence Training" seminar to "smooth out those rough edges caused by too much assertiveness training," as the brochure put it. Then she took a refresher course in home economics, with a focus on Sock Ironing and Football Appreciation to give it contemporary relevance. At the advice of her instructor, she substituted needlepoint for aerobics as her principal form of exercise and quickly dropped two or three pounds of unladylike upper-body musculature. Finally, she purged her bookshelves of emasculating titles like *Sisterhood Is Powerful* and replaced them with more comforting fare like *How to Make Love to a Man* and *The American Heritage Cookbook*.

It must have worked because she called me not long ago to announce, in the hushed and proud tone of someone who has just acquired a thoroughbred whippet, "I've got one! Would you like to come over and see him?" When I got there, she waved excitedly toward a pudgy figure sprawled on the living-room couch, listening to something that might have been music or might have been Led Zeppelin, it was hard to tell at that volume.

There were crumpled back issues of *Car and Driver* all over the floor and cigarette butts in the potting soil with Dawn's prized ficus plants. The source of this disorder was staring fixedly at his toenails. He had a two-day stubble and a look of extreme

emotional inaccessibility on his face. Otherwise, he bore no re-
semblance to Don Johnson. "Well," I said as politely as possible,
"he's, uh, certainly cute." "Forget it!" Dawn snarled in sudden
fury. "I'm not into sharing!"

I couldn't help wondering, as she rushed off to freshen up his
Diet Coke, whether there might not be more humane solutions
to the man shortage. Surely there must be some way to find a
husband or, for that matter, merely an escort, without sacrificing
one's privacy, self-respect, and interior decorating scheme. For
example, men could be imported from the developing countries,
many parts of which are suffering from a man excess, at least in
relation to the local food supply. There's already a brisk business
in mail-order brides for American men, so why shouldn't a
woman be able to dial an 800 number and have a fiancé delivered
to her doorstep? It wouldn't have to be a scrawny, desperate
refugee. Think of Bronson Pinchot on *Perfect Strangers*. Think of
Dondi. Personally, I can't see why it would be any less romantic
to find a husband in a nice four-color catalogue than in the average downtown bar at happy hour.

Or, if there is a premium on English-speaking men, we might
be able to find some way to tap into the U.S. prison system,
which presently houses 500,000 adult males, many of whom are
single and only a minority of whom are rapists or serial killers.
According to the latest crime statistics, one out of four American
men serves a jail sentence at some point in his life anyway. If
you're going to rule out 25 percent of the available man supply
just because they are, or are about to be, convicted criminals,
you might as well sell your hope chest to Goodwill right now.
We're not talking quality here, just sheer statistical odds.

There is another solution, especially if you're interested in a
man who may someday be capable of holding down a job. Quit
your own job—it's probably infested with females anyway—and
get retrained for a male-rich work setting. I'm thinking of off-
shore oil rigs, for example, or even your local organized crime
subsidiary. (Not an equal opportunity employer, I realize, but
an employer nonetheless.) Or, if you don't mind investing in a

few more years of education, you might try one of the obscure, male-oriented medical specialties, such as proctology. Probably the very best place to work, though, is on a missile-bearing nuclear submarine. These are underwater for months at a time and represent the closest thing we have to canned men.

Seriously, though, as I tried to explain to Dawn, there wouldn't even be a man shortage if women would simply go for younger men. The entire hype, including the scientific study that involves the Croatian terrorist, is based on the assumption that women marry men three years older than themselves. That in itself wouldn't be a problem except for the famous population bulge called the baby boom. If you're in the middle of it, that is, if you're in your thirties, there just aren't enough men three years older than you to go around. But as you start dipping into the younger age groups—where the population bulge is really big—you hit pay dirt: an actual excess of single, marriageable males.

"How young?" you are probably wondering. Well, I am not entirely sure. But once you've gotten over the ancient prejudice that a husband should be older, taller, smarter, and richer—then the field is wide open. In fact, if you're willing to consider a very short male who is incontinent, illiterate, and incapable of handling eating utensils, you may have found the best possible solution to the man shortage: growing your own.

And we do have to come up with some solutions. Otherwise, sooner or later, some smart editor or talk show guest is going to decide that the problem isn't a man shortage, but a woman excess. The old-fashioned methods of dealing with "excess women" were female infanticide and witch burnings. More likely, being civilized, we'd start seeing articles like "Rotten Beauty Advice to Give Your Girlfriends (Tee-Hee!)," and even "Is There a Wife in Your Way? Easy-to-Prepare Herbal Remedies That Leave No Trace!"

Needless to say, men are already taking full advantage of the situation. On a first or second date, just when things are warming

up enough for a woman to begin inquiring about her date's history of sexually transmitted diseases and the possibility of getting
a photocopy of his latest blood test results, it's now common for
the fellow to snap back with: "Are you now or have you ever
been an admirer of Gloria Steinem, Sally Ride, or any of those
other twisted, man-hating women's libbers? Do you believe in
'equal pay for equal work' or any similar subversive, anti-male
propaganda?" (The correct answer is "Nooo!" with a dainty
shudder.)

It would be a sickening irony if all the bright, ambitious young
women among us were to be defeated—not by men—but by a
shortage of them. And we women would only have ourselves to
blame. I mean, we must be suffering from a terminal case of
"fear of success" if we're going to let a numerical advantage for
our side turn into a reason for a full-scale retreat back to the
kitchens and typing pools.

Instead, maybe we ought to be figuring out how to beat them
while we still outnumber them. Here's our chance, it seems to
me, to mobilize to get pay equity, strict child-support laws, subsidized child care, paid parental leave, and a few other items that
have been of only incidental interest to the minority sex. In the
end, they'll probably thank us and claim they would have done
all that themselves if there'd only been enough of them. And
we'll just smile back prettily.

In the meantime, there are plenty of men out there if you
know where to look. And as for those petted darlings among the
dwindling supply of single males aged twenty-five to forty-five:
I say, let them learn to fetch their own Diet Cokes.

[1986]

Talking in Couples

●··●··●··●··●··●··●

SOME TIME AGO, *Ms* magazine carried an article on how to talk to a man in bed. My only disappointment was that it was not followed up by a series of articles on how to talk to a man in other settings and on other items of furniture: "Talking in Living Rooms," for example, "Talking in Dinettes," and "Talking on Straight-Backed Chairs." For it is my conviction, based on years of what sociologists call participant observation, that far more male-female relationships die in the dining room than in the bedroom. And the problem is not the cuisine, it's the conversation.

The fact is that we are going through a profound Crisis in Intersex Conversation, and that this crisis has been the subject of a vast, systematic coverup. I am not referring to the well-known difficulty of maintaining equity in public discourse—meetings, cocktail parties, seminars, and the like—a problem amply documented by our feminist foresisters in the late sixties. I am referring to the much more insidious problem of intimate conversation between consenting adults of different sexes. Television evangelists alert us daily to new threats to the family, ranging from sex education to secular humanism. No one, however, mentions the crisis in conversation, which is far more serious. It threatens not only the family, but also the casual affair, the illicit liaison, and possibly the entire institution of heterosexuality.

I can understand that there are solid artistic and commercial reasons for the coverup. If art were forced to conform to conversational reality, *A Man and a Woman* would have been done as a silent film, and the Broadway hit *The Lunch Hour* would have been condensed, quite adequately, into *The Coffee Break*. Imagine, for example, what would happen if Gothic novels were required to meet truth-in-conversation standards:

> *She:* Now that we are alone, there is so much to talk about! I am filled with such confusion, for I have never told you the secret of my origins. . . .
>
> *He:* Hmmm.
>
> *She:* The truth about my identity and my true relationship to the Earl of D'Arcy, not to mention the real reason why the uppermost room in the far turret of Weathermore Manor has been sealed for thirty years!
>
> *He:* Uh-huh.
>
> *She:* You know the room at the top of the spiral staircase over the stables? Well, there's something so terrifying, so abominable, so *evil* . . .
>
> *He:* Hey, will you look at that? It stopped raining.

Nevertheless, the truth about male-female conversations have been leaking out. In her book *On Loving Men*, Jane Lazarre recounts a particularly disastrous conversational attempt with one of the objects of her love. Jane has just spent a long phone call consoling her recently widowed mother-in-law, who is hysterical with grief. She tells her husband about the call (after all, it was *his* mother), "after which we both lie there quietly." But she is still—understandably—shaken, and begins to fantasize losing her own husband:

> Crying by now, due to the reality of my fantasy as well as the full comprehension of my mother-in-law's pain, I turn

to James, then intrude upon his perpetual silence and ask, "What are you thinking?" hoping for once to be answered from some vulnerable depth. . . . And he admitted (it was an admission because he was incredulous himself at the fact): "I was thinking about the Knicks. Wondering if they were going to trade Frazier."

Jane Lazarre attributes her husband's talent for aborting conversations to some "quality of character" peculiar to him and, in the book, goes off in search of more verbose companionship. Thousands of other women have also concluded that theirs was an individual problem: "*He* just doesn't listen to me." "I just can't talk to him," and so forth. This, however, is a mistake. We are not dealing with individual problems—unfortunate conversational mismatches—but with a crisis of genderwide proportions.

Much of the credit for uncovering the crisis must go to a few stealthy sociologists who have devoted themselves to listening in on male-female conversations. Pamela Fishman planted tape recorders in the homes of three couples and recorded (with their permission) more than fifty hours of real-life chitchat. The picture that emerges from Fishman's work is that of women engaged in a more or less solitary battle to keep the conversational ball rolling. Women nurture infant conversations—throwing out little hookers like "you know?" in order to enlist some help from their companions. Meanwhile, the men are often working at cross-purposes, dousing conversations with "ummms," non sequiturs, and unaccountable pauses. And, in case you're wondering, the subjects that Fishman's women nourished and men killed were neither boringly trivial nor threateningly intimate: they were frequently about current events, articles read, work in progress. Furthermore, the subjects of Fishman's research were couples who described themselves as "liberated" from sex roles. One can only wonder what she might have found by leaving her tape recorder in the average Levittown breakfast nook.

The problem is not that men are so taken with the strong, silent look that they *can't* talk. Sociologists Candace West and Donald

Zimmerman did some extensive eavesdropping at various sites around the University of California campus at Santa Barbara and found that men interrupt women much more often then they interrupt other men and that they do so more often than women interrupt either men or other women. In analyzing her tapes of men and women who live together, Pamela Fishman found that topics introduced by men "succeeded" conversationally 96 percent of the time, while those introduced by women succeeded only 36 percent of the time and fell flat the rest of the time. Men can and will talk—if they can set the terms.

There are all kinds of explanations for the conversational mismatch between the sexes, none of which require more than a rudimentary feminist analysis. First, there's the fact that men are more powerful as a class of people, and expect to dominate in day-to-day interactions, verbal or otherwise. Take any intersex gathering and—unless a determined countereffort is undertaken—the basses and tenors quickly overpower the altos and sopranos.

For most men, public discourse is a competitive sport, in which points are scored with decisive finger jabs and conclusive table poundings, while adversaries are blocked with shoulder thrusts or tackled with sudden interruptions. This style does not, of course, carry over well to the conversational private sector. As one male informant admitted to me, albeit under mild duress, "If you're just with a woman, there's no real competition. What's the point of talking?"

Male dominance is not the only problem. There's also male insecurity. When men have talked honestly about talking (or about not talking), either under psychiatric pressure or the lure of royalties, they tell us they are *afraid* to talk to women. Marc Feigen Fasteau confessed in *The Male Machine* that a "familiar blankness" overcame him in conversations with his wife, resulting from an "imagined fear that spontaneous talk will reveal unacceptable feelings—almost anything that would show vulnerability or indicate that the speaker doesn't 'measure up' to the masculine ideal."

Given the cultural barriers to intersex conversation, the amazing thing is that we would even expect women and men to have anything to say to each other for more than ten minutes at a stretch. The barriers are ancient—perhaps rooted, as some paleontologist may soon discover, in the contrast between the occasional guttural utterances exchanged in male hunting bands and the extended discussions characteristic of female food-gathering groups. History does offer a scattering of successful mixed-sex conversational duos—Voltaire and Madame Du Châtelet, Marie and Pierre Curie—but the *mass* expectation that ordinary men and women should engage in conversation as a *routine* activity probably dates back no further than the 1950s and the era of "togetherness." Until then, male-female conversation had served principally as an element of courtship, sustained by sexual tension and easily abandoned after the nuptials. After suburbanization threw millions of couples alone together in tiny tract houses for whole weekends at a stretch, however, media pundits decided that conversation was not only a healthy but a necessary marital activity, even if the topic never rose above the level of septic tanks and aluminum siding. While I have no direct evidence, the success of these early mixed-sex conversational endeavors may perhaps be gauged by the mass influx of women into the work force and the explosive spread of feminism in the 1960s and 1970s.

It was feminism, of course, that raised women's conversational expectations. In consciousness-raising groups and National Organization for Women chapters, women's centers and caucuses, women discovered (or rediscovered) the possibilities of conversation as an act of collective creativity: the intimate sharing of personal experience, the weaving of the personal into the general and political, the adventure of freewheeling speculation unrestrained by academic rules or boundaries.

As men became aware of the heightened demands being placed upon them, their intellectual spokesmen quickly displaced the problem into the realm of sexuality. Thus Christopher Lasch, in discussing men's response to feminism, never even touches upon the conversational crisis, but tells us that "women's sexual demands terrify men," evoking images of "the vagina which threatens to eat them alive." But we could just as well invert this overwrought Freudiana and conclude that it is women's verbal demands that terrify men and that the dread *vagina dentata* (devouring, toothed vagina) of male fantasy is in fact a *mouth* symbol, all set to voice some conversational overture such as "Don't you think it's interesting that . . . ?"

Now that the crisis is out in the open, what do we do about it? Is there any way to teach a grown man, or short of that, a little one, how to converse in a manner that is stimulating, interesting, and satisfying to women? One approach might be to work through the educational system, introducing required mixed-gender courses in English Conversation. Or we might take a clinical approach, setting up therapeutic centers to treat Male Conversational Dysfunction. Various diagnostic categories leap to mind: "Conversational Impotence" (total inability to get a subject off the ground); "Premature Ejaculation" (having the answer to everything before anybody else gets a chance to utter a sentence); "Conversus Interruptus"; and so forth. It may even be necessary, in extreme cases, to provide specially trained female Conversational Surrogates.

My own intuition is that the conversational crisis will be solved only when women and men—not just women—together realize their common need for both social and personal change. After all, women have discovered each other and the joy of co-operative discourse through a common political project—the feminist movement. So struck was I with this possibility that I tried it out on a male companion: "Can you imagine women and men working together in a movement that demands both social and personal transformation?" There was a long, and I hoped pregnant, pause. Then he said, "Hmmmmm."

[1981]

At Last, a New Man

•··•··•··•··•··•··•··•

THERE HAVE BEEN WAVES of "new women" arriving on cue almost every decade for the last thirty years or so—from the civic-minded housewife, to the liberated single, to the dressed-for-success executive. But men, like masculinity itself, were thought to be made of more durable stuff. Change, if it came at all, would come only in response to some feminine—or feminist—initiative.

In the 1970s, for example, it had become an article of liberal faith that a new man would eventually rise up to match the new feminist woman, that he would be more androgynous than any "old" variety of man, and that the change, which was routinely expressed as an evolutionary leap from John Wayne to Alan Alda, would be an unambiguous improvement.

Today a new man is at last emerging, and I say this as someone who is not much given to such announcements. A new man, like a new sexuality or a new conservatism, is more likely to turn out to be a journalistic artifact than a cultural sea change.

But this time something has happened, both to our common expectations of what constitutes manhood and to the way many men are choosing to live.

I see the change in the popular images that define masculinity, and I see it in the men I know, mostly in their thirties, who are conscious of possessing a sensibility and even a way of life that is radically different from that of their fathers. These men have been, in a word, feminized, but without necessarily becoming more feminist. In fact, I do not think that those of us who are feminists either can or, for the most part, would want to take credit for the change.

If we had not all been so transfixed by the changes in women in the last fifteen or twenty years, far more attention would have been paid to the new man by this time. We can recall—with nostalgia or relief—the feminine ideal of less than a generation ago: the full-time homemaker who derived her status as well as her livelihood from her husband and considered paid employment a misfortune visited only on the opposite sex or the unwed. So sudden was her demise, at least as an ideal for most girls to aspire to, that we sometimes forget the notion of manhood that went along with that "feminine mystique."

I think of the men of my father's generation, men who came of age in the 1950s and who, like my own father, defined their masculinity, if not their identity, in terms of their ability to make a living and support a family. This was a matter of convention as much as of choice, for the man who failed to marry and become a reliable provider was considered a failure, and those who failed to marry at all (that is, by the age of thirty or so) were candidates for the stigma of "latent homosexual." Men of this generation were encouraged to equate effeminacy with un-Americanism and to use their leisure to escape—into sports, hunting, or simply the basement—from women and all things feminine.

We recognize that for the most part men aren't like that anymore and those who are seem grievously out of style. Usually, we think of the change simply as a movement away from the old norm—an opening up of possibilities. But the new man emerging today is not simply the old one minus the old prohibitions and anxieties. There is a new complex of traits and attitudes that has come to define manhood and a kind of new masculine gentility.

Taking his mid-1950s progenitor as a benchmark, the most striking characteristic of the new man is that he no longer anchors his identity in his role as family breadwinner. He may *be* the family breadwinner, or imagine becoming one someday, but his ability to do so has ceased to be the urgent and necessary proof of his maturity or of his heterosexuality. In fact, he may postpone or avoid marriage indefinitely—which is why the women's magazines complain so much about the male "lack of commitment" and "refusal to grow up."

But if the old responsibilities have declined, the pressure is not off: the old man expressed his status through his house and the wife who presided over it; the new man expects to express his status through his own efforts and is deeply anxious about the self he presents to the world. Typically, he is concerned— some might say obsessed—with his physical health and fitness. He is an avid and style-conscious consumer, not only of clothes but of food, home furnishings, and visible displays of culture. Finally, and in a marked reversal of the old masculinity, he is concerned that people find him, not forbearing or strong, but genuine, open, and sensitive.

These traits do not always occur together; in individual men, in fact, we are probably more used to encountering them separately, scattered among men of the middle and upper-middle classes. For example, on a spring lunch hour in the nation's capital, you will find scores of ruddy, middle-aged men, jogging resolutely on the banks of the Potomac, and I doubt that many of them are practitioners of the new sensitivity. On the other hand, sensitivity is now fairly well dispersed throughout the male population, so that it is not uncommon to encounter it in married breadwinners with children, where it may take the form of a somewhat fatuous volubility on the subject of fathering. Then, too, rejection of the breadwinner role—at least as reflected in the scandalously high rate of default on child-support payments —is so endemic that it cannot be confined to a special new type of man. There are men who are otherwise old-fashioned but have taken up a formerly feminine activity like cooking; just as there must be (though I have not met one) upscale bachelors who eschew physical exercise and designer shirts.

But it is possible, increasingly, to find men who qualify as prototypical new males. They are likely to be from twenty-five to forty years old, single, affluent and living in a city, for it is among such men that the most decisive break in the old masculine values is occurring. In these men, the traits that define the new masculinity are beginning to form a pattern and even to frame a new kind of conformity—one that is vastly different, however, from the gray-flannel blues that bedeviled an earlier generation of middle-class American men.

Jeffrey A. Greenberg was one of a number of young men interviewed by me and my assistant, Harriet Bernstein, a market researcher, who helped me locate single affluent men who were willing to discuss their interests and values. Greenberg is a thirty-two-year-old resident in neurosurgery who lives and works in Washington. He puts in eighty to a hundred hours a week as a doctor, works out in a gym three times a week, and otherwise devotes himself to "the study and acquisition of art." Cooking is his latest enthusiasm: "I thought I wasn't creative in that aspect, but I found that I'm definitely OK. I know what tastes good and I'm able to do that." He entertains at least once a week, which gives him a chance to show off his paintings and eclectic music collection. He indicated that, while there were women in his life, he did not yet "have the ability to make a firm commitment."

Thirty or even twenty years ago, a man like Jeffrey Greenberg would have been a self-conscious minority of "older" bachelors —probably envied by his married friends, and, at the same time, faintly suspected for his "effeminate" tastes.

Today he is part of a demographic trend that fascinates market researchers and delights the purveyors of upscale consumer goods. There are 7.5 million men living alone (twice as many as there were in 1970). And as the home-furnishings expert Joan Kron observes in her recent book *Home Psych*, single men are less likely to view their condition as one of temporary deprivation, marked by canned-hash dinners and orange-crate furniture. They cook; they furnish; they may even decorate. *Home Furnishings Daily* has declared them the "New Target," and the magazines that guide their consumption decisions are proliferating and expanding. Significantly, the genre of men's magazine that has done the best in the last few years is the one (represented by *Esquire, GQ,* and *M*) that does not depend on the lure of sexy female images, only page after page of slender, confident-looking male models.

What accounts for this change in men? Or, perhaps I should ask more broadly, for this change in our notion of masculinity— a change that affects not only single, affluent young men but potentially the married, middle-aged, and financially immobile male? Sheldon Kotel, a Long Island accountant in his early forties, who was my host on a local radio talk show, attributes any change in men to a prior revolution among women. From the early 1970s, he says, "you could see what was happening with women, and we had to get our act together, too. They didn't want to be in their traditional role anymore, and I didn't want to go on being a meal ticket for some woman."

Certainly the new man's unwillingness to "commit himself," in the old-fashioned sense, could be interpreted as a peevish reaction to feminist women—just as his androgynous bent could be interpreted as a positive adjustment, an attempt, as the advocates of men's liberation would say, to "get in touch with one's feminine side." Spokesmen for men's liberation, from Warren Farrell in the early 1970s to Donald H. Bell, whose book *Being a Man: The Paradox of Masculinity,* was published in 1982, depict themselves and their fellows as wrestling with the challenge of feminism—giving up a little privilege here, gaining a little sensitivity there, to emerge more "whole" and "self-nurturing."

But for the most part, the new men one is likely to encounter today in our urban singles' enclaves (or on the pages of a men's fashion magazine) bear no marks of arduous self-transformation. No ideological struggle—pro or antifeminist—seems to have shaped their decision to step out of the traditional male role; in a day-to-day sense, they simply seem to have other things on their minds. Stephen G. Dent, for example, is a twenty-nine-year-old member of a private New York investment firm who was also interviewed by Harriet Bernstein. Dent defines his goals in terms of his career and making money, "because that's how the score is kept." To this end, he rations his time carefully: more than ten hours a day for work and approximately half an hour a day for calisthenics and running. Women definitely figure in his life, and he is pleased to have reduced the time spent arranging dates to an efficient five minutes a day.

Dent feels that "sensitivity is very important to being a man. It's easy for people to become so caught up in their career challenges that they don't stop to be sensitive to certain things." By that he said he meant "being able to appreciate things that girls appreciate. Like being able to window-shop, for example. An insensitive guy probably won't stop and look at a dress in a window."

For Brian Clarke, like Stephen Dent, the pressures of upward mobility have pushed marriage into the distant future. He is thirty-three and works fourteen hours a day as a production assistant for a major network television show.

Feminism has not figured much in his life; he discussed it respectfully, but as if it were an idiosyncracy he had not encountered before. Yet he agreed enthusiastically to being identified as a new man. "I'm going uphill, and I don't see the top of the hill yet. So for now there is no one woman in my life. . . . I say it on the first date, 'No commitments!' " He is, furthermore, an ardent and tasteful consumer who remains au courant by reading *GQ*, *M*, *Interior Design*, and *Playboy*, this last, he reassured me, "for the fashions."

So I do not think there is a one-word explanation—like feminism —for the new manhood. Rather, I would argue, at least a part of what looks new has been a long time in the making and predates the recent revival of feminism by many decades. Male resistance to marriage, for example, is a venerable theme in American culture, whether in the form of low humor (Li'l Abner's annual Sadie Hawkins Day escape from Daisy Mae) or high art (the perpetual bachelorhood of heroes like Ishmael or the Deerslayer). As Leslie Fiedler argued in 1955 in *An End to Innocence,* the classics of American literature are, by and large, propaganda for boyish adventure rather than the "mature heterosexuality" so admired by mid-twentieth-century psychoanalysts.

The sources of male resentment are not hard to find: in a frontier society, women were cast as the tamers and civilizers of men; in an increasingly urban, industrial society, they became, in addition, the financial dependents of men. From a cynical male point of view, marriage was an arrangement through which men gave up their freedom for the dubious privilege of supporting a woman. Or, as H. L. Mencken put it, marriage was an occasion for a man "to yield up his liberty, his property, and his soul to the first woman who, in despair of finding better game, turns her appraising eye upon him." After all, the traditional female contributions to marriage have been menial, like housework, or intangible, like emotional support. The husband's traditional contribution, his wage or at least a good share of it, was indispensable, measurable, and, of course, portable—whether to the local tavern or the next liaison.

But before male resentment of marriage could become anything more than a cultural undercurrent of grumbling and misogynist humor, three things had to happen. First, it had to become not only physically possible but reasonably comfortable for men to live on their own. In nineteenth-century homes, even simple tasks like making breakfast or laundering a shirt could absorb long hours of labor. Bachelorhood was a privileged state, sustained by servants or a supply of maiden sisters; the average man either married or settled for boardinghouse life. As a second condition for freedom from marriage, men had to discover better ways of spending their money than on the support of a family. The historic male alternatives were drinking and gambling, but these have long been associated, for good reason, with precipitate downward mobility. Third, the penalties levied against the nonconforming male—charges of immaturity, irresponsibility, and latent sexual deviancy—had to be neutralized or inverted.

Within the last few decades, all of these conditions for male freedom have been met. Domestic appliances, plus a rapid rise in the number of apartment dwellings and low-price restaurants made it possible for a man of average means to contemplate bachelorhood as something other than extended vagrancy. As Phillip Roth observed of the 1950s in *My Life as a Man*, it had become entirely feasible—though not yet acceptable—for a young man to "eat out of cans or in cafeterias, sweep his own floor, make his own bed, and come and go with no binding legal attachments." In addition, that decade saw two innovations that boosted the potential autonomy of even the most domestically incompetent males—frozen foods and drip-dry clothes.

Perhaps more important, the consumer-goods market, which had focused on a bland assemblage of family-oriented products, began to show the first signs of serious segmentation. *Playboy*'s success in the 1950s instigated a revival of sophisticated men's magazines (sophisticated, that is, compared with *True, Police Gazette*, or *Popular Mechanics*) that delivered an audience of millions of independent-minded men to the advertisers of liquor, sports cars, stereo equipment, and vacations.

In *Playboy*'s case, the ads were complemented by editorial exhortations to male revolt and feature articles portraying wives as "parasites" and husbands as "slaves." There were better ways to spend money than on power mowers and patio furniture, as Hugh Hefner insinuated in his magazine's very first issue: "We like our apartment. . . . We enjoy mixing up cocktails and an hors d'oeuvre or two, putting a little mood music on the phonograph, and inviting in a female acquaintance for a quiet discussion of Picasso, Nietzsche, jazz, sex." And in case that sounded suspiciously effete for 1953, the centerfolds testified to an exuberant, even defiant, heterosexuality.

No sooner had the new, more individualistic male life-style

become physically possible and reasonably attractive than it began also to gain respectability. Starting in the 1960s, expert opinion began to retreat from what had been a unanimous endorsement of marriage and traditional sex roles. Psychology, transformed by the human-potential movement, switched from "maturity" as a standard for mental health to the more expansive notion of "growth." "Maturity" had been a code word, even in the professional literature, for marriage and settling down; "growth" implied a plurality of legitimate options, if not a positive imperative to keep moving from one insight or experience to the next. Meanwhile, medicine—alarmed by what appeared to be an epidemic of male heart disease—had begun to speak of men as the "weaker sex" and to hint that men's greater vulnerability was due, in part, to the burden of breadwinning.

The connection was scientifically unwarranted, but it cast a lasting shadow over conventional sex roles: the full-time homemaker, who had been merely a parasite on resentful males, became a potential accomplice to murder, with the hardworking, role-abiding breadwinner as her victim. By the 1970s, no salvo of male resentment—or men's liberation—failed to mention that the cost of the traditional male role was not only psychic stagnation and sexual monotony, but ulcers, heart disease, and an early death.

Today, the old aspersions directed at the unmarried male have largely lost their sting. Images of healthy, hard-working men with no apparent attachments abound in the media, such as, for example, the genial-looking bicyclist in the advertisement for *TV Guide*, whose caption announces invitingly, "Zero Dependents."

Perhaps most important, a man can now quite adequately express his status without entering into a lifelong partnership with a female consumer. The ranch house on a quarter acre of grass is still a key indicator of social rank, but it is not the only one. A well-decorated apartment, a knowledge of wines, or a flair for cooking can be an equally valid proof of middle-class (or upper-middle-class) membership, and these can now be achieved without the entanglement of marriage or the risk of being thought a little "queer."

Certainly feminism contributed to the case against the old style of male conformity. On the ideological front, the women's movement popularized the sociological vocabulary of "roles"—a linguistic breakthrough that highlighted the social artifice involved in masculinity, as we had known it, as well as femininity. More practically, feminists envisioned a world in which neither sex would be automatically dependent and both might be breadwinners. Betty Friedan speculated that "perhaps men may live longer in America when women carry more of the burden of the battle with the world, instead of being a burden themselves," and Gloria Steinem urged men to support the cause because they "have nothing to lose but their coronaries." Yet feminism only delivered the *coup de grâce* to the old man, who married young, worked hard, withheld his emotions, and "died in the harness." By the time of the feminist revival in the late 1960s and '70s, American culture was already prepared to welcome a new man, and to find him—not caddish or queer—but healthy and psychologically enlightened.

But if the new man's resistance to commitment grows out of longstanding male resentment, there are other features of the new manhood that cannot be explained as a product of the battle of the sexes, no matter which side is presumed to have taken the initiative. Married or single, the preoccupations of these men suggest anxiety rather than liberation, and I think the anxiety stems from the very real and relatively recent insecurities about class.

The professional-managerial middle class, which is the breeding ground for social ideals like the new man or new woman, has become an embattled group. In the 1950s and '60s, young men of this class could look forward to secure, high-status careers, provided only that they acquired some credentials and showed up for work. Professional-level job slots were increasing, along with the expansion of corporate and governmental administrative apparatuses, and jobs in higher education increased to keep pace with the growing demand for managerial and "mental" workers.

Then came the long economic downturn of the 1970s and whole occupations—from public administration to college history teaching—closed their ranks and lost ground. One whole segment of formerly middle-class, educated youth drifted downward to become taxi drivers, waiters, or carpenters. As other people crowded into the most vocationally promising areas— medicine, law, management—those too became hazardously overpopulated. According to recent studies of the "disappearing middle class," the erstwhile middle-class majority is tumbling down and out (both because of a lack of jobs and because those that remain have not held their own against inflation), while a minority is scrambling up to become the new high-finance, high-tech gentry. Our new men are mainly in the latter category, or are at least holding on by their fingernails.

Times of rapid class realignment magnify the attention paid to class insignia—the little cues that tell us who is a social equal and who is not. In the prosperous 1960s and early '70s, the counterculture had temporarily blurred class lines among American men, mixing Ivy League dropouts with young veterans, hip professionals with unschooled street kids. Avant-garde male fashion was democratic: blue jeans, gold chains, and shoulder-length hair could equally well be affected by middle-aged psychiatrists, young truck drivers, or off-duty tax lawyers. Thanks to Army-surplus chic and its rock-star embellishments, there was no sure way to distinguish the upward bound from the permanently down and out.

In the insecure 1980s, class lines are being hastily redrawn, and many features of the new manhood can best be understood as efforts to stay on the right side of the line separating "in" from "out," and upscale from merely middle-class. The new male consumerism, for example, is self-consciously elitist: Italian-knit sweaters and double-breasted blazers have replaced the voluntary simplicity of flannel shirts and denim jackets. Esquire announced a "return to elegant dressing" that excludes not only the polyester set but the rumpled professor and any leftover bohemians.

Food fashions, too, have been steadily gentrified, and the traditional masculine culinary repertory of chili and grilled meats would be merely boorish today. A recent issue of *GQ* magazine gave its readers the following advice, which I would have thought almost too precious for the pages of *Gourmet:* To turn dinner for two into an affair, break open the caviar again—this time over oysters or spooned into baked potatoes with melted butter, a dollop of crème fraîche and a sprinkling of minced green onion. Or offer truffles—black or white . . . tossed with pasta, cream and butter." Real men may not eat quiche—which has been adopted by the proletariat anyway—but new men are enthusiasts of sushi and cold pasta salads, and are prepared to move on as soon as these, too, find their way to more plebeian palates. As *M* magazine half-facetiously warned its readers, sushi may already be "out," along with pesto dishes and white-wine spritzers.

Consumer tastes are only the most obvious class cues that define the new man and set him off, not only from the old white-collar man but from the less fortunate members of his own generation. Another is his devotion to physical exercise, especially in its most solitary and public form—running. Running is a new activity, dating from the 1970s, and it is solidly upscale. Fred Lebow, the president of the New York Road Runners Club, describes the average marathon runner as a male, "34 years old, college-educated, physically fit and well-off," and a *New York Times* poll found that 46 percent of the participants in the 1983 New York City Marathon earned more than $40,000 a year (85 percent of the participants were male). The old man smoked, drank martinis to excess, and puttered at golf. The new man is a nonsmoker (among men, smoking is becoming a blue-collar trait), a cautious drinker, and, if not a runner, a patron of gyms and spas.

I would not argue that men run in order to establish their

social status—certainly not at a conscious level. Running is one manifestation of the general obsession with fitness that gripped the middle class in the 1970s and for which there is still no satisfactory sociological explanation. On one level, running is a straightforward response to the cardiac anxiety that has haunted American men since the 1950s; it may also be a response to the occupational insecurity of the 1970s and '80s. Then, too, some men run to get away from their wives—transforming Rabbit Angstrom's cross-country dash in the final scene of John Updike's *Rabbit Run* into an acceptable daily ritual. Donald Bell says he took up running (and vegetarianism) "to escape somewhat from the pain and frustration which I felt in this less than perfect marriage."

But whatever the individual motivations, running has become sufficiently identified as an upper-middle-class habit to serve as a reliable insignia of class membership: running is public testimony to a sedentary occupation, and it has all but replaced the more democratic sports, such as softball and basketball, that once promoted interclass male mingling.

Finally, there is that most promising of new male traits— sensitivity. I have no hesitation about categorizing this as an upscale class cue if only because new men so firmly believe that it is. For more than a decade, sensitivity has been supposed to be the inner quality that distinguishes an educated, middle-class male from his unregenerate blue-collar brothers: "they" are Archie Bunkers; "we" are represented by his more liberal, articulate son-in-law. As thoughtful a scholar as Joseph H. Pleck, program director of the Wellesley College Center for Research on Women, who has written extensively on the male sex role, simply restates (in a 1976 *Journal of Social Issues*) the prejudice that blue-collar men are trapped in the "traditional" male role, "where interpersonal and emotional skills are relatively undeveloped."

No one, of course, has measured sensitivity and plotted it as a function of social class, but Judith Langer, a market researcher, reports that, in her studies, it is blue-collar men who express less "traditional" or "macho" values, both in response to products and in speaking of their relationships with women. "Certainly I'm not suggesting that *only* blue-collar men show such openness," she concludes, "but rather that the stereotype of blue-collar workers can be limited."

To the extent that some special form of sensitivity is located in educated and upwardly mobile males, I suspect it may be largely a verbal accomplishment. The vocabulary of sensitivity, at least, has become part of the new masculine politesse; certainly no new man would admit to being insensitive or willfully "out of touch with his feelings." Quite possibly, as sensitivity has spread, it has lost its moorings in the therapeutic experience and come to signify the heightened receptivity associated with consumerism: a vague appreciation that lends itself to aimless shopping.

None of these tastes and proclivities of the new man serve to differentiate him from the occasional affluent woman of his class. Women in the skirted-suit set tend to postpone marriage and childbearing; to work long hours and budget their time scrupulously; to follow fashions in food and clothing, and to pursue fitness, where once slimness would have sufficed. As Paul Fussell observes in *Class: A Guide Through the American Status System*, the upper middle class—and I would include all those struggling to remain in the upper part of the crumbling middle class—is "the most 'role reversed' of all." And herein lies one of the key differences between the old and the new versions of the American ideal of masculinity: the old masculinity defined itself against femininity and expressed anxiety—over conformity or the rat race—in metaphors of castration. The new masculinity seems more concerned to preserve the tenuous boundary between the classes than to delineate distinctions between the sexes. Today's upper-middle-class or upwardly mobile male is less terrified about moving down the slope toward genderlessness than he is about simply moving downscale.

The fact that the new man is likely to remain single well into his prime career years—or, if married, is unlikely to be judged by his wife's appearance and tastes—only intensifies his status consciousness. The old man of the middle class might worry about money, but he could safely leave the details of keeping up with the Joneses to his wife. He did not have to comprehend casseroles or canapés, because she would, nor did he have to feel his way through complex social situations, since sensitivity also lay in her domain. But our new man of the 1980s, married or not, knows that he may be judged solely on the basis of his own savoir-faire, his ability to "relate," his figure and possibly his muscle tone. Without a wife, or at least without a visible help-mate, he has had to appropriate the status-setting activities that once were seen as feminine. The androgynous affect is part of making it.

The question for feminists is: is this new man what we wanted? Just a few years ago, feminists were, on the whole, disposed to welcome any change in a direction away from traditional man-hood. Betty Friedan, in *The Second Stage*, saw "the quiet move-ment of American men" as "a momentous change in their very identity as men, going beyond the change catalyzed by the women's movement," and she suggested that it might amount to a "massive, evolutionary development."

That was written in a more innocent time, when feminists were debating the "Cinderella complex," as Colette Dowling termed women's atavistic dependencies on men, rather than the "Peter Pan syndrome," which is how another best-seller de-scribes the male aversion to commitment. In recent months, there has been a small flurry of feminist attacks on the new male or on assorted new-male characteristics.

The *Washington City Paper* carried a much-discussed and thor-oughly acid article on "Wormboys," described by writer Debo-rah Laake as men who are "passive" in relation to women, who "shrink from marriage" and children, and "cannot be depended on during tough times." According to one woman she quotes, these new men are so fearful of commitment that they even hesitate to ask a woman out to dinner: "They're more interested in saying, 'Why don't you meet me for a drink?' because it implies so much less commitment on their part." I wouldn't exaggerate the extent of the backlash, but it has been sufficient to send several male colleagues my way to ask, with nervous laughter, whether I was writing a new contribution to the "war on wimps."

I don't blame them for being nervous. My generation of feminists insisted that men change, but we were not always directive —or patient—enough to say how. We applauded every sign of male sensitivity or growth as if it were an evolutionary advance. We even welcomed the feminization of male tastes, expecting that the man who was a good cook and a tasteful decorator at twenty-five would be a devoted father and partner in midlife. We did not understand that men were changing along a trajectory of their own and that they might end up being less like what we *are* than like what we were once expected to be—vain and shallow and status-conscious.

But since these are times when any hint of revisionism easily becomes grist for conservatism, it is important to emphasize that if we don't like the new male, neither are we inclined to return to the old one. If the new man tends to be a fop, the old man was (and is), at worst, a tyrant and a bully. At best, he was merely dull, which is why, during the peak years of male conformity, when the test of manhood lay in being a loyal breadwinner, so many of us lusted secretly for those few males—from James Dean and Elvis Presley to Jack Kerouac—who represented unattainable adventure. In our fantasies, as least, we did not want to enslave men, as *Playboy*'s writers liked to think, but to share the adventure.

Today, thanks to the women's movement, we have half a chance: individualism, adventure—that "battle with the world" that Friedan held out to women more than twenty years ago—is no longer a male prerogative. But if it is to be a shared adventure, then men will have to change, and change in ways that are not, so far, in evidence. Up until now, we have been content to ask them to become more like women—less aggressive, more emotionally connected with themselves and others. That message, which we once thought revolutionary, has gotten lost in the androgynous drift of the consumer culture. It is the marketplace that calls most clearly for men to be softer, more narcissistic and receptive, and the new man is the result.

So it is not enough, anymore, to ask that men become more like women; we should ask instead that they become more like what both men and women *might* be. My new man, if I could design one, would be capable of appreciation, sensitivity, intimacy—values that have been, for too long, feminine. But he would also be capable of commitment, to use that much-abused word, and I mean by that commitment not only to friends and family but to a broad and generous vision of how we might all live together. As a feminist, I would say that vision includes equality between men and women and also—to mention a social goal that seems almost to have been forgotten—equality among men.

[1984]

Wimps

SOMEONE HAS TO STAND UP for wimps. It used to be that the worst you could say about a man was that he was a brute, a Neanderthal, and possibly out of touch with his feelings. Then, with the swiftness of cultural change in the microchip age, disapproval shifted to the man who appeared to be too sensitive, soft, and accommodating to the interests of others. "Wimp," which must be one of the creepiest little syllables in the language, leaped from obscurity to become the ultimate term of masculine derogation.

It was no more than a year and a half ago that the media first set aside the issue of sensitivity and began to fret about the danger of wimpiness. I recall my own first encounter with the problem, when a radio talk show host asked me, in the solemn tones of a newscaster covering an epidemic of wasting disease "Why are American men turning into wimps?" Since the show emanated from somewhere like Bozeman, Montana, rather than Los Angeles, I knew he must be referring to a trend that was already well under way. Indeed, in the weeks that followed I came across dozens of media references to wimps—as disappointing dates, ineffective politicians, health-spa wallflowers—in effect, white-collar trash.

.   .   .

All this commentary offered the same explanation for the threatened erosion of American masculinity: American men, once cut from the same mold as Clint Eastwood, had been trying to redo themselves to meet feminist demands for a new, more sensitive and caring male. Unfortunately, they had gone too far. They had become so sensitive and obliging that now not even women could stand their company. A female columnist in one of the high-priced men's magazines claimed to long for the crude attentions of a man like LBJ. A therapist in California announced a new program to help overly softened males get back in touch with their "primal maleness," as if it were a little animal suffocating in men's chests. Male friends who had once taken me aside to inquire anxiously whether they might have been sexists now wanted to know whether I thought they were sissies.

As history would have it, the 1984 presidential race coincided with a peak of antiwimp hysteria. We all recall the spectacle of the male candidates variously cussing, arm-wrestling, and boasting about their ability to lick all comers in the foreign policy arena. In fact, it was fortunate for all of us that the race ended when it did, before any of them resorted to cruder, though possibly more objective, measures of manhood.

It took me a while to see the sinister side to this latest fashion in verbal roughhousing. Of course, there have been no more "wimps"—or genuinely nice, sensitive men for that matter—in the last couple of years than in the years before. There has been no sudden decline in the incidence of rape or wife-battering, and no documented increase in male participation in housework. All that is happening is that our collective values are shifting away from the liberal, unisex ideals of the seventies toward something more belligerent. The national wimp hunt, I have concluded, is an attempt to press men into line for the postdetente militarism of the eighties—just as the Salem witch hunt was, among other things, a powerful object lesson in why girls should be good.

The truth is, I had never warmed to the more fatuous and self-indulgent products of "men's liberation," if the men's liberationists are indeed the prototypical wimps. Like many other women, I could not understand why every man who changed a diaper has felt impelled, in recent years, to write a book about it. Nor is it clear to me why a man should want to get in touch with his feminine side if that means being able to cry: far better, I should think, to have nothing to cry about. Men's support groups and conferences also made me uneasy: a careful study of the world's great religious and military hierarchies would show, I am sure, that men alone, whatever their stated ideals, are in bad company.

But perhaps I am too intolerant. Suppose, say, white Southerners, when first faced with the civil rights movement thirty years ago, had begun to organize consciousness-raising groups and white-lib conferences in order to help themselves cope graciously with change. Imagine their holding workshops on "getting in touch with your Afro-American side," writing long confessional articles on what it is like to sit in the back of a bus (or, for that matter, to have to use a bus at all), undergoing group therapy to eradicate that deep, subconscious expectation that every black man who approaches on the street is either a brigand or a Jehovah's Witness, and so forth. Surely blacks would have been thorougly disgusted, and rightly so. But would we still be arguing about basics like affirmative action today? Probably not.

The real problem with men's liberation is that it never went far enough: a few men's conferences, a dozen or so books on male angst, a few good cries and hugs all around—and then all the good intentions of the seventies seem to have gone into a slow fade. The counterparts of the young middle-class men who once struggled against their sexism and racism—however pompously and noisily—are now straining against the weights in the Nautilus machines. Overcoming the ancient grip of sex roles is somehow less urgent to men who can cook their own gourmet meals and who will probably not bother to marry until they find a woman they can effectively "network" with. The only real residue of men's liberation may be that it is finally possible for men who admire a John Wayne style in public policy to dress and dine in a fashion that the grizzled old cowboy would have found indecently effete.

Yet surely there is plenty more for the men's liberationists to work on. Women, for example, are still waiting for the mass arrival of a new man: someone who can perform a simple, menial household chore and manage to keep his mouth shut about it. Someone who will not define ambition, when it occurs in a woman, as "aggression." Someone who has the inner resources to realize—despite what the men's magazines tell him these days—that he is more than just a pretty face and a nice set of pectorals. Someone with tough enough convictions to be able to cross over to the liberal side of a gender gap now and then. If men were to remold themselves along these lines, the gratitude of women would be touching to behold.

With equal urgency, though, men should be rising up in their own self-interest to combat the antiwimp backlash. Any man with any backbone at all ought to be outraged by this latest attempt to hector him back to paleolithic styles of masculinity— and he shouldn't need a feminist to tell him so. Real men, in my judgment, may eat quiche and wear cologne, but they won't stand for wimp-baiting.

[1985]

STRIDENT WOMEN

●··●··●··●··●··●··●

Stop Ironing the Diapers

●··●··●··●··●··●··●··●

I WAS SADDENED to read, a few weeks ago, that a group of young women is planning a conference on that ancient question: is it possible to raise children and have a career at the same time? A group of young *men*—now that would be interesting. But I had thought that among women the issue had been put to rest long ago with the simple retort, Is it possible to raise children *without* having some dependable source of income with which to buy them food, clothing, and Nintendo?

Of course, what the young women are worried about is whether it's possible to raise children *well* while at the same time maintaining one's membership in the labor force. They have heard of "quality time." They are anxious about "missing a stage." They are afraid they won't have the time to nudge their offsprings' tiny intellects in the direction of the inevitable SATs.

And no wonder they are worried: while everything else in our lives has gotten simpler, speedier, more microwavable and user-friendly, child-raising seems to have expanded to fill the time no longer available for it. At least this is true in the trendsetting, postyuppie class, where it is not uncommon to find busy young lawyers breast-feeding until the arrival of molars, reserving entire weekdays for the company of five-year-olds, and feeling guilty about not ironing the diapers.

This is not only silly but dangerous. Except under the most

adverse circumstances—such as homelessness, unsafe living conditions, or lack of spouse and child care—child-raising was not *meant* to be a full-time activity. No culture on earth outside of mid-century suburban America has ever deployed one woman per child without simultaneously assigning her such major productive activities as weaving, farming, gathering, temple maintenance, and tent building. The reason is that full-time, one-on-one child-raising is not good for women *or* children. And it is on the strength of that anthropological generalization, as well as my own two decades of motherhood, that I offer you my collected tips on *how to raise your children at home in your spare time*.

1. *Forget the "stages."* The women who are afraid to leave home because they might "miss a stage" do not realize that all "stages" last more than ten minutes. Sadly, some of them last fifteen years or more. Even the most cursory parent, who drops in only to change clothes and get the messages off the answering machine, is unlikely to miss a "stage." Once a "stage" is over— and let us assume it is a particularly charming one, involving high-pitched squeals of glee and a rich flow of spittle down the chin—the best thing you can do is *forget it* at once. The reason for this is that no self-respecting six-year-old wants to be reminded that she was once a fat little fool in a high chair; just as no thirteen-year-old wants to be reminded that she was ever, even for a moment, a six-year-old.

I cannot emphasize this point strongly enough: the parent who insists on remembering the "stages"—and worse still, bringing them up—risks turning that drool-faced little darling into a *lifelong enemy*. I mean, try to see it from the child's point of view: suppose you were condemned to being two and a half feet tall, unemployed, and incontinent for an indefinite period of time. Would you want people reminding you of this unfortunate phase for the rest of your life?

2. *Forget "quality time."* I tried it once on May 15, 1978. I know because it is still penciled into my 1978 appointment book.

"Kids," I announced, "I have forty-five minutes. Let's have some quality time!" They looked at me dully in the manner of rural retirees confronting a visitor from the Census Bureau. Finally, one of them said, in a soothing tone, "Sure, Mom, but could it be after *Gilligan's Island?*"

The same thing applies to "talks," as in "Let's sit down and have a little talk." In response to that—or the equally lame "How's school?"—any self-respecting child will assume the demeanor of a prisoner of war facing interrogation. The only thing that works is *low-quality* time: time in which you—and they—are ostensibly doing something else, like housework. Even a two-year-old can dust or tidy and thereby gain an exaggerated sense of self-importance. In fact, this is the only sensible function of housework, the other being to create the erroneous impression that you do not live with children at all.

Also, do not underestimate the telephone as a means of parent-child communication. Teenagers especially recognize it as an instrument demanding full disclosure, in infinite detail, of their thoughts, ambitions, and philosophical outlook. If you want to know what's on their minds, call them from work. When you get home, they'll be calling someone else.

3. *Do not overload their intellects.* Many parents, mindful of approaching nursery-school entrance exams, PSATs, GREs, and so forth, stay up late into the night reading back issues of *Scientific American* and the *Cliff's Notes* for the *Encyclopaedia Britannica.* This is in case the child should ask a question, such as "Why do horses walk on their hands?" The *overprepared* parent answers with a twenty-minute disquisition on evolution, animal husbandry, and DNA, during which the child slinks away in despair, determined never to ask a question again, except possibly the indispensable "Are we there yet?"

The part-time parent knows better, and responds only in vague and elusive ways, letting her voice trail off and her eyes wander to some mythical landscape, as in: "Well, they don't when they fight. . . . No, then they rear up. . . . Or when they fly . . . like Pegasus . . . mmmm." This system invariably elicits a stream of eager questions, which can then be referred to a more reliable source.

4. *Do not attempt to mold them.* First, because it takes too much time. Second, because a child is not a salmon mousse. A child is a temporarily disabled and stunted version of a larger person, whom you will someday know. Your job is to help them overcome the disabilities associated with their size and inexperience so that they get on with being that larger person, and in a form that you might *like* to know.

Hence the part-time parent encourages self-reliance in all things. For example, from the moment my children mastered Pidgin English, they were taught one simple rule: Never wake a sleeping adult. I was mysterious about the consequences, but they became adept, at age two, at getting their own cereal and hanging out until a reasonable hour. Also, contrary to widespread American myth, no self-respecting toddler enjoys having wet and clammy buns. Nor is the potty concept alien to the one-year-old mind. So do not make the common mistake of withholding the toilet facilities until the crisis of nursery-school matriculation forces the issue.

5. *Do not be afraid they will turn on you, someday, for being a lousy parent.* They *will* turn on you. They will also turn on the full-time parents, the cookie-making parents, the Little League parents, and the all-sacrificing parents. If you are at work every day when they get home from school, they will turn on you, eventually, for being a selfish, neglectful careerist. If you are at home every day, eagerly awaiting their return, they will turn on you for being a useless, unproductive layabout. This is all part of the normal process of "individuation," in which one adult ego must be trampled into the dust in order for one fully formed teenage ego to emerge. Accept it.

Besides, a part-time parent is unlikely to ever harbor that most poisonous of all parental thoughts: "What I gave up for you . . . !" No child should have to take the rap for wrecking a grown woman's brilliant career. The good part-time parent convinces her children that they are positive assets, without whose wit and insights she would never have gotten the last two promotions.

6. *Whether you work outside the home or not, never tell them that being a mommy is your "job."* Being a mommy is a relationship, not a profession. Nothing could be worse for a child's self-esteem than to think that you think that being with her is *work*. She may come to think that you are involved in some obscure manufacturing process in which she is only the raw material. She may even come to think that her real mom was switched at birth, and that you are the baby-sitter. Which leads to my final tip:

7. Even if you are not a part-time parent, even if you haven't the slightest intention of entering the wide world of wage earning, *pretend that you are one.*

[1989]

Why We Lost the ERA

●··●··●··●··●··●··●

SHORTLY AFTER the defeat of the ERA in 1982, a magazine editor asked me to travel to the capitals of states that had rejected the ERA, exhume old testimony, interview lobbyists on both sides, investigate the key legislators, and come up with the "smoking gun" that had killed the ERA. Payoffs from the insurance industry were widely suspected, or from "big business" generally, if not some sort of cabalistic intervention by the New Right. After all, when a measure starts out as vigorous and healthy as the ERA was in 1972—fairly breezing through Congress and thirty-five state legislatures—only to sicken a few years later and die ignominiously, it is hard not to suspect foul play.

Though strongly tempted, I did not take the assignment, chiefly because I thought I already knew who had killed the ERA: not men in business suits, passing money under the table in provincial Holiday Inns, but the women of Phyllis Schlafly's Stop ERA. That *women* had spoiled their own chance for an honorable mention in the Constitution of the United States was, it seemed to me, mystery and irony enough. But with Jane Mansbridge's splendid and eye-opening study *Why We Lost the ERA*, we find the irony to be deeper and more disturbing. The ERA, she argues, was defeated not only by the women who opposed it, with their gifts of homemade bread for legislators and speeches on the glories of homemaking, but by the feminists who so ardently supported it.

Why We Lost the ERA is not, I should explain, the latest addition to the new genre of I-told-you-so feminist-bashing books, such as Germaine Greer's *Sex and Destiny: The Politics of Human Fertility* or Sylvia Ann Hewlett's *A Lesser Life: The Myth of Women's Liberation in America.* Mansbridge is both a fine scholar and a feminist whose credentials, which go back to the sixties, include months of fruitless toil for the passage of the ERA in her home state of Illinois. When she says that feminists did something wrong, it's because she wants them to get it right next time. Where they went wrong, according to Mansbridge, was in believing that the fifty-two-word ERA would literally and bloodlessly decree the gender revolution. That was the implication, for example, of the classic pro-ERA button, which said only "59¢": the amount that women earn, on the average, for every dollar men earn—an injustice that would, presumably, be redressed after those fifty-two innocuous words were inserted into the law of the land.

The nation's legislators, most of whom are men and few of whom are revolutionaries, might well have approved the ERA as an abstract statement of rights, a kind of collective good intention—which is what it was. But, as Mansbridge argues, you cannot sustain a volunteer movement on the strength of good intentions and symbolic gains. To keep the volunteers mobilized, the pro-ERA side tended to inflate the amendment's probable impact, and each inflation of its impact gave the anti-ERA side and the undecided more cause for alarm. If the ERA could dissolve the historical inequity represented by "59¢," then it could, the anti-ERAers imagined, destroy the family, integrate rest rooms, and encourage female toplessness in public places. Confronted with the exaggerated claims of both sides, the legislators decided—perhaps understandably—not to write such a wild and risky venture into the two-hundred-year-old Constitution.

As Mansbridge sees it, the pro-ERA side's most damaging

exaggeration arose over the question of whether the ERA would require women to be drafted and, once drafted, to fight alongside men. The reassuring and no doubt correct answer would have been no, that even if the Supreme Court became gender-blind as a result of the ERA, it would still be up to the president, Congress, and ultimately the military to determine who went into combat, and there was little chance that they would pick their wives and daughters. But in some Amazonian excess of purity, the lawyers who advised the pro-ERA movement, and then the leaders of the movement, decided that the easy answer was a sellout. Instead, they argued that the ERA would require women to fight, that this was what equality meant, and besides, as one pro-ERA debater ventured, "Women are smaller, they'll fit well in tanks."

It was this refusal to compromise on the principle of equality that probably doomed the ERA. Whether the principle outweighs the loss is still a matter of debate. On the one hand, as Mansbridge points out, much of what had been expected from the ERA in 1972 had already been accomplished by other means by the time the deadline for ratification came up, ten years later. On the other hand, the ERA would certainly have emboldened women, and perhaps also the judiciary, in such matters as pay equity, or equal pay for work of comparable worth. But if the net effect of the ERA was, by the early eighties, so tentative and insubstantial, then one has to ask whether the entire pro-ERA campaign—eleven woman-years of marching, lobbying, fasting, boycotting, and general hell-raising—was worth the trouble.

I had my doubts in the mid-seventies, and, thanks to Mansbridge, my doubts are deeper now. True, the pro-ERA campaign did result in some real gains. It brought a sharp focus to the complex and utopian ideology of feminism and drew thousands of women into their first experience of political activism. But the ERA became in its own way complex and utopian, promising everything but having almost nothing concrete to say on the daily issues of housework, child-raising, and low-wage "women's work." Many loyal feminists who wore green ERA buttons, paid dues to NOW, and abstained from commerce with the unratified states, came to resent NOW's increasingly single-minded focus on the ERA. NOW is not the women's movement, but it is the movement's mightiest institution; and while NOW was obsessed with the ERA, other issues—from abortion to welfare rights—went begging for far too long.

Perhaps the best the pro-ERA forces can do, as they stand around the shallow grave of the ERA, is not to apportion blame but to reconsider the ancient feminist conundrum of *equality* versus *difference*. Put simply, women's movements historically have had two choices. One is to downplay gender differences and to insist on entering, rough and tumble, the games that men are playing. The other is to underscore the differences—weakness, nurturance, spirituality, what have you—and press them for every possible advantage. The "first-wave" feminists took the latter course, basing their arguments for suffrage on the inherent nobility of the "mothers of the race." They won the vote but lost the larger struggle, and were left standing on their pedestals while the twentieth century rushed by them.

The second wave of feminism chose equality, in part because men themselves were now becoming less and less willing to be conned by the old insistence on difference. Those of us in the second wave had no choice but to get out into the world and support ourselves, and we figured we would rather be paid for it than merely flattered. But our insistence on equality became, at times, an uncritical rush to assimilation. We wanted to be doctors and lawyers, and soon we wanted to be executives in the corporations that manufacture cosmetics and missiles and toxic wastes. We forgot, at times, that some differences, particularly those forged in women's long exclusion from the world of men, cannot be instantly overcome, and that some, such as women's slightly greater skepticism about war and profit, probably should not be overcome.

The ERA brought out the weaknesses of a purely egalitarian approach. First, it alarmed many of those women—financially dependent homemakers—who have little to gain from assimilation except for a barely adequate job at the minimum wage. The bread-baking activists of Stop ERA may have been dupes of the far right, but they genuinely feared that they would lose the one great "privilege" that rests on difference: the right to be supported by a man. Sadly, we still have no solution for their appalling vulnerability. In addition, the single-mindedly egalitarian approach led to moral confusion on the issue of combat. You cannot say that "war is senseless," as a 1980 NOW position paper did, and in almost the next sentence demand the right to be warriors. Participation is, after all, the heartiest form of approval.

Yet, having said all that, I confess I also fear that feminists may now go too far in the other direction, back to a strategy based on difference. Mansbridge hails the signs of new ferment in feminist thought, now that the ERA is no longer around to enforce a "party line." But there is a faintly sinister side to this little venture too. Carol Gilligan's insightful study of moral decision-making by girls and boys, *In a Different Voice: Psychological Theory and Women's Development,* is being used, willy-nilly, to reopen the old case for women's absolute moral superiority. Some advocates for women's economic rights are, in understandable desperation, resorting to arguments based solely on motherhood and the needs of children. And the feminist antipornography movement, no less than the feminist movement of a century ago, encourages the assumption that male and female sexuality, and possibly morality, are as unlike as yin and yang.

There is a dialectic here, but hardly a paradox. The original idea of feminism as I first encountered it, in about 1969, was twofold: that nothing short of equality will do *and* that in a society marred by injustice and cruelty, equality will never be good enough. That idea does not lend itself to condensation into three letters of the alphabet or two-digit button inscriptions, but it is still the best idea, I believe, that women have ever had.

[1986]

Their Dilemma and Mine

●··●··●··●··●··●··●

QUITE APART FROM blowing up clinics and terrorizing patients, the antiabortion movement can take credit for a more subtle and lasting kind of damage: it has succeeded in getting even prochoice people to think of abortion as a "moral dilemma," an "agonizing decision," and related code phrases for something murky and compromising, like the traffic in infant formula mix. In liberal circles, it has become unstylish to discuss abortion without using words like "complex," "painful," and the rest of the mealy-mouthed vocabulary of evasion. Regrets are also fashionable, and one otherwise feminist author writes recently of mourning, each year following her abortion, the putative birthday of her discarded fetus.

I cannot speak for other women, of course, but the one regret I have about my own abortions is that they cost money that might otherwise have been spent on something more pleasurable, like taking the kids to movies and theme parks. Yes, that is abortions, plural (two in my case)—a possibility that is not confined to the promiscuous, the disorderly, or the ignorant. In fact, my credentials for dealing with the technology of contraception are first rate: I have a Ph.D. in biology that is now a bit obsolescent but still good for conjuring up vivid mental pictures of zygotes and ova, and I was actually paid, at one point in my life, to teach other women about the mysteries of reproductive biology.

. . .

Yet, as every party to the abortion debate should know, those methods of contraception that are truly safe are not absolutely reliable no matter how reliably they are used. Many women, like myself, have felt free to choose the safest methods because legal abortion is available as a backup to contraception. Anyone who finds that a thoughtless, immoral choice should speak to the orphans of women whose wombs were perforated by Dalkon shields or whose strokes were brought on by high-estrogen birth-control pills.

I refer you to the orphans only because it no longer seems to be good form to mention women themselves in discussions of abortion. In most of the antiabortion literature I have seen, women are so invisible that an uninformed reader might conclude that fetuses reside in artificially warmed tissue culture flasks or similar containers. It must be enormously difficult for the antiabortionist to face up to the fact that real fetuses can only survive inside women, who, unlike any kind of laboratory apparatus, have thoughts, feelings, aspirations, responsibilities, and, very often, checkbooks. Anyone who thinks for a moment about women's role in reproductive biology could never blithely recommend "adoption, not abortion," because women have to go through something unknown to fetuses or men, and that is pregnancy.

From the point of view of a fetus, pregnancy is no doubt a good deal. But consider it for a moment from the point of view of the pregnant person (if "woman" is too incendiary and feminist a term) and without reference to its potential issue. We are talking about a nine-month bout of symptoms of varying severity, often including nausea, skin discolorations, extreme bloating and swelling, insomnia, narcolepsy, hair loss, varicose veins, hemorrhoids, indigestion, and irreversible weight gain, and culminating in a physiological crisis which is occasionally fatal and almost always excruciatingly painful. If men were equally at risk for this condition—if they knew that their bellies might swell as if they were suffering from end-stage cirrhosis, that they would have to go for nearly a year without a stiff drink, a cigarette, or even an aspirin, that they would be subject to fainting spells and unable to fight their way onto commuter trains—then I am sure that pregnancy would be classified as a sexually transmitted disease and abortions would be no more controversial than emergency appendectomies.

Adding babies to the picture does not make it all that much prettier, even if you are, as I am, a fool for short, dimpled people with drool on their chins. For no matter how charming the outcome of a pregnancy that is allowed to go to term, no one is likely to come forth and offer to finance its Pampers or pay its college tuition. Nor are the opponents of abortion promising a guaranteed annual income, subsidized housing, national health insurance, and other measures that might take some of the terror out of parenthood. We all seem to expect the individual parents to shoulder the entire burden of supporting any offspring that can be traced to them, and, in the all-too-common event that the father cannot be identified or has skipped town to avoid child-support payments, "parent" means mother.

When society does step in to help out a poor woman attempting to raise children on her own, all that it customarily has to offer is some government-surplus cheese, a monthly allowance so small it would barely keep an adult male in running shoes, and the contemptuous epithet "welfare cheat." It would be far more reasonable to honor the survivors of pregnancy and childbirth with at least the same respect and special benefits that we give, without a second thought, to veterans of foreign wars.

But, you will object, I have greatly exaggerated the discomforts of pregnancy and the hazards of childbearing, which many women undergo quite cheerfully. This is true, at least to an extent. In my own case, the case of my planned and wanted pregnancies, I managed to interpret morning sickness as a sign of fetal tenacity and to find, in the hypertrophy of my belly, a voluptuousness ordinarily unknown to the skinny. But this only proves my point: a society that is able to make a good thing out of pregnancy is certainly free to choose how to regard abortion.

We can treat it as a necessary adjunct to contraception, or as a vexing moral dilemma, or as a form of homicide—and whichever we choose, that is how we will tend to experience it.

So I will admit that I might not have been so calm and determined about my abortions if I had had to cross a picket line of earnest people yelling "baby-killer," or if I felt that I might be blown to bits in the middle of a vacuum aspiration. Conversely, though, we would be hearing a lot less about ambivalence and regrets if there were not so much liberal head-scratching going on. Abortions will surely continue, as they have through human history, whether we approve or disapprove or hem and haw. The question that worries me is: How is, say, a sixteen-year-old girl going to feel after an abortion? Like a convicted sex offender, a murderess on parole? Or like a young woman who is capable, as the guidance counselors say, of taking charge of her life?

This is our choice, for biology will never have an answer to that strange and cabalistic question of when a fetus becomes a person. Potential persons are lost every day as a result of miscarriage, contraception, or someone's simple failure to respond to a friendly wink. What we can answer, with a minimum of throat clearing and moral agonizing, is the question of when women themselves will finally achieve full personhood: and that is when we have the right, unquestioned and unabrogated, to *choose* not to be pregnant when we decide not to be pregnant.

[1985]

The Lesson of Mary Beth

●··●··●··●··●··●··●

WHEN I FIRST HEARD about the Baby M case, it was being presented as a cautionary tale about the perils of high-tech biology. But a clean glass and a syringe were all that had been required for the chaste transfer of semen from one Bill Stern to the surrogate mother, Mary Beth Whitehead of Bricktown, New Jersey. High tech wasn't at issue so much as a greviously low variety of economics. Baby M had been produced, so to speak, for sale. And the economic revelation was that neither party to this unholy transaction seemed to think that $10,000 was a bad price to pay—or be paid—for a small but otherwise perfect human being.

Mentally, I filed the story under "class injustice." Bill and Betsy Stern, the "buyers" in this case, are at the upper end of the class spectrum—double-income professionals for whom the acquisition of a baby must rank financially somewhere near the purchase of a second Audi. Mary Beth Whitehead and her then-husband Rick represent the declining blue-collar working class, where steady work is scarce and the bills just keep on coming. The Baby M case showed just how far these two groups have grown apart—to the point where the children of the wage-earning class could become discretionary purchases for the yuppie class.

The other angle, it quickly emerged, was gender injustice.

Biologically speaking, Baby M is the daughter of Mary Beth and
Bill, just as if she had been conceived in adulterous passion in
the local Travelodge.

But when Mary Beth decided to back out of the deal and
keep the baby, she discovered that the court didn't see her as a
mother—and barely as a human being. In the media, she was
only a "surrogate mother," although she had endowed the baby
with her genes, carried her to term, and nursed her for four
months. To world-class psychologist Lee Salk, who testified on
behalf of the Sterns, Mary Beth wasn't any kind of mother, only
a "surrogate uterus."

That kind of talk doesn't sit well with women, and during the
court proceedings hundreds of them, from Gloria Steinem to the
Whiteheads' working-class neighbors, rallied to Mary Beth's support. The issues seemed clear-cut: if Mary Beth lost and the
practice of surrogacy was given the blessing of the law, then the
way would be open for the mass exploitation of poor women
doing rent-a-womb service for the rich.

But no matter how strongly you felt about the abstract dimensions of class and gender—no matter how powerfully you em-
pathized with a woman whose baby had been snatched, almost
literally, from her breast—there was still one gnawing, treason-
ous little question. It's the same question that registers silently
in my mind every time I look at poor Hedda Nussbaum's punch-
drunk features: How does a woman—an apparently sane, job-
holding or home-making type of woman—get into something
like this in the first place? What kind of woman, in particular,
contracts to bear and sell a child?

Unfortunately, *A Mother's Story*, which covers Mary Beth's life
through the Baby M case and right up to her recent remarriage,
suffers from the flat, distracted tone of an "as-told-to" story, so
it takes some effort on the reader's part to get to know her and
begin to grasp her motives. Born the sixth and apparently not
the most favored of eight children, she carved out a place in the
family by mothering her youngest siblings.

At an age when most girls are collecting Bon Jovi albums or

their generational equivalent, she hit upon motherhood as a career option and dropped out of high school. In no time, she met Rick Whitehead, fresh back from Vietnam with a drinking problem and a meager future as a truck driver. Marrying him was like taking a vow of poverty. He lost jobs, smashed up the family car, and spent too many evenings courting amnesia in the local bars.

Two children and Rick's vasectomy later, Mary Beth, still only twenty-nine, developed a premature case of empty-nest syndrome. Her son had been sent to live with grandparents in Florida, where the schools seemed to agree with him better than those in New Jersey—leaving her with only one child (and Rick) to mother. Mary Beth needed a project, and a newspaper ad placed by surrogacy entrepreneur Noel Keane seemed like the answer.

Why not a job, or a crack at high-school equivalency? Mary Beth is not much given to self-analysis, but two things stand out. One, she did not understand that a surrogate mother is an actual, genetic mother. All through her months of inseminations with Bill Stern's semen—produced fresh for each occasion while Mary Beth waited in another room—she believed she was being injected with fertilized eggs, courtesy of Bill and Betsy Stern. Only in the throes of childbirth did it dawn on her that she was the "real," biological mother all along. If nothing else, *A Mother's Story* should stand as a potent argument for sex education.

The second, and to me the most surprising, feature of her decision was that she seems to have been motivated less by money than by a feeling she describes as "religious." I don't think this mitigates the economic injustice of the situation: affluent women—those who inhabit the same socioeconomic category as Betsy Stern, for example—do not automatically hit upon "surrogate" childbearing when they need a change of pace. Mary Beth does mention the distant eventuality of college tuition for her children, but basically—and this must be the saddest secret in the book—she chose surrogacy because she wanted to *please*.

She doesn't quite say this herself. And I don't say this to add to the weight of psychiatric judgment already passed against

Mary Beth by the Sterns' hired "experts," who demeaned their professions by testifying that she was, among other things, "immature, narcissistic, impulsive, and histrionic."

On the contrary. Although Mary Beth would not aggrandize herself in quite these terms, she seems to have decided to bear someone else's baby because this was a noble and generous thing to do—perhaps the most noble and generous option that *could* present itself to a woman of limited means and even more limited expectations.

Why, then, didn't she carry out her end of the bargain and surrender the baby without a fuss? The darling reality of the baby was part of it. But perhaps even more decisive was the Sterns' response to Mary Beth's quasi-religious "gift" of her own flesh and blood: "When they came to my hospital room, they seemed cold and standoffish. It seemed as though they just wanted to take my baby, leave, and forget that I existed."

Mary Beth had imagined that she was establishing a deep human connection with the Sterns—sealed with the most precious offering one person can make to another. But to the Sterns, those exemplars of middle-class rationality, a deal was a deal. You take the money; we'll take the baby; end of story.

Their coldness drained all the glory out of Mary Beth's one great, magnanimous gesture. But, strangely, it did not destroy her notion of how people related by parenthood—even "surrogate" parenthood—should treat each other. At first, she could not bring herself to tell them of her decision to keep the baby, only slowly realizing that "I was going to let two strangers take my baby simply because I couldn't bear to hurt them." Even at the bitter height of the court proceedings, Mary Beth regretted that "we had come to this point. And that all of us were in so much pain."

Only in retrospect—speaking of Bill Stern's pointed silences during their drives to the insemination sessions—does she realize that "what I'd assumed was a friendship was only a financial relationship to him."

To the psychiatric experts who testified for the Sterns, Mary

Beth's desire to keep the baby despite the contract she had signed was an example of "magical thinking," implying a primitive and irrational mentality. But one can't help conclude that it was the Sterns who were guilty of believing in magic: the idea of getting a baby for cash, coldly and bloodlessly, is a state-of-the-art yuppie fantasy. It is also as old as the fairy stories in which wishes are granted on a witch's whim. Mary Beth's way of thinking, in which human ties count for more than law or money, was more human and, ultimately, more rational.

The Sterns of course "won." In part because of Mary Beth's initial reluctance to hurt them, they gained the legal advantage —and the baby. But in a larger sense, the triumph was Mary Beth's. In an appeal to the Supreme Court, she was reinstated as Baby M's legal mother and given ample visitation rights. More important, the practice of surrogacy was outlawed in New Jersey and, soon after, in five other states.

This was not the noble and generous gift that Mary Beth Whitehead had originally set out to offer. But it is—both through her original mistakes and her eventual determination—what she has ended up giving us all: a renewed understanding that the value of human life cannot be negotiated by contract or computed in cash. For this alone, her story deserves to be read.

[1989]

Strategies of Corporate Women

•··•··•··•··•··•··•··•··•

Some of us are old enough to recall when the stereotype of a "liberated woman" was a disheveled radical, notoriously braless, and usually hoarse from denouncing the twin evils of capitalism and patriarchy. Today the stereotype is more likely to be a tidy executive who carries an attaché case and is skilled in discussing market shares and leveraged buy-outs. In fact, thanks in no small part to the anger of the earlier, radical feminists, women have gained a real toehold in the corporate world: about 30 percent of managerial employees are women, as are 40 percent of the current MBA graduates. We have come a long way, as the expression goes, though clearly not in the same direction we set out on.

The influx of women into the corporate world has generated its own small industry of advice and inspiration. Magazines like *Savvy* and *Working Woman* offer tips on everything from sex to software, plus the occasional instructive tale about a woman who rises effortlessly from managing a boutique to being the CEO of a multinational corporation. Scores of books published since the mid-1970s have told the aspiring managerial woman what to wear, how to flatter superiors, and when necessary, fire subordinates. Even old-fashioned radicals like myself, for whom "CD" still means civil disobedience rather than an 8 percent interest rate, can expect to receive a volume of second-class mail inviting them to join their corporate sisters at a "networking brunch" or to share the privileges available to the female frequent flier.

But for all the attention lavished on them, all the six-figure promotion possibilities and tiny perks once known only to the men in gray flannel, there is a malaise in the world of the corporate woman. The continuing boom in the advice industry is in itself an indication of some kind of trouble. To take an example from a related field, there would not be a book published almost weekly on how to run a corporation along newly discovered oriental principles if American business knew how to hold its own against the international competition. Similarly, if women were confident about their role in the corporate world, I do not think they would pay to be told how to comport themselves in such minute detail. ("Enter the bar with a briefcase or some files. . . . Hold your head high, with a pleasant expression on your face. . . . After you have ordered your drink, shuffle through a paper or two, to further establish yourself [as a businesswoman]," advises *Letitia Baldridge's Complete Guide to Executive Manners*.)

Nor, if women were not still nervous newcomers, would there be a market for so much overtly conflicting advice: how to be more impersonal and masculine (Charlene Mitchell and Thomas Burdick's *The Right Moves*) or more nurturing and intuitive (Marilyn Loden's *Feminine Leadership*); how to assemble the standard skirted, suited uniform (de rigueur until approximately 1982) or move beyond it for the softness and individuality of a dress; how to conquer stress or how to transform it into drive; how to repress the least hint of sexuality, or alternatively, how to "focus the increase in energy that derives from sexual excitement so that you are more productive on the job" (Leslie Aldridge Westoff's *Corporate Romance*). When we find so much contradictory advice, we must assume that much of it is not working.

There is a more direct sign of trouble. A small but significant number of women are deciding not to have it all after all, and are dropping out of the corporate world to apply their management skills to kitchen decor and baby care. Not surprisingly, these retro women have been providing a feast for a certain "I told you so" style of journalism; hardly a month goes by without a story about another couple that decided to make do on his $75,000 a year while she joins the other mommies in the playground. But the trend is real. The editors of the big business-oriented women's magazines are worried about it. So is Liz Roman Gallese, the former *Wall Street Journal* reporter who interviewed the alumnae of Harvard Business School, class of '75, to write *Women Like Us.*

The women Gallese interviewed are not, for the most part, actual dropouts, but they are not doing as well as might have been expected for the first cohort of women to wield the talismanic Harvard MBA. Certainly they are not doing as well as their male contemporaries, and the gap widens with every year since graduation. Nor do they seem to be a very happy or likable group. Suzanne, the most successful of them, is contemptuous of women who have family obligations. Phoebe, who is perhaps the brightest, has an almost pathological impulse to dominate others. Maureen does not seem to like her infant daughter. Of the eighty-two women surveyed, thirty-five had been in therapy since graduation; four had been married to violently abusive men; three had suffered from anorexia or bulimia; and two had become Christian fundamentalists. Perhaps not surprisingly, given the high incidence of personal misery, two-fifths of the group were "ambivalent or frankly not ambitious for their careers."

What is happening to our corporate women? The obvious antifeminist answer, that biology is incompatible with business success, is not borne out by Gallese's study. Women with children were no less likely to be ambitious and do well than more mobile, single women (although in 1982, when the interviews were carried out, very few of the women had husbands or children). But the obvious feminist answer—that women are being discouraged or driven out by sexism—does gain considerable support from *Women Like Us.* Many of the women from the class of

'75 report having been snubbed, insulted, or passed over for promotions by their male coworkers. Under these circumstances, even the most determined feminist would begin to suffer from what Dr. Herbert J. Freudenberger and Gail North (in their book *Women's Burnout*) call "business burnout." For nonfeminists, or, more precisely, postfeminists—like Gallese and her informants, sexism must be all the more wounding for being so invisible and nameless. What you cannot name, except as apparently random incidents of "discrimination," you cannot hope to do much about.

Gallese suggests another problem, potentially far harder to eradicate than any form of discrimination. There may be a poor fit between the impersonal bureaucratic culture of the corporation and what is, whether as a result of hormones or history, the female personality. The exception that seems to prove the rule is Suzanne, who is the most successful of the alumnae and who is also a monster of detachment from her fellow human beings. In contrast, Gallese observes that men who rise to the top are often thoroughly dull and "ordinary"—as men go—but perhaps ideally suited to a work world in which interpersonal attachments are shallow and all attention must focus on the famed bottom line.

To judge from the advice books, however, the corporate culture is not as impersonal, in a stern Weberian sense, as we have been led to believe. For example, *The Right Moves*, which is a good representative of the "how to be more like the boys" genre of books for corporate women, tells us to "eliminate the notion that the people with whom you work are your friends"—sound advice for anyone who aspires to the bureaucratic personality. But it also insists that it is necessary to cultivate the "illusion of friendship," lest coworkers find you "aloof and arrogant." You must, in other words, dissemble in order to effect the kind of personality—artificially warm but never actually friendly—that suits the corporate culture.

Now, in a task-oriented meritocratic organization—or, let us just say, a thoroughly capitalist organization dedicated to the maximization of profit—it should not be necessary to cultivate "illusions" of any kind. It should be enough just to get the job done. But as *The Right Moves* explains, and the stories in *Women Like Us* illustrate, it is never enough just to get the job done; if it were, far more women would no doubt be at the top. You have to impress people, win them over, and in general project an aura of success far more potent than any actual accomplishment. The problem may not be that women lack the capacity for business-like detachment, but that, as women, they can never entirely fit into the boyish, glad-handed corporate culture so well described three decades ago in *The Lonely Crowd*.

There may also be a deeper, more existential, reason for the corporate woman's malaise. It is impossible to sample the advice literature without beginning to wonder what, after all, is the point of all this striving. Why not be content to stop at $40,000 or $50,000 a year, some stock options, and an IRA? Perhaps the most striking thing about the literature for and about the corpo-rate woman is how little it has to say about the purposes, other than personal advancement, of the corporate "game." Not one among the Harvard graduates or the anonymous women quoted in the advice books ever voices a transcendent commitment to, say, producing a better widget. And if that is too much to expect from postindustrial corporate America, we might at least hope for some lofty organizational goals—to make X Corp. the biggest damn conglomerate in the Western world, or some such. But no one seems to have a vast and guiding vision of the corporate life, much less a fashionably conservative belief in the moral purpose-fulness of capitalism. Instead, we find successful corporate women asking, "Why am I doing what I'm doing? What's the point here?" or confiding bleakly that "something's missing."

In fact, from the occasional glimpses we get, the actual con-tent of an executive's daily labors can be shockingly trivial. Con-sider Phoebe's moment of glory at Harvard Business School. The class had been confronted with a real-life corporate problem to solve. Recognizing the difficulty of getting catsup out of a bottle, should Smucker and Co. start selling catsup out of a wide-mouthed container suitable for inserting a spoon into? No, was Phoebe's answer, because people like the challenge of pounding catsup out of the bottle; a more accessible catsup would never sell. Now, I am not surprised that this was the right answer, but I am surprised that it was greeted with such apparent awe and amazement by a professor and a roomful of smart young students. Maybe for a corporate man, the catsup problem is a daunting intellectual challenge. But a woman must ask herself: Is *this* what we left the kitchen for?

Many years ago, when America was more innocent but everything else was pretty much the same, Paul Goodman wrote, "There is nearly 'full employment' . . . but there get to be fewer jobs that are necessary or unquestionably useful; that require energy and draw on some of one's best capacities; and that can be done keeping one's honor and dignity." Goodman, a utopian socialist, had unusually strict criteria for what counted as useful enough to be "man's work," but he spoke for a generation of men who were beginning to question, in less radical ways, the corporate work world described by William H. Whyte, David Riesman, Alan Harrington, and others. Most of the alienated white-collar men of the 1950s withdrew into drink or early coronaries, but a few turned to Zen or jazz, and thousands of their sons and daughters eventually joined with Goodman to help create the anticorporate and, indeed, anticareerist counterculture of the 1960s. It was the counterculture, as much as anything else, that nourished the feminist movement of the late 1960s and early 1970s, which is where our story began.

In the early years, feminism was torn between radical and assimilationist tendencies. In fact, our first sense of division was between the "bourgeois" feminists who wanted to scale the occupational hierarchy created by men, and the radical feminists who wanted to level it. Assimilation won out, as it probably must among any economically disadvantaged group. Networks replaced consciousness-raising groups; Michael Korda became a more valuable guide to action than Shulamith Firestone. The old radical, anarchistic vision was replaced by the vague hope (well articulated in *Feminine Leadership*) that, in the process of assimilating, women would somehow "humanize" the cold and ruthless world of men. Today, of course, there are still radical feminists, but the only capitalist institution they seem bent on destroying is the local adult bookstore.

As feminism loses its critical edge, it becomes, ironically, less capable of interpreting the experience of its pioneer assimilationists, the new corporate women. Contemporary mainstream feminism can understand their malaise insofar as it is caused by sexist obstacles, but has no way of addressing the sad emptiness of "success" itself. Even the well-worn term "alienation," as applied to human labor, rings no bells among the corporate feminists I have talked to recently, although most thought it an arresting notion. So we are in more or less the same epistemological situation Betty Friedan found herself in describing the misery—and, yes, alienation—of middle-class housewives in the early 1960s; better words would be forthcoming, but she had to refer to "the problem without a name."

Men are just as likely as women to grasp the ultimate pointlessness of the corporate game and the foolishness of many of the players, but only women have a socially acceptable way out. They can go back to the split-level homes and well-appointed nurseries where Friedan first found them. (That is assuming, of course, they can find a well-heeled husband, and they haven't used up all their childbearing years in the pursuit of a more masculine model of success.) In fact, this may well be a more personally satisfying option than a work life spent contemplating, say, the fluid dynamics of catsup. As Paul Goodman explained, with as much insight as insensitivity, girls didn't have to worry about "growing up absurd" because they had intrinsically meaningful work cut out for them—motherhood and homemaking.

There is no doubt, from the interviews in *Women Like Us* as well as my own anecdotal sources, that some successful women are indeed using babies as a polite excuse for abandoning the rat race. This is too bad from many perspectives, and certainly for the children who will become the sole focus of their mothers' displaced ambitions. The dropouts themselves would do well to take a look at Peggy J. Berry's *Corporate Couple*, which advises executive wives on the classic problems such as: how to adjust to the annual relocation, how to overcome one's jealousy of a husband's svelte and single female coworkers, and how to help a husband survive his own inevitable existential crisis.

Someday, I believe, a brilliantly successful corporate woman will suddenly look down at her desk littered with spread sheets and interoffice memos and exclaim, "Is this really worth my time?" At the very same moment, a housewife, casting her eyes around a kitchen befouled by toddlers, will ask herself the identical question. As the corporate woman flees out through the corporate atrium, she will run headlong into the housewife, fleeing into it. The two will talk. And in no time at all they will reunite those two distinctly American strands of radicalism—the utopianism of Goodman and the feminism of Friedan. They may also, if they talk long enough, invent some sweet new notion like equal pay for . . . meaningful work.

[1986]

The Mommy Test

●··●··●··●··●··●··●··●

MY, MY GIRLS, what's all the fuss over the new "mommy test"? Hundreds of eager young female job-seekers have written to me in the last few weeks alone, confident of being able to pass the drug test, the polygraph test, Exxon's new breathalyzer test —but panicked over the mommy test. Well, the first thing you have to grasp if you hope to enter the ranks of management is that corporations have a perfect *right* to separate the thieves from the decent folk, the straights from the druggies, and, of course, the women from the mommies.

For starters, you should know that thousands of U.S. women, even those afflicted with regular ovulatory cycles and patent fallopian tubes, have been taking—and *passing*—the mommy test for decades. In fact, it used to be almost the first question (just after "Can you type?") in the standard female job interview: "Are you now, or have you ever, contemplated marriage, motherhood, or the violent overthrow of the U.S. government?"

Today, thanks to women's lib, you won't be out on the street even if you fail. All right, there are disadvantages to the mommy track: mandatory milk and cookies at ten, quiet time at three, and so forth. But many women are happy to get a paycheck of any kind, even if it is a gift certificate to Toys 'R' Us. And if you *still* want to be on the fast track, with the grown-ups and the men, here are a few simple tips for acing the mommy test:

1. Be prepared for tricky psychological questions, such as: Would you rather (a) spend six straight hours in a windowless conference room with a group of arrogant, boorish men fighting over their spread sheets, or (b) scrape congealed pabulum off a linoleum floor? (The answer, surprisingly, is *a*.) Or try this one: Would you rather (a) feed apple juice to a hungry baby, or (b) figure out how to boost profits by diluting the company's baby apple-juice product with wastewater from the local nuclear power plant? But you get the idea. . . .
2. Bring proof of infertility: your uterus in a mason jar, for example. Alternatively, tell the interviewer that you already had a child, but—and at this point you stare pensively into space —it didn't work out. . . .
3. Your interviewer will no doubt have framed photos of his own wife and children displayed prominently on his desk. Do not be misled; this is *part of the test*. Be sure to display appropriate levels of disgust and commiseration. You might ask, in a pitying tone, "Oh, did you marry a *mommy?*"
4. If you actually are a mommy, and have small children of your own who, for some reason, are still living with you, the case is almost hopeless. Unless you can prove that, as a result of some bioengineering feat or error on their birth certificates, you are actually their daddy and hence have no day-to-day responsibility for their care.

But the key thing is *attitude*. If you go for your job interview in a hostile, self-pitying mood, if you're convinced that the mommy test is an example of discrimination or prejudice, believe me, it will show. And there isn't prejudice against mommies today, not really. They're no longer subject to the extreme residential segregation imposed in the fifties, when mommies were required to live in special suburban compounds, far from the great centers of commerce. Today, you'll find them living just about everywhere, even in jaunty little cardboard structures within walking distance of Wall Street.

Today it is no longer necessary (as it was for poor Nancy

Reagan) for a woman who aspires to public recognition to renounce all knowledge of, and contact with, her children. We even have a special day devoted to the distribution of flowers on the graves of dead mothers, as well as to those mothers who, for some reason, still linger on.

However, even if we acknowledge all the tremendous contributions mothers have made—and there were mommies at Plymouth Rock, at Gettysburg, possibly even at the Republican National Convention—we must admit that they have, as a race, shown remarkably little aptitude for the fine points of corporate management. When have you ever seen a get-rich-quick book titled *Leveraged Buyouts: A Mother's Secrets,* or *Swimming with the Sharks: A Mommy's Guide to Eating the Competition (And Finishing Every Last Bite)?*

But the bottom line (not to be confused, gals, with the mark left by overly tight Pampers!) is: even if you respect mommies, like mommies, and are aware of the enormous diversity among them, would you really want to work with one? This is the question that thousands of top U.S. male managers have had to face: would you want to be at a hundred-dollar power lunch and risk being told to polish your plate? Hence the mommy track. It just makes *sense* to segregate them in special offices equipped with extra umbrellas, sweaters, raincoats, and toothbrushes—for their own sake as much as anything.

Personally, I think the mommy track may be just the first step in a new wave of corporate cost cutting. There's a new approach based on the experience of a brilliant young fast-track executive who got pregnant unbeknownst to herself and handily delivered in the ladies' room during a break in the third-quarter sales conference. The baby was raised on phenobarbital and take-out food until it outgrew the lower right-hand desk drawer, at which point our fast-tracker hired a baby-sitter—to take over her corporate responsibilities!

For the truth is, all you eager young job-seekers, that no one knows for sure what the management of top U.S. corporations does all day or well into the night. Sitting at desks has been observed. Sitting at meetings has been observed. Initialing memos has been observed. Could a woman—even a mommy—do all this? Certainly, and with time left over for an actual job of some sort. So the question that our corporate leaders must ultimately face is: what does our vast army of pin-striped managers do anyway, and could it be done by a reliable baby-sitter?

[1989]

ACROSS THE
CLASS DIVIDE

●••●••●••●••●••●••●

Small Talk

●··●··●··●··●··●··●

ONE OF MY FAVORITE SOCIOLOGISTS, Richard Sennett, has warned that we are losing the art of impersonal civility, without which urban life can only be nasty, brutish, etc. In particular, in the absence of a blackout or a major garbage strike, we have nothing to talk to strangers about—a fact that is tragically illustrated by Bernhard Goetz and his intemperate behavior on the IRT. Reportedly, one of the victims approached him with the one acceptable interstranger conversational opener: "Got the time?" When that subject was exhausted, either because Goetz lacked a watch or had not read Sennett's book *The Fall of Public Man,* the victims-to-be were left with the one other question suitable for use between strangers of vastly different social classes: "Got five bucks?" Goetz pulled a gun because, as far as he could tell, the conversational possibilities had been used up.

In the suburbs, there is less violence because we still have the weather to talk about. For example, one of my neighbors is a known political conservative and a dealer in seven-figure real estate, but despite the yawning social gap between us, neither of us has ever drawn a gun on the other. Instead, we each make a point of inquiring graciously whether it is cold enough for the other one yet—a question that implies nothing more hostile than that the other may have perverse tastes in temperatures. Nor do weather conversations have to be trite and unfeeling. Just the other night in a takeout pizza place, in response to the usual query on snow, a harried-looking woman waiting for two sausage specials announced with great vehemence: "I wouldn't mind if it snowed if it would just snow once and get it over with! One day, that's it, then finish. No more. Enough!" Everyone was stirred by the strong stand she had taken and everyone, including the ordinarily sullen young men behind the counter, joined in a chorus of hearty approbation.

Under conditions where we cannot talk about the weather, the suburbs become as dangerous as the Canarsie line is said to be at 2 A.M. These breakdowns in civility occur primarily on the roads and highways, where we spend most of the time that we are not at home watching news reports of urban mayhem. The problem is that there is simply no way to engage the driver of a car sideswiping you at seventy miles an hour in a speculative dialogue about the prospects for another nice weekend. Even a bumper sticker with an unobjectionable personal statement like I'D RATHER BE IN PHILADELPHIA has no power to distract a station wagon bent on tailgating until you consent to drive off into a ditch and give it the road. If there has been less attention to this problem than to, say, subway crime, it is probably because the politicians are intimidated by the class of people who are capable of assault with a $35,000 Jaguar or Mercedes.

The lesson for the cities is that there is an urgent need to institute some form of universally understood, content-free, urban small talk. Unfortunately, the weather will not do; for one thing, because it is not a very prominent feature of urban life, at least not compared with crime or the price of real estate. Furthermore, city dwellers do not have a sufficiently shared experience of the weather to enable them to discuss it at a common level of expertise. Some people live in climate-controlled condos where the windows cannot even be opened from the inside; others live in doorways. Some people spend their winters in the Caribbean; others go to the steam pipes under Times Square. With such a diversity of habitats and life-styles, the weather is a far too politically charged subject to safely undertake with strangers. Men in fleece-lined outerwear, for example, should avoid opening with such remarks as: "I wonder if that plastic garbage bag is as warm as it looks."

If the weather is out, we will probably have to make do with the time. "Got the time?" should not be ruled out just because it fell flat with Goetz. As an opener, it has the virtue of creating an ephemeral framework of equality: it establishes the person being questioned as a potential authority in the matter, while at the same time establishing that the questioner is busy and important enough to need to know the time, although perhaps too free-spirited to bother with a watch. (In contrast, "Cold enough for you?" invites only a subjective impression—generally a weak grimace—and does not enhance the status of either party.) But the best feature of "Got the time?" is that it refers to a shared condition—perhaps the only condition that a randomly selected pair of Manhattanites can be sure of having in common.

I never really saw the possibilities in the time as a subject of conversation until several months ago when I happened to see some news footage of President Reagan attempting to chat with a group of rather surly-looking construction workers. He approached them, tucked his chin down, and gave that rueful little smile he uses when explaining that he did not know the deficit was so big or realize that missiles cannot be recalled in flight, and pointing to the ground, announced that it was a different day in China, where he had recently been or was soon to go. The workers looked at the ground, appeared to consider this odd feature of Sino-American relations, then chuckled obligingly; and the conversation apparently continued along the same themes. In much the same way, visiting relatives from Idaho can make a week fairly whiz by with remarks like, "I don't know why you people look so tuckered out—it's only 8 P.M. my time."

I am not saying that the IRT tragedy could definitely have been averted if Goetz had given a civil answer to "Got the time?" It takes two at least to make a conversation work, and some responsibility would have fallen on the young men, in this case, to come up with suitable follow-up remarks. For example, if Goetz had said it was three, someone might have said: "That late? I would have thought two, two forty-five max. I don't know where the time goes." To which an amiable Goetz might have offered: "It's been like that all day. The so-called lunch hour seemed like forty minutes, if you know what I mean." This would have invited that all-purpose verbal gesture of solidarity: "Geez, what are they going to think up next?" Instead of a shoot-out, the encounter would have ended in that warm feeling, so well known to discussants of subway crime or suburban weather, of shared antagonism to a common oppressor.

Even with the best of wills, small talk may not be enough to save our cities. Some of us will feel our blood pressure drop and our eyes glaze over at the thought of sustaining a discourse on the time, or even on that far richer topic, the weather. But those who don't, as the expression goes, have the time of day for their fellow citizens should brace themselves for further barbarism. For if "Got the time?" doesn't work, there will be only one question to hurl across the chasm of urban class divisions, and that is, "Got five bucks?"

[1985]

Two, Three, Many Husbands

●··●··●··●··●··●··●

IT IS MIDSUMMER and a soft sound of concupiscent lip-smacking rises from the Potomac valley, for it is all right, once again, for important men to talk about the Family, and especially its most fascinating and recalcitrant form, the Black Family. Not so long ago, poverty was believed to be the result of unemployment, discrimination, low wages, and other dreary economic factors, the mere reciting of which would cause a whole seminar full of modern-day social thinkers to slump forward in profound slumber. It was further thought, in the old days, to be impolite to blame poverty on the sleeping arrangements of the poor, just as no one would have thought of blaming plant closings on the personal hygiene of American's blue-collar workers. In those days, white men felt inhibited about castigating the black family, more or less as they hesitated to approach a random young man of color with amusing speculations about the sexual proclivities of his mama.

But, hey, this is the eighties and it sure is fun to reflect on what the poor are doing in the privacy of their tenements or street-side cardboard shelters, as the case may be. Are they married, single, promiscuous, underage, depraved? Whole books, conferences, and sonorous speeches are now devoted to these questions, which some believe may hold the key to every social problem from infant malnutrition to subway graffiti. If you wish to appear au courant in the postliberal set, just cast your eyes downward and mutter knowingly about the Black Family. White folks should still be a little circumspect when in mixed company, perhaps adding modestly, "It's up to *you people* to do something about it, of course. . . ."

Actually, the problem is not a new one. It's been tossed back and forth like a hot potato between Daniel Patrick Moynihan and various members of the black intelligentsia for over twenty years now. When he first suggested that black poverty was caused by black "matriarchy"—i.e., that the very existence of so many single mothers was "emasculating" black men—the intelligentsia wisely suggested that his mouth be washed out with soap. But time passed. Moynihan transmogrified himself from a liberal into a neoconservative and finally into a neoliberal. The black intelligentsia mellowed too, produced their own crop of neoconservatives, and perhaps—sensing that a righteous distance had at last grown up between themselves and the wretched underclass—decided to reclaim the Problem of the Black Family for themselves. And recently, with just the tiniest trace of a smirk on his face, Moynihan has come out with a book *(Family and Nation)* reminding everyone that he thought of the whole thing first.

So what is the problem of the Black Family, now that you have surely grasped that it is not someone's idea of a catchy title for a *Cosby Show* spin-off? The problem, to simplify volumes of sociological folderol, is that the black family does not have enough grown-ups in it. Almost half of all black families—43 percent—contain only one grown-up, the mother; and the fact that so many black female-headed families—over 50 percent—are poor, is taken as prima facie evidence that a mother is not enough. That, plus the wisdom of seven thousand years of patriarchy, seventy years of Freudian psychology, and forty years of Parsonian sociology, establishes conclusively that the black family is short one person, and that person should be an adult male.

Or so the experts think. But I have come to believe that this formulation seriously understates the problem. Most of us would agree that a family consisting of *zero* grown-ups—say a fifteen-year-old girl and her baby—is probably not viable either as an economic unit or as a fundamental building block of civilization. Add one grown-up—the closest one at hand usually being an adult mother—and all we get is the feminization of poverty. But can we assume that adding a husband will solve the problem? And this is really the most challenging question that the black family confronts us with: Are two parents really enough?

It takes just a few simple calculations to reveal the inadequacy of the two-parent black family. First we observe that the median black male income is $9,448, which is approximately $1,000 less than the official poverty level for a family of four. So adding one median-type black male to a preformed family unit consisting of a mother and two children leaves us with a black family that still has a problem, namely, poverty. Adding two black males is still not much of an improvement; only by adding three can we hope to clear the median U.S. family income, which is about $28,000. If our hypothetical black family is to enter the middle-class mainstream, which means home ownership, it will need at least $36,596—or four black men.

I can hear the objections already. The morally squeamish will point out that polyandry contradicts the policies of Judaism, Islam, and even Mormonism. The overly sensitive will fret about the possibilities of "intimacy" and "commitment" in a five-way relationship involving at least four heterosexual males. The nit-pickers will say I have neglected certain diseconomies of scale—e.g., that each man we add will take up a certain amount of spending money and space—so that it may actually take six or seven husbands to produce the problem-free black family.

But I am convinced the upper-middle-class whites (the politically pivotal group in our society) are already warming to the notion of the six-parent black family. Just days ago, at a wine-and-Brie reception for some worthy cause, I overheard a young blond woman in linen suit and Reeboks opine, to general mutters of approval, that "blacks really haven't gotten anywhere, considering all that's been *done* for them. Why, just look at the Orientals—but of course they have these really wonderful, big extended families!"

This is not the place to take on the myth of the Asian family, which, as the story goes, escaped from Saigon with only a suitcase full of bullion from the national treasury, a few keys of heroin, and a dozen hardworking aunts and grandmothers, set up a modest asparagus and kiwi dealership on Sunset Boulevard, and now has six sons at MIT. The point is that—just as we have learned to look to the East for clues about how to run corporations, assemble VCRs, and manufacture automobiles—we have begun to look to the Orient for the model family, especially the model poor-but-striving family. It must have been easier for the black family when the model for comparison was the two-parent European immigrant family. But standards are rising. Implicitly, the upper middle class has come to believe that a family that is *really* trying will include a half dozen or more breadwinners all willing to work at least twelve hours a day at minimum wage.

There is another solution, one that may not go down quite so well with the wine-and-Brie set. It occurred to me only after many hours of poring over the dour statistics made available by the U.S. Census Bureau, when I came across a fact so striking, so curious, that it is hard to believe that it has escaped the notice of all those worthy scholars who muse about the Problem of the Black Family. The fact is that the number of white *single* men who have never married and earn more than the median *family* income (i.e., the number of really *prime* bachelors) is almost the same, give or take a hundred thousand or so, as the number of poor, black single mothers!

Could this be a coincidence, a meaningless convergence of unrelated digits? I very much doubt it. To all those single white males earning far more than they need, we must say firmly, "Shape up, fellas, for demography is destiny! Go forth to the welfare hotels, the day-old bread shops, the emergency rooms of the public hospitals, and find a single mom to woo!"

Some will find this an unfeeling solution, a heavy-handed attempt to reduce a complex issue to mere dollars and cents. After all, a family income does not a family make.

Just look at that other great sociological conundrum—the Problem of the White Family. Even when it is not poor (and space does not permit us to deal with the doleful fact that white poverty is numerically still a far greater problem than black poverty), the White Family has long been a nesting place for social ills too numerous to list: alcoholism, incest, organized crime, senior abuse, pediatric stress diseases—not to mention, in many cases, national chauvinism, racism, and militant religious intolerance. No wonder that white families by the millions have turned to the black gentry, represented by Bill Cosby and the Huxtables, to learn the elementary principles of domestic nonviolence.

But if economics isn't everything, neither should it be forgotten in our search for a solution to poverty. Money helps, and it is especially helpful to those who have very little of it. In the absence of all the old-fashioned ways of redistributing wealth—progressive taxation, job programs, adequate welfare, social services, and other pernicious manifestations of pre-Reaganite "big government"—the rich will just have to marry the poor.

[1986]

On the Street Where You Live

•··•··•··•··•··•··•··•

THERE WAS A TIME, I am old enough to recall, when homelessness was thought to be a result of poverty, which was in turn believed to arise from a shortage of money. But that interesting and arcane theory has long since been abandoned for two new ones: the conservative theory, that homelessness is voluntary, and hence no one should be discouraged from the outdoor life. And the liberal theory, that anyone who refuses to avail him or herself of a nice condo or town house is a nutcase, and deserves immediate housing in a locked ward.

The conservative theory no doubt reflects the fact that many conservatives have had bad experiences with homes. I am thinking of clogged gutters, defective siding, property taxes, and pool scum, which are enough to make any reasonable person want to pack a change of underwear and take up residency in a nearby dumpster. Or consider, if you will, the frustrations of the 3 million Americans who have *more than one* home, and are always asking themselves, "Where did I put that little brush attachment to the vacuum cleaner, the one for getting the dust balls off the windowsills? Aspen? Palm Springs? Westhampton?"

The liberal theory, on the other hand, reflects the fact that many liberals have had bad experiences with the homeless. They are—let us be honest about it—an unsightly bunch, due largely to the difficulties of maintaining a freshly pressed wardrobe in a plastic garbage bag. New York's Mayor Koch, for example, launched his plan to round up the homeless and put them in mental hospitals after observing a poor street dweller who had defecated on herself.

The Koch plan is to have little teams of mental-health professionals going door-to-door, as it were, among the city's homeless, testing for signs of mental illness. Naturally, the mental-health professionals heralded this plan with squeals of delight. A few years ago, you will recall, they lost considerable face when it was discovered that the hundreds of thousands of inpatients in their care were receiving no more psychiatric help than one normally gets when checked in at a Quality Inn. The patients were discharged, the shrinks were exposed as shills of the Thorazine industry, and many of them were reduced to treating neurotic pets and glitched-out computer programs.

So, it's quite a coup—a vote of confidence, really—for the mental-health professionals to get the nation's homeless people to work on. In fact, inside sources tell me that the American Psychiatric Association already has designated homelessness as a committable offense and has hopes of reclassifying poverty itself as a mental illness, probably under the "self-defeating personality" category.

But there are problems with the liberal approach, and I am not referring to that self-serving quibble the mental-health professionals keep bringing up: "There just aren't enough beds," they say, meaning mental hospital beds, "for the homeless." This is true, but neither are there enough coffee tables, chaise lounges, love seats, or breakfast nooks. If the homeless are not going to get homes, if they are only going to get one ingredient of a home, then better it should be a bed than (as Koch was originally considering) a toilet. But this does not mean that each homeless person needs his or her own private bed. As Hugh Hefner once demonstrated, it is possible to live for many years without leaving one's bed (a giant, mirror-lined one, in his case), and still find room for any number of impoverished young people in need of a place to stay.

No, the real problem is, first, what will the little teams of mental-health professionals use for a street-side mental-health test? We trust they will dispense with embarrassing questions like, "Name and address?" But what about that standard neurological question: "Who is the president of the United States?" Many people inside homes do not know for sure, or whether he is still with us; and it would be a terrible thing if the homeless were penalized for good guesses, like "Howard Baker" or "Nancy Reagan."

Then there is the potential problem of backlash from the homed and multiple-homed, who are bound to become resentful and start demanding free mental-health care for themselves. You, for example, if you are reading this inside a home, are probably thinking, When was the last time a little team of mental-health professionals came to my door to inquire as to whether I was using the toilet and knew who the president was? Already, a group of militant California homeowners is demanding free psychiatric house calls with a choice of rolfing, color therapy, or channeling to the deceased person of one's choice.

I hate to say it, but the conservatives probably will come up with a better solution. The far right, for example, believes that giving the homeless beds, even in mental hospitals, is an invitation to immorality and sloth. They suggest that, if the homeless are to be given anything, they should be given addresses, presumably for post office boxes so that they will no longer be excluded from Richard Viguerie's mailing lists. Another proposal, from a group of Republican charity ball organizers, is to let the homeless continue their al-fresco existence but give them each something decent to wear—a little bubble skirt, for eample, or one of the new minisuits from Donna Karan's collection.

I have my own theory of homelessness, of course. It has to do with some elaborate calculations I have made involving the ratio between the average rent for an urban studio apartment and the median monthly wage. Or the price of a suburban ranch house compared to the mean annual family income. I would love to tell you about it, but I can say no more, because I have just learned that there is a new plan afoot to institutionalize anyone found on the street mumbling the words "housing crisis."

[1987]

Profile of a Welfare Cheat

●··●··●··●··●··●··●··●

I WAS NOT OFFENDED by the amount of money that Nancy Reagan reportedly spent for her inaugural wardrobe, $46,000, because I know that this sum would barely be enough to buy the Pentagon a screwdriver. Since I can buy a screwdriver for $2.95 at the local hardware store, I appreciated the ingenuity Mrs. Reagan had shown in finding a way to cover herself, head to toe, at an equivalent price. What sets my teeth on edge is not the administration's extravagance, but its apparent hostility to the female poor, who form a majority of the population known colloquially as "welfare cheats." The average family on welfare receives a good deal less than $4,600 a year, which, at official Washington prices, would not even finance a set of shoelaces— and even this sum is due for further cuts.

I used to think that the administration was stingy and meanspirited, but the latest academic thinking on welfare is that it is positively unkind to shower the poor with largesse, even in the low four-figure range. Give an unemployed and bankrupt person a little help, according to welfare critics George Gilder and Charles Murray, and he or she will lapse into the psychic slough known as demoralization—from which few ever venture forth again to seek honest employment at an hourly wage. The implication for public policy is that it would be much kinder to spare the poor the misery of demoralization, which is after all only a product of big government and other human errors, and let them experience the hunger that is natural to their condition.

There is someone I would like to introduce to the aforementioned gentlemen. She is a friend and former neighbor of mine, who will have to remain anonymous until public opinion takes a more generous turn. "Lori," let us call her, makes an excellent first impression. She is vivacious, smart, and, although it shouldn't matter, disconcertingly pretty. She is also on welfare —and those who imagine the average welfare recipient as a slatternly mother of six or a young man apprenticing in street crime should know that Lori is a far more representative case: she is a single mother, as are close to 90 percent of recipients; she has only one child, which puts her among the 70 percent that have two or fewer; and, although this shouldn't matter either, she is white, as are a majority of welfare recipients.

Lori is no more demoralized by welfare than I am by an unexpected royalty check. True, she resents the days spent in the welfare office, the long waits, the interrogations about her limited inventory of household possessions. But she feels that she and her daughter have rights in the matter, like the right to a standard of living on some level exceeding vagrancy. She was not always, she will tell you, so assertive—certainly not in the two years when she was married to a man who routinely beat her and had once chased her around the house with a gun. Only welfare had made it possible to leave him, a move she says was like being born again, "as a human being this time."

In one way, though, Lori fits the worst stereotypes: she is a "cheat." That is to say, she has sources of income that she does not report to the welfare office. When she can find a friend to watch her daughter (welfare doesn't provide funds for child care), she rushes out to whatever job she can find: baby-sitting, waitressing, cleaning other people's houses, anything so long as it's off the books. I wouldn't want to swear to it in court, but she sometimes brings in close to $100 a week in this manner—not enough to enable to her to get off welfare, but a useful supple-

ment, along with the occasional house plant or pizza pie she
accepts from an admirer.

If I was made of sterner stuff, if, for example, I was tough
enough to disport myself in thousand-dollar-plus outfits while,
only blocks away, my fellow citizens were warming themselves
over bonfires in vacant lots, then I suppose I would turn Lori in.
And if I were a welfare critic of the stature of Gilder or Murray,
I suppose I would tell her I was doing it for her own good.
Instead, I merely sit back and reflect on what Lori's case reveals
about welfare. The worst problem with it is not that it causes
demoralization, atrophy of the work ethic, or craven dependency. The worst problem is that welfare doesn't pay enough.

This, I have realized, is the true cause of the demoralization
critics are so concerned about: It is one thing to spend a day
queueing up in a crowded stuffy room if the setting is OTB and
you end up winning $50,000 in cash. But it is dispiriting to do
the same thing for no greater reward than a $17 allowance for a
child's winter jacket. And, as should be obvious, it is inadequate
benefits, rather than depravity, that are the cause of cheating.
Lori, for example, does not use her illicit income to build up a
fleet of Cadillacs, but to buy little things that some pebble-
hearted bureaucrat has determined are inessential to a welfare
recipient's well-being: deodorant, hand lotion, an occasional
commercial haircut.

The only question, then, is how much welfare benefits should
be increased. Bearing in mind that the primary purpose of welfare is to support mothers and young children, we might use an
estimate offered in *Newsweek*'s recent cover story on yuppies, in
which a young woman said she ordinarily required $200,000 to
live on, but would of course need more if she were to have a
baby. If $300,000 or so seems high, we might just go with the
market value of the average mother's work: approximately $7 an
hour, for both child care and housekeeping, for what is mini-
mally a ten-hour day, or about $26,000 a year.

·   ·   ·

Now, I can imagine the objections of the welfare critics, who will speak out manfully against this latest proposal to drive the poor beyond demoralization to outright despondency. Well, if they cannot understand that it feels better to have some money rather than none and more than less, I will base my argument on middle-class self-interest: Welfare, as it is now, is degrading to the middle class. It makes us mean and petty, bad neighbors and worse citizens. In fact, the more miserly welfare is, the more anxious we feel, deep inside, about our own economic security. And the more anxious we feel, the more we are inclined to bluster about "not taking any handouts," and the nastier we get toward those who most need our understanding and support. It is a terrible cycle that we, the taxpayers and breadwinners, have entered into, and perhaps far more debilitating in the long run than any "cycle of dependency" experienced by the poor. Never mind the welfare recipients, *we* can't afford to go on like this.

Then there is the inevitable question, asked by the well-meaning as well as the mean-willed, of where the money is supposed to come from. Awed as I am by the federal deficit—and who cannot help but wonder when some international banking cabal will lose patience and set a collection agency loose on our nation's capital?—I have little patience for this question. Surely a nation that tolerates $46,000 wardrobes and equally overpriced screwdrivers can figure out how to support the poor at some level of dignity and comfort. Why, the president could hold a fund-raising dinner and invite a few dozen of his intimate friends and supporters. Or, as we say in the suburbs, the Pentagon could hold a garage sale.

[1985]

Is the Middle Class Doomed?

●··●··●··●··●··●··●

MOST OF US are "middle-class," or so we like to believe. But there are signs that America is becoming a more divided society: over the last decade, the rich have been getting richer; the poor have been getting more numerous; and those in the middle do not appear to be doing as well as they used to. If America is "coming back," as President Reagan reassured us in the wake of the economic malaise of the early 1980s, it may be coming back in a harsh and alien form.

It was in the late sixties that American society began to lurch off the track leading to the American dream. No one could have known it at the time, but, according to the economists Bennett Harrison, Chris Tilly, and Barry Bluestone, those were the last years in which economic inequality among Americans declined. Since then, in a sharp reversal of the equalizing trend that had been under way since shortly after World War II, the extremes of wealth have grown further apart and the middle has lost ground. In 1984, according to a report by Congress's Joint Economic Committee, the share of the national income received by the wealthiest 40 percent of families in the United States rose to 67.3 percent, while the poorest 40 percent received 15.7 percent (the smallest share since 1947); the share of the middle 20 percent declined to 17 percent. The tax-revision bill will be of some help to low-income families, but it will by no means alter the overall pattern of income distribution in their favor—or, critics say, halt the trend toward greater inequality.

Some economists have even predicted that the middle class, which has traditionally represented the majority of Americans and defined the nation's identity and goals, will disappear altogether, leaving the country torn, like many Third World societies, between an affluent minority and a horde of the desperately poor.

At least in the area of consumer options, we seem already in the process of becoming a "two-tier society." The middle is disappearing from the retail industry, for example. Korvettes and Gimbels are gone. Sears, Roebuck and J.C. Penney are anxiously trying to reposition themselves to survive in an ever more deeply segmented market. The stores that are prospering are the ones that have learned to specialize in one extreme of wealth or the other: Nordstrom's and Neiman-Marcus for the affluent; K Mart for those constrained by poverty or thrift. Whether one looks at food, clothing, or furnishings, two cultures are emerging: natural fibers versus synthetics; handcrafted wood cabinets versus mass-produced maple; David's Cookies versus Mister Donuts.

The political implications of the shift toward a two-tier society —if this is what is really happening—are ominous. Felix Rohatyn, the investment banker and civic leader, has observed: "A democracy, to survive, must at the very least appear to be fair. This is no longer the case in America." We may have outgrown the conceit that America is a uniformly "middle-class" society, but we have expected the extremes of wealth and poverty to be buffered by a vast and stable middle class. If the extremes swell, and if the economic center cannot hold, then our identity and future as a nation may be endangered.

Because the stakes are so high, the subject of class polarization has itself become bitterly polarized. On what could be called the "pessimistic" side is a group of mostly young, though highly acclaimed, economists who tend to be based in the relatively prosperous state of Massachusetts. The other side, which is represented at two research organizations, the Brookings Institution, in Washington, and the Conference Board, in New York City, argues that there are no fundamental flaws in the economy, and that the shift toward greater inequality will be short-lived.

Though much of the debate has been numbingly technical, the differences sometimes seem to have more to do with ideology than statistics. Fabian Linden of the Conference Board, for example, says of "the pessimists": "There are always people who think that this is an imperfect world and has to be changed. . . . It's awfully arrogant, if you think about it."

But no one, however humble, denies that there has been a profound change in the class contours of American society. No matter how you slice up the population—whether you compare the top fifth to the bottom fifth, or the top 40 percent to the poorest 40 percent—and no matter whether you look at individual earnings or household earnings, the have-nots are getting by on less and the haves are doing better than ever.

The change is particularly striking when families with children are compared over time. In 1968, the poorest one-fifth of such families received 7.4 percent of the total income for all families; in 1983, their share was only 4.8 percent, down by one-third. During the same period, the richest fifth increased its share from 33.8 percent to 38.1 percent. The result, according to the Census Bureau, is that the income gap between the richest families and the poorest is now wider than it has been at any time since the bureau began keeping such statistics in 1947.

So far, the middle class is still a statistical reality. At least a graph of income distribution still comes out as a bell-shaped curve, with most people hovering near the mean income rather than at either extreme. (If the middle class disappeared, the curve would have two humps rather than one in the middle.) But in the last decade, the income distribution curve has slumped toward the lower end and flattened a little on top, so that it begins to look less like a weathered hill and more like a beached whale. To the untrained eye, the shift is not alarming, but as economist Jeff Faux, president of the Economic Policy

Institute in Washington, says: "These numbers are very slow to move, really glacial. So when you do get a change you better pay attention."

The optimists in the debate attribute the downward shift in earnings chiefly to the baby boomers—the 78-million-member generation that began to crowd into the labor market in the 1960s and '70s, presumably driving down wages by their sheer numbers. As the boomers age, the argument goes, their incomes will rise and America will once again be a solidly middle-class society. But a recent analysis by the economists Bennett Harrison and Chris Tilly at the Massachusetts Institute on Technology and Barry Bluestone at Boston College suggests that the bulge in the labor force created by the baby boom and business-cycle effects can account for less than one-third of the increase in income inequality that has occurred since 1978.

In fact, baby boomers may find it much more difficult to make their incomes grow over time than did their parents' generation. A study by the economists Frank S. Levy and Richard C. Michel shows that, in earlier decades, men could expect their earnings to increase by about 30 percent as they aged from forty to fifty. But men who became forty in 1973 saw their earnings actually decline by 14 percent by the time they reached fifty. If this trend continues, the baby boomers, the oldest of whom are just now turning forty, will find little solace in seniority.

The fate of the baby boomers is central to the debate about America's economic future in another way, too. Contrary to the popular stereotype, the baby boomers are not all upwardly mobile, fresh-faced consumers of mesquite cuisine and exercise equipment. The baby boom is defined as those born between 1946 and 1964, and only 5 percent of them qualify as "yuppies" (young urban professional or managerial workers earning over $30,000 a year each, or $40,000 or more for a couple). Most of them, like most Americans, are "middle-class," in the limited sense that they fall somewhere near the middle of the income distribution rather than at either extreme. But they are also young, and whether they can hold on to, or achieve, middle-class status—however defined—is a test of whether the American middle class is still capable of reproducing itself from one generation to the next.

"Middle-class" can be defined in several ways. Statistically, the middle class is simply the part of the population that earns near the median income—say, the 20 percent that earns just above the median income plus the 20 percent whose earnings fall just below it. But in colloquial understanding, "middle-class" is a matter of status as well as income, and is signaled by subtler cues—how we live, what we spend our money on, what expectations we have for the future. Since the postwar period, middle-class status has been defined by home ownership, college education (at least for the children), and the ability to afford amenities such as a second car and family vacations.

In the matter of home ownership, the baby boomers are clearly not doing as well as their parents. Levy and Michel calculate that the typical father of today's boomers faced housing costs that were equivalent to about 14 percent of his gross monthly pay. In 1984, a thirty-year-old man who purchased a median-priced home had to set aside a staggering 44 percent of his income for carrying charges. The recent decline in interest rates has helped some, but it has been largely offset by continuing inflation in the price of homes. The problem is not only that housing costs have escalated, but that the median income has actually been declining. According to the National Association of Homebuilders, a family today needs an income of approximately $37,000 to afford a median-priced home. In 1985, according to newly released census figures, the median family income was $27,735—almost $10,000 short.

If the baby-boom bulge in the work force is not the cause—or sole cause—of America's slide toward greater economic inequality, what is? Public policy is one obvious contributing factor. In the 1960s and early '70s, public policy—and political rhetoric—favored a downward redistribution of wealth. Ronald Reagan reversed the trend and instituted policies that resulted in the government's first major upward redistribution of wealth since World War II. As a result of the combination of reduced taxes for the better-off and reduced social spending for the poor, the richest one-fifth of American families gained $25 billion in disposable income between 1980 and 1984, while the poorest one-fifth lost $7 billion. The current tax-revision bill would correct some of these inequities. But at the same time, according to a number of the bill's critics including Richard A. Musgrave, professor emeritus of political economy at Harvard, it also represents a retreat from the very principle of progressivity in taxation in that it reduces the maximum rate of taxation for the very rich.

The drift toward a two-tier society actually began before the Republicans took office in 1981, and must have been set in motion by changes that go deeper than political trends. Some of these changes may be more social than economic; divorce, for example, can have the effect of splitting the members of individual families into different social classes. In most cases, the woman ends up with the children and most of the responsibility for supporting them. As a result, according to Lenore J. Weitzman, author of *The Divorce Revolution,* an ex-wife's disposable income is likely to fall by 73 percent in the year following divorce, while her ex-husband's *rises* by 42 percent. Single mothers now account for almost half the household heads in poverty.

But if divorce is a factor in the emerging pattern of inequality, so is marriage. Mimi Lieber, a New York–based marketing consultant who has been following the impact of class polarization on consumer choices, says that we are seeing "a changing pattern of marriage; today, the doctor marries another doctor, not a nurse." The result is that marriage is less likely to offer women a chance at upward mobility.

On the whole, however, marriage is probably a stabilizing factor, at least if it is a "nontraditional" form of marriage. Seventy percent of baby-boom women are in the work force—compared with about 30 percent in their mothers' generation—and the earnings of working wives are all that hold a growing number of families in the middle class. A study prepared by Sheldon

Danziger and Peter Gottschalk for the Joint Economic Committee of Congress shows that most of the income gains made by
white two-parent families with children since 1967 can be accounted for by increased earnings by wives. On a husband's
earnings alone, the average family (of any race) would fall below
the median income; on the wife's earnings alone, it would fall to
the poverty level of $10,990 for a family of four.

Whatever else is changing in our patterns of marriage and
divorce, something has happened to the average American's ability to support a family. According to Bluestone and Harrison, the
economy is simply not generating enough well-paying jobs anymore: between 1963 and 1978, only 23 percent of all new jobs
paid poverty-level or "near-poverty-level" wages; but of the new
jobs generated between 1978 and 1984, almost half—48 percent
—paid near-poverty-level wages. Here again, public policy is
partly to blame. The minimum wage has not gone up since 1981,
and now amounts to $6,700 for full-time, year-round work—
almost $4,000 short of the poverty level for a family of four.

There are no doubt deeper—or, as the economists say,
"structural"—reasons for the average American's sagging earning power. For one thing, the economy has been "globalized."
In some industries, such as garments, toys, and electronics,
American workers are competing—directly or indirectly—with
Third World workers whose wages are a few dollars per day,
rather than per hour. In a related development, the American
economy has been "deindustrializing," or shifting from manufacturing to services, fast enough to displace 11.5 million Americans from blue-collar jobs (many in highly paid industries, such
as auto and steel) since 1979. For the most part, service jobs
tend to be lower-paying and nonunionized. Finally, there has
been the technological revolution. Computers are eating away at
many skilled, mid-level occupations—middle managers, department store buyers, machinists—as well as traditionally low-paid
occupations such as bank teller and telephone operator.

It is on the role of the "structural" changes that the economists are most fiercely divided, and, it seems to me, confused.

The optimists insist that the causes of class polarization are more ephemeral than structural—if not the baby-boom bulge, then the strong dollar, or some other factor equally likely to go away by itself. Not long ago, the pessimists were convinced that polarization was the straightforward result of globalization, deindustrialization, and high technology, the combination of which, at least theoretically, could be expected to produce a nation of low-skilled helots dominated by a tiny technical-managerial elite.

Now some of them are not so sure. "It's incontestable," says David Smith, an economist on Senator Edward M. Kennedy's staff, "that as a service economy, we won't be able to sustain the level of growth required to maintain our standard of living." But, he says, recent data suggest that high technology does not necessarily bring about occupational polarization. As for international competition, he asks sarcastically, "Who the hell are we competing with in the insurance industry?"

There is no question, though, that American workers are less able than they were in the recent past to hold their own at the bargaining table—and most of them (the more than 80 percent who are not union members) never even get to the bargaining table. In the last decade, citing the need to compete in the newly global marketplace, employers have launched an aggressive campaign to cut labor costs, demanding—and frequently getting—wage give-backs, two-tier contracts, and other concessions. While wage-earning workers tighten their belts, top executives are reaping salaries that might once have been considered provocatively high. According to the social critic Michael Harrington: "We're seeing a savage attack on workers' wages and living standards. In the long run, no one's going to win because a low-wage society cannot be an affluent society."

Whatever the reasons for the growing polarization of American society, polarization creates its own dynamics, and perversely, they tend to make things worse, not better. For one thing, the affluent (say, the upper fifth or those with family incomes over $48,000 a year) do what they can to avoid contact with the desperate and the downwardly mobile. They abandon public services and public spaces—schools, parks, mass transit—which then deteriorate. One result is that the living conditions and opportunities available to the poor (and many in the middle range of income) worsen. And, of course, as the poor sink lower, the affluent have all the more reason to withdraw further into their own "good" neighborhoods and private services.

As the better-off cease to utilize public services, they also tend to withdraw political support for public spending designed to benefit the community as a whole. If you send your children to private school, commute to work by taxi, and find your clean air at Aspen, you are likely to prefer a tax cut to an expansion of government services. This may be one reason for the decline of liberalism among America's upper middle class. The liberal "effete snobs" that Spiro T. Agnew railed against are as rare today as Republicans on the welfare rolls.

There is another way in which class polarization tends to become self-reinforcing. As the Columbia University economist Saskia Sassen-Koob says: "The growth of the new urban upper middle class stimulates the proliferation of low-wage jobs. We're seeing the growth in the cities of a kind of 'servant class' that prepares the gourmet take-out food for the wealthy, stitches their designer clothes, and helps manufacture their customized furniture."

Traditional middle-class patterns of consumption, she notes, had a more egalitarian impact. "When everyone bought their furniture at Sears and their food at the A & P, they were generating employment for workers in mass-production industries that were likely to be unionized and to pay well." In contrast, today's upscale consumer shops are boutique-scale outlets for items that are produced, or prepared, by relatively small, nonunionized companies.

The polarization of the extremes—the urban upper-middle class versus the "underclass"—inevitably makes it harder for those in the middle range of income to survive. As the rich get richer, they are able to bid up the costs of goods that middle-income people also consume, particularly housing. Wildly inflated housing costs hurt the affluent upper fifth, too, but they are far more likely than middle-income people to be able to command salary increases to match their escalating cost of living. For those in the "new collar class," as Ralph Whitehead, Jr., a University of Massachusetts professor, terms the nonyuppie plurality of baby boomers, a mortgage may be out of reach, much less a designer style of consumption. But we are all subjected to the blandishments of the booming market for upscale goods.

To be demonstrably "middle-class" in today's culture, a family needs not only the traditional house and car, but at least some of the regalia of the well-advertised upscale life-style—beers that cost five dollars a six-pack for guests, and sixty-dollar sweatshirts for the teenage and preteen children. In order to be "middle-class" as our culture is coming to understand the term, one almost has to be rich.

So far, the hard-pressed families in the middle range of income have found a variety of ways to cope. They delay childbearing; and, even after the children come, both spouses are likely to hold jobs. They are ingenious about finding K Mart look-alikes for Bloomingdale's status goods; and, for the really big expenditures, they are likely to turn to parents for help. But these stratagems have their own costs, one of them being leisure for the kind of family life many of us were raised to expect. "We are seeing the standard two-income family," says Ethel Klein, a Columbia University political-science professor, "and the next step will probably be the three-income family, with the husband having to take a second job in order to keep up."

Karl Marx predicted that capitalist society would eventually be torn apart by the conflict between a greedy bourgeoisie and a vast, rebellious proletariat. He did not foresee the emergence, within capitalism, of a mass middle class that would mediate between the extremes and create a stable social order. But with that middle class in apparent decline and with the extremes diverging further from each other, it would be easy to conclude that the Marxist vision at last fits America's future.

But America is unique in ways that still make any prediction foolhardy. For one thing, Americans are notorious for their lack of class consciousness or even class awareness. In the face of the most brutal personal dislocations, we lack a vocabulary to express our dismay. Furthermore, at least at this point, we seem to lack political leadership capable of articulating both the distress of the have-nots and the malaise in the middle.

Thus there is no sure way to predict which way America's embattled middle class will turn. Some groups that are being displaced from the middle class seem to be moving leftward. Downwardly mobile single mothers, for example, may have helped create the gender gap that emerged, for the first time, in 1980 and was still prominent in the 1984 election, in which a greater proportion of women than men voted for the losing Democratic ticket. But the nation's debt-ridden farmers, another formerly middle-class group, have gone in all directions: some responding to Jesse Jackson's liberal populist message; others moving toward extreme right-wing fringe groups. The financially squeezed middle-income baby boomers are perhaps the most enigmatic of all. After much lush speculation as to their political inclinations, we know only that they tend to be liberal on social issues and more conservative on economic issues, and that they admire both Ronald Reagan and Bruce Springsteen.

Only at the extremes of wealth is political behavior becoming true to Marxist form. Thomas Byrne Edsall, author of *The New Politics of Inequality,* has documented an "extraordinary intensification of class-voting" in the eighties as compared with the previous two decades. For example, in 1956 Dwight D. Eisenhower won by nearly the same margin in all income groups, but in 1980 Reagan won among the rich but was soundly rejected by those in the bottom 40 percent of the income distribution. Party affiliation is becoming equally polarized, with the haves more monolithically Republican than at any time since the 1930s, and the have-nots more solidly Democratic.

It is not clear that either party, though, is willing to advance the kinds of programs that might halt America's slide toward a two-tier society. Admittedly, it will be hard to get at the fundamental causes of class polarization until we know what they are. But there is no question that the dominant policy direction of the last few years has only exacerbated the trend. If we want to avert the polarization of American society, there is no choice, it seems to me, but to use public policy to redistribute wealth, and opportunity, downward again: not from the middle class to the poor, as Lyndon B. Johnson's Great Society programs tended to do, but from the very rich to everyone else.

We could start, for example, by raising the minimum wage, which would not only help the working poor but would also have a buoyant effect on middle-level wages. We could enact long-overdue measures, such as national health insurance and a system of subsidized child care, to help struggling young families. We could institute tax reforms that would both generate income for federal spending *and* relieve those in the middle brackets. A truly progressive income tax, combined with more generous public spending for education and social-welfare programs, would go a long way toward smoothing out the widening inequalities of opportunity.

Everyone has a stake in creating a less anxious, more egalitarian society. In fact, from the point of view of the currently affluent, the greatest danger is not that a class-conscious, left-leaning political alternative will arise, but that it will not. For without a potent political alternative, we are likely to continue our slide toward a society divided between the hungry and the overfed, the hopeless and the have-it-alls. What is worse, there will be no mainstream, peaceable political outlets for the frustration of the declining middle class or the desperation of those at the bottom. Instead, it is safe to predict that there will be more crime, more exotic forms of political and religious sectarianism, and ultimately, that we will no longer be one nation, but two.

[1986]

Marginal Men

●··●··●··●··●··●··●

CRIME SEEMS TO CHANGE character when it crosses a bridge
or a tunnel. In the city, crime is taken as emblematic of the vast
injustices of class and race. In the suburbs, though, it's intimate
and psychological—resistant to generalization, a mystery of the
individual soul. Recall the roar of commentary that followed the
murderous assault on a twenty-eight-year-old woman jogging in
Central Park. Every detail of the assailants' lives was sifted for
sociological significance: Were they poor? How poor? Students
or dropouts? From families with two parents or one? And so on,
until the awful singularity of the event was lost behind the impersonal grid of Class, Race, and Sex.

Now take the Midtown Tunnel east to the Long Island Expressway, out past the clutter of Queens to deepest suburbia,
where almost every neighborhood is "good" and "social pathology" is something you learn about in school. Weeks before the
East Harlem youths attacked a jogger, Long Islanders were
shaken by two murders which were, if anything, even more
inexplicably vicious than the assault in Central Park. In early
March, the body of thirteen-year-old Kelly Tinyes was found in
the basement of a house just down the block from her own. She
had been stabbed, strangled, and hit with a blunt instrument
before being mutilated with a bayonet. A few weeks later, four-
teen-year-old Jessica Manners was discovered along the side of a

road in East Setauket, strangled to death, apparently with her own bra, and raped.

Suspects have been apprehended. Their high-school friends, parents, and relatives have been interviewed. Their homes and cars have been searched; their photos published. We know who they hung out with and what they did in their spare time. But on the scale of large social meanings, these crimes don't rate. No one is demanding that we understand—or condemn—the white communities that nourished the killers. No one is debating the roots of violence in the land of malls and tract homes. Only in the city, apparently, is crime construed as something "socioeconomic." Out here it's merely "sick."

But East Setauket is not really all that far from East Harlem. If something is festering in the ghetto, something very similar is gnawing away at Levittown and East Meadow. A "way of life," as the cliché goes, is coming to an end, and in its place a mean streak is opening up and swallowing everything in its path. Economists talk about "deindustrialization" and "class polarization." I think of it as the problem of *marginal men:* they are black and white, Catholic and Pentecostal, rap fans and admirers of technopop. What they have in common is that they are going nowhere—nowhere legal, that is.

Consider the suspects in the Long Island murders. Twenty-one-year-old Robert Golub, in whose basement Kelly Tinyes was killed, is described in *Newsday* as an "unemployed bodybuilder." When his high-school friends went off to college, he stayed behind in his parents' home in Valley Stream. For a while, he drove a truck for a cosmetics firm, but he lost that job, in part because of his driving record: his license has been suspended twelve times since 1985. At the time of the murder, he had been out of work for several months, constructing a life around his weight-lifting routine and his dream of becoming an entrepreneur.

Christopher Loliscio, the suspect in the Manners case, is nineteen, and, like Golub, lives with his parents. He has been in trouble before, and is charged with third-degree assault and "menacing" in an altercation that took place on the campus of the State University at Stony Brook last December. Loliscio does not attend college himself. He is employed as a landscaper.

The suburbs are full of young white men like Golub and Loliscio. If they had been born twenty years earlier, they might have found steady work in decent-paying union jobs, married early, joined the volunteer fire department, and devoted their leisure to lawn maintenance. But the good blue-collar jobs are getting sparser, thanks to "deindustrialization"—which takes the form, in Long Island, of cutbacks in the defense and aerospace industries. Much of what's left is likely to be marginal, low-paid work. Nationwide, the earnings of young white men dropped 18 percent between 1973 and 1986, according to the Census Bureau, and the earnings of male high-school dropouts plunged 42 percent.

Landscaping, for example—a glamorous term for raking and mowing—pays four to five dollars an hour; truck driving for a small firm is in the same range: not enough to pay for a house, a college education, or even a mid-size wedding reception at the VFW hall.

And even those modest perquisites of life in the subyuppie class have become, in some sense, "not enough." On Long Island, the culture that once sustained men in blue-collar occupations is crumbling as more affluent settlers move in, filling the vacant lots with their new, schooner-shaped, $750,000 homes. In my town, for example, the last five years saw the bowling alley close and the blue-collar bar turn into a pricey dining spot. Even the volunteer fire department is having trouble recruiting. The prestigious thing to join is a $500-a-year racquetball club; there's just not much respect anymore for putting out fires.

So the marginal man lives between two worlds—one that he aspires to and one that is dying, and neither of which he can afford. Take "Rick," the twenty-two-year-old son of family friends. His father is a machinist in an aerospace plant which hasn't been hiring anyone above the floor-sweeping level for years now. Not that Rick has ever shown any interest in his father's trade. For one thing, he takes too much pride in his appearance to put on the dark green company-supplied work clothes his father has worn for the past twenty years. Rick has his kind of uniform: pleated slacks, high-tops, Italian knit cardigans, and a $300 leather jacket, accessorized with a gold chain and earring stud.

To his parents, Rick is a hard-working boy for whom things just don't seem to work out. For almost a year after high school, he worked behind a counter at Crazy Eddie's, where the pay is low but at least you can listen to rock and roll all day. Now he has a gig doing valet parking at a country club. The tips are good and he loves racing around the lot in the Porsches and Lamborghinis of the stockbroker class. But the linchpin of his economic strategy is living at home, with his parents and sisters, in the same room he's occupied since third grade. Rick is a long way from being able to afford even a cramped, three-bedroom house like his family home; and, given the choice, he'd rather have a new Camaro anyway.

If this were the seventies, Rick might have taken up marijuana, the Grateful Dead, and vague visions of a better world. But like so many of his contemporaries in the eighties, Rick has no problem with "the system," which, in his mind, embraces every conceivable hustle, legal or illegal. Two years ago, he made a tidy bundle dealing coke in a local dance club, bought a $20,000 car, and smashed it up. Now he spends his evenings as a bouncer in an illegal gambling joint—his parents still think he's out "dancing"—and is proud of the handgun he's got stowed in his glove compartment.

Someday Rick will use that gun, and I'll probably be the first to say—like Robert Golub's friends—"but he isn't the kind of person who would hurt *anyone*." Except that even now I can sense the danger in him. He's smart enough to know he's only a cut-rate copy of the upscale young men in *GQ* ads and MTV commercials. Viewed from Wall Street or Southampton, he's a peon, a member of the invisible underclass that parks cars, waits on tables, and is satisfied with a five-dollar tip and a remark about the weather.

He's also proud. And there's nowhere for him to put that pride except into the politics of gesture: the macho stance, the seventy-five-mile-per-hour takeoff down the expressway, and eventually maybe, the drawn gun. Jobs are the liberal solution; conservatives would throw in "traditional values." But what the marginal men—from Valley Stream to Bedford-Stuyvesant— need most of all is *respect*. If they can't find that in work, or in a working-class life-style that is no longer honored, they'll extract it from someone weaker—a girlfriend, a random jogger, a neighbor, perhaps just any girl. They'll find a victim.

[1989]

MONEY AND
MAYHEM

●··●··●··●··●··●··●··●

Welcome to Fleece U.

●··●··●··●··●··●··●

THIS FALL, my lovely and brilliant daughter will matriculate at a famous Ivy League college. Naturally, I am brokenhearted. You see, this fabulously prestigious institution, which for purposes of anonymity, I will call "Fleece U.," charges $20,000 a year—or more than two-thirds the median annual family income—to provide one's child with a bunk bed, cafeteria meals, and a chance to socialize with the future arbitrageurs and racehorse breeders of America.

Like any thrifty parent, I had done everything I could to discourage her from turning into "college material." I hid her schoolbooks. I tried to interest her in cosmetology, teen pregnancy, televison viewing. I even took her to visit a few campuses in the hope that she would be repelled by the bands of frat boys chasing minority students and beating on them with their marketing textbooks. I warned her that collegiate sexism has gotten so bad that the more enlightened colleges are now offering free rape crisis counseling as part of the freshman advising package. "Oh, Mom," is all I got, "why don't you lighten *up?*"

When the college acceptance letters started pouring in last April, I sent them back stamped "Addressee Unknown," little realizing how determined these places can be when they're closing in on a sale. Brooke Shields called from Princeton to invite my daughter to a taffy pull. Henry Kissinger dropped by in a

Lear jet to discuss the undergraduate curriculum at Harvard. Benno Schmidt offered her a 15 percent discount at Yale and a date with a leading literary deconstructionist. I was flattered, but I could see I was trapped, like the time I accepted a coupon for a free margarita and found out I had obligated myself to attend a six-hour presentation on time-sharing options in the Poconos.

And don't tell me about financial aid. I had high hopes for that until I started filling out the application form. Question 12 inquired whether I had, in addition to my present income and home furnishings, any viable organs for donation. Question 34 solicited an inventory of the silverware. Question 92 demanded a list of rock stars who could plausibly be hit with a paternity suit.

Why does college cost so much? Or, more precisely, just where is the money going? The mystery deepens when you consider that $20,000 a year is approximately what it would cost to live full-time in a downtown hotel with color TV and complimentary Continental breakfast. Yet Fleece U., I happen to know, does not even offer room service. Alternatively, $20,000 is what it would cost to institutionalize some poor soul in a facility providing twenty-four-hour nursing service. Yet Fleece U., as everyone knows, has extraordinarily high standards and accepts only those students who have already learned to wash and dress themselves with a minimum of help.

Certainly, the money is not going to enrich the faculty. Except for a few celebrity profs, who have their own gene-splicing firms on the side or who moonlight as Pentagon consultants, most college faculty are a scruffy, ill-nourished lot, who are not above supplementing their income by panhandling on the steps of the student union. Nor can the money be going to the support staff. Even at venerable Fleece U., which has an endowment the size of the federal deficit, secretaries' wages are calculated on the basis of the minimum daily caloric requirement of the human female—any larger sum being considered an incitement to immorality.

Finally, we can rule out the possibility that the money is being used to support poor students who might otherwise go straight into burger flipping. With tuition rising twice as fast as inflation, poor students are no longer welcome at places like Fleece U., even in token numbers. Nationwide, the enrollment of black students peaked in 1980 but is now in decline due to cutbacks in federal aid programs. Meanwhile, the upper middle class is fleeing the private colleges and beginning to crowd the working class out of state universities, which—at the astonishingly low price of $10,000 or so a year—are the best bargain since double coupons.

This leaves two possibilities: one is that the money is finding its way into the Iran-contra-Brunei triangle, from which no money has ever been known to reemerge. Of course, I have no logical reason for suspecting this. It is just that so much money these days starts out in the checkbooks of wealthy Connecticut widows or the royal family of Saudi Arabia and ends up hovering inaccessibly between Panama, Georgetown, and Zurich—perhaps to turn up someday as an Italian silk suit for Adolfo Calero or a spray of gardenias for Fawn Hall.

The second possibility, and the one that I personally consider more likely, is that the money is going to Don Regan. Not just Don Regan, of course, but G. Gordon Liddy, H. R. Haldeman, and possibly, in a year or two, Oliver North. For what do these fellows do after a period of public service followed, in some cases, by a relaxing spell in a minimum security prison? They repair to the college lecture circuit where, as I read recently, Don Regan pulls down $20,000 a night—the exact amount of my daughter's tuition at Fleece U.!

You can imagine how I feel about paying a sum of this magnitude to the man who almost drove Nancy Reagan to join a feminist support group. Yet I am gradually beginning to believe that the college experience will be important for my daughter. I realize that, even if she never opens a book, college will give her an opportunity I was never able to provide in our home: the chance to be around rich people—almost all of them young and attractive—continuously, twenty-four hours a day. Nor do I have to fear that she will lose the common touch. By the time she graduates, there will be at least one desperately poor person in her circle of acquaintances—myself.

[1987]

How You Can Save
Wall Street

●··●··●··●··●··●··●

WAY BACK WHEN the Dow Jones first melted down, dozens
of important men in pinstriped suits gathered outside the White
House to chant: "Wake up, sir! Give us leadership! Quickly,
please, before we go back to our fortieth-story offices and hurl
our well-nourished bodies onto the Street!" This was foolish,
and not just because President Reagan was tied up in his office,
memorizing the names of his close friends and cabinet members.

It was foolish because in a free-enterprise system, the economy is none of the president's business. In fact, that is the very
definition of the free-enterprise system, which should perhaps
be called the "free-president system," since it leaves the president free of all responsibility for the economically anguished,
whether they appear at the White House gates in pinstripes or
overalls or second-hand blankets.

A free-enterprise economy depends only on *markets*, and according to the most advanced mathematical macroeconomic theory, markets depend only on *moods:* specifically, the mood of the
men in the pinstripes, also known as the Boys on the Street.
When the Boys are in a good mood, the market thrives; when
they get scared or sullen, it is time for each one of us to look into
the retail apple business. For as Franklin Delano Roosevelt once
said, "We have nothing to be moody about except a bad mood
itself, especially when it strikes someone richer than us."

And what is responsible for the mood of the Boys on the Street? Their wives, their valets, their blood-sugar levels? No; *you* are responsible, because in free enterprise, individual is paramount. What you do in the next few hours will determine whether a few thousand key men on Wall Street have, as we like to say, a nice day. And if *they* don't have a nice day, it'll be 1933 all over again, and you might as well head to the freight yards and check into a nice clean boxcar before the crowd gets there.

Abbie Hoffman had the right idea in 1967, when he and some fellow Yippies gathered in the gallery of the New York Stock Exchange and tossed dollar bills into the pit. At the time, this gesture was widely interpreted as guerrilla theater—some crazed radical attempt at social satire. Actually, it was a desperate and earnest effort to save the economy by propitiating the gods of the market—that is, the Boys in the pit—with their favorite substance. And it worked! They were pleased! They picked up the bills and used them to wipe the perspiration from their furrowed brows. Then they smiled; and they bought low, and they sold high, and the economy surged ahead.

I would say, do it again—change your savings into small bills and toss them like confetti at the men in the pit. Only today it wouldn't work, because although dollars fall very fast, these days they are practically weightless, and the Boys on the Street might be depressed to be in a blizzard of paper worth only pennies in yen or deutsche marks. No, you have to be more clever these days, more subtle—which is why I have prepared the following guidelines on What You Can Do to Stabilize World Markets and Guarantee Global Prosperity:

Rule 1: Spend. Now is the time to buy everything you have ever needed or wanted, from a two-dollar porn magazine to a dwarf-shaped hitching post for the front lawn. The reason is that every dollar you spend is a vote of confidence for our free-enterprise economy. Every dollar you spend helps employ someone —in the pornography or lawn-statuary industry or wherever—so that they, too, are enabled to spend. Then the men on Wall

Street, sensing the groundswell of confidence around them, will feel happy and confident themselves. Except that . . .

Reckless consumer spending created our scandalous $2.5 trillion level of personal debt, which alarms certain key men in Tokyo and Bonn, who in turn are likely to call the men on Wall Street and say, "Whaddya got going there, fellas, a Third World country?" which will bring gloom to Wall Street and penury to the rest of us. Which brings us to:

Rule 2: Save. Sell all your belongings and put the money into a bank, where it will quickly become available to the Boys on the Street for the purposes of leveraged buy-outs, corporate take-overs, and other activities that keep them distracted. If you feel queasy about giving up your furniture to provide a larger kitty for those jumpy fellows on the Street, stuff all your assets into a cookie jar. This will help drive up interest rates and make America a more attractive investment to Bonn. However . . .

The merest upward flutter of interest rates could savage the bond market and reduce the Boys on the Street to craven terror, so it would probably be better to:

Rule 3: Invest all assets in an export-oriented industry—such as TOW missiles or infant-formula mix. This will shift the balance of trade in our favor and bring cheer to the Boys on the Street. If you have trouble thinking of something that American corporations still know how to produce that someone in the world still might want to buy, remember the pioneering example of pet rocks and the great untapped market of southern Sudan. But be careful not to:

Shift the balance of trade so far in our favor that you upset Toshiba and Mercedes, which means Tokyo and Bonn, so . . .

"But wait!" you say. "Why should two hundred million people pander to the mood swings of a few thousand addicted gamblers?" But that's free enterprise, friends: freedom to gamble and freedom to lose. And the great thing—the truly democratic thing about it—is that you don't even have to be a player to lose.

[1988]

Sanity Clause

●··●··●··●··●··●··●

AS TAX TIME approaches, many Americans—who are normally content to applaud any high crime or misfeasance committed by their elected officials—suddenly become testy, irritated, defensive. Even the most saintly among us—the vegetarians and residents of contemplative religious orders—are bound to ask themselves that familiar question: Why should 52 percent (that's right, *52* percent!) of my tax dollars go to the Pentagon rather than to *personal* weapons systems such as, for example, a semiautomatic Smith and Wesson designed to take out a mediumweight tax auditor at fifty yards?

Well, there's no *need* for all that anger, which only produces stress, which leads to multiple illnesses which will, in the end, be worth only minute deductions in next year's accounting. Try to see tax time as a *joyous* occasion, which is located right next to the great Judeo-Christian celebrations of Easter and Passover for a very good *reason:* it's meant to be a time for growth and personal reassessment, a time to ask ourselves such questions as: Who am I as a person? Where have I been? How did I get there? Do I have a receipt?

Although no one at 1-800-424-1040 will admit it, this is the real function of the IRS: it's a form of mass, mail-order therapy. And damn cheap, I say! In fact, as far as the IRS goes, the money is really incidental—it just shows that you're paying *attention*.

But, you say, the *form*—it's so impersonal! Where are the essay questions? Let me explain: just because they don't ask doesn't mean they're not *interested*. Consider the criterion for deducting travel expenses incurred while carrying out charitable works: the trip must have entailed "no significant element of personal pleasure." But how much is "significant"? A sunset fleetingly savored while digging graves for homeless paupers? And what if you are the sort of person who derives intense, orgiastic pleasure from acts of simple altriusm, such as throwing coins at beggars and watching the ensuing melee?

You see what I mean. Even the simplest question can be an invitation to profound reflection and searching self-analysis, leading to lengthy addenda, which may then be stapled to your form, along with philosophical digressions and clippings of interest to the Treasury Department. In fact, that estimable tract, modestly entitled *1040—Forms and Instructions*, specifically invites "privately designed and printed substitute tax forms" from those who feel restrained by the mass-produced, federally subsidized variety.

And there are more happy surprises awaiting you in *1040—Forms and Instructions*. For example, on Form 2441, p. 2, we find that a spouse may have entered the category of a "dependent" if he "is mentally or physically unable to care for himself." Who says feminists haven't penetrated the highest ranks of the federal bureaucracy? For what husband, even in the well-known two-income marriage, is capable of performing simple acts of daily self-care without the constant assistance of a watchful and fully able spouse?

Of course, the tax process won't work if you're *holding back*. Did you receive income from manufacturers' rebates (up to two dollars on a fifth of Kahlua), double coupons, deposits on soda-pop cans? Well, declare it, itemize it, document it! You'll feel better!

My advice is: approach every potential deduction in the same spirit of openness and absolute candor. Take the "business lunch," which is not the same as the "businessman's lunch" (brisket and mashed potatoes in a venue such as the "Shamrock Inn"). A "business lunch" (80 percent deductible) is a situation in which you throw aside appetite, friendship, and innocent conviviality for the grim imperatives of greed. Nothing less will do. Thus each "business lunch" you intend to claim can be a prod to agonizing self-examination: What if you did indeed discusss "business" and nothing but business from club soda to coffee but you *weren't really paying attention?* What if the person you lunched with doesn't *know* you weren't paying attention and intends to deduct his or her share of the bill? Should you alert the IRS to this potential tax fraud on his or her part? What if you earnestly attempted to talk business but the other person grew restless and called you a callow yuppie fool? It is for questions such as these that thousands of professionals stand ready at 1-800-424-1040. Call early and often!

But, you may say after many hours of toiling through Form 1040A, searching for insight and opportunities for growth—why does the subject keep coming back to *money?* Is money perhaps a metaphor for some nobler aspect of the human condition? Are instructions such as "if line 7 is $45,000, enter $5859 on line 8, otherwise multiply line 7 by 1302" meant to be taken in the spirit of zen, as a whimsical puzzle posed by some Higher Mind?

No, the tax process is indeed about money: for it is the great ebb and flow of money, cascading in tidal waves about the fortunate and splashing now and again even on the destitute, that unites us as a people. Think of it: each year the U.S. government produces a fresh supply of cash, which moves around at dizzying speed, much of it flowing uphill into the deep pockets and waiting vaults of the rich. This is known as "the economy," and also as "our way of life."

Then each year, near the time of the Resurrection, the U.S. government undertakes to harvest some of the money it has sent forth into circulation. Since the abolition of progressive taxation in the Reagan era, most of this vast harvest must come from people like you and me, the nonrich. And most of it (52 percent anyway) goes, of course, to defend "our way of life."

If you find something odd about this, something sick, mean, and ultimately futile, then you have reached the state of enlightenment known mundanely as "mental health." If not, return to Form 1040A. It will help, believe me.

[1989]

Socialism in One Household

•··•··•··•··•··•··•··•

ONE OF THE MOST PECULIAR MYTHS to come out of the New Right is the one about the compatibility of free enterprise and the family. For one thing, free enterprise has not been too kind to the family; otherwise it would have provided each able-bodied adult with wages sufficient to support one. Less frequently recognized is the fact that the family—even the relatively slender family of two—is a positive hazard to the free enterprise system.

Consider the standard two-person married couple, and consider them, for a moment, not as a bastion of heterosexuality or a living witness to Jesus or any other such high-minded abstraction. Rather, consider them in relation to what Karl Marx would have called the "realm of commodities" and George Carlin would call "their *stuff*." They will possess, at least if they are affluent enough to matter to the economy at all, one VCR, one microwave oven, one electric knife sharpner, one stationary bicycle, and, of course, one house or apartment. Among other things too numerous to mention. The point is, that they will *share* a VCR, a microwave oven, etc. This is not a matter of ideology or even personal inclination. It is practically the definition of marriage: marriage is socialism among two people.

Now, as a mental exercise, let us send this standard two-person family to the divorce court. How sad, you may be think-

ing; they were such a nice couple. Well, pull yourself together
and take a clear-headed capitalist view of things. After we have
put asunder what God had rather hastily joined, they will *each*
need a VCR, a microwave, and so forth. What has happened, as
viewed from the turrets of corporate America, is that the market
for VCRs, dwelling units, and knife sharpeners has suddenly
doubled! The population remains the same, advertising budgets
remain the same, but the market is now *twice* as big as it used to
be.

It was the director of market research at one of the *Fortune*
500 companies, a humble and scholarly man, who explained the
whole thing to me more than a decade ago. Singleness, he said,
is "good because it means you sell more products." Divorce is
the next best thing, he said, because it generates singles. A faraway look came into his eyes, perhaps in contemplation of an obligatory second divorce per lifetime or the prospect of sending the
hapless children off, one by one, to their own studio apartments.

There was a time, not so long ago, when free enterprise and
the family were on better terms. Back in the fabled fifties, as
John Godwin once wrote, Madison Avenue "regarded singleness
as akin to halitosis, and anyone lacking offspring as either an
invert or a Communist." For some reason, the consumption of
anything more substantial than a pack of Luckies or a shot of rye
was considered to require a group effort, preferably by a 4.3-
member family dwelling in Levittown.

Sometime in the sixties, Madison Avenue discovered that singles, no less than their married counterparts, were capable of
exceeding their credit limits and in general disporting themselves like all-American consumers. My own theory is that much
of the credit for this discovery belongs to James Bond in his Sean
Connery days, since he was the first well-known bachelor on the
American scene who was not a drifter or a degenerate and did
not eat out of cans. If you did not allow yourself to be distracted
by the ski chases and the sharkfeeding scenes, there was a hidden message for American capitalists: namely, that one sybaritic
single could outspend and outconsume an entire block full of

standard-issue suburban families. This is the true meaning of Bond, the first man to *have it all* without having a wife to do the shopping for him.

At first, Madison Avenue approached the singles market gingerly, as if it were something exotic and specialized. Families, it was well known, lived in houses and consumed power mowers, dishwashers, deep freezers, and Froot Loops. Singles, as far as anyone knew, consumed only Campari, sports cars, stereo equipment, designer clothes, and airplane tickets. Perhaps the first singles lived in caves—no one knows for sure—or in tiny one-room apartments that they used chiefly for storing their credit cards. But well into the seventies, they were believed to have led fairly furtive existences, eschewing furniture and other big-ticket items until the glorious day when they ceased to be single.

Today all that has changed. Singleness is no longer "a period of marking time or making do. It's a period of acquisition," according to the *Wall Street Journal.* "You can see the change in the numbers of single people buying single-family homes, china, silver, and all the other goodies." The only known product the modern single does not consume is wedding cake. But who knows? Wedding cake may be about to replace mesquite-grilled oysters as the latest yuppie snack food.

The emergence of the single as a well-rounded, grown-up consumer casts an ugly light on those who willfully marry or remain married. In fact, we may come to see them as selfish, unpatriotic, and disrespectful of the GNP. I would not go so far as to say they are subversive. But many states do not countenance sodomy between married heterosexuals, and I do not think we will long put up with the secret practice of socialism—even when committed by two consenting adults in the privacy of their own home. We know that they should be in their own *two* homes.

Sooner or later, members of the New Right are going to have to choose between the family and free enterprise. I know that this will be painful. But in the end they will all look into their hearts and ask: who has done more to finance the PACs and the

think tanks and the single-issue campaigns of the New Right—
the family or free enterprise? Then, without further ado or even
a pause for silent prayer, they will put their mouths where the
money is.

[1987]

How to Help the Uptrodden

●··●··●··●··●··●··●

EVERYONE BY NOW is familiar with the "culture of poverty," that regrettable syndrome which, the conservatives say, causes far more misery than any mere shortage of cash: the key traits are promiscuity, alcoholism, an "inability to defer gratification," family breakdown, and crime—not to mention a propensity to dine at public trash cans. It is because of the culture of poverty, we are told, that money won't help the poor. What they need, supposedly, is a kick in the pants—in the form of reduced welfare payments, a stint at "workfare," or a bracing encounter with the penal system.

But let's not focus solely on the poor. Gazing upward to the top of the income distribution chart (and trying not to strain our necks in the process), we are confronted with a problem of even more daunting proportions, namely, the rich. While the rest of us were going "tsk, tsk" over the poor, the rich were up there breeding and multiplying, eating and gobbling, fattening themselves to the collective proportions of a pre-farm-crisis hog at the county fair.

We all know the alarming statistics. The number of billionaires on *Forbes* magazine's 1986 list was almost twice that of the year before. The richest 2 percent of American families now controls half of all personal wealth in the economy. And so forth. And they are everywhere—starring in every witless miniseries, featured in every single magazine except conceivably *Bowling Age.*

Can anything be done about this ghastly bloating at the topmost reaches of the socioeconomic scale? Well, it will not be easy, because the "overclass," like the underclass, suffers from a complex psychosocial syndrome related only indirectly to material circumstances. I call it the "culture of profligacy."

Consider your run-of-the-mill rich folks: for example, Nancy Reagan and her friends, the kind of people you see in the style section embracing Ralph Lauren while raising money to send the multiply disabled to Swiss ski resorts. It is among such people that the symptoms of the culture of profligacy stand out with tragic clarity: a life-style centered on alcohol, adultery, garments, gluttony, and gambling. In the case of that last item, we are not talking about church bingo. We are talking about "speculation," a game in which the chips are entire corporations, Third World nations, and medium-sized midwestern cities.

It is this life-style that spawns the characterological traits associated with the culture of profligacy, and it is fascinating to note how similar they are to those found in the culture of poverty. Take the inability to defer gratification. It is a well-known fact that American corporate leaders are incapable of thinking beyond the quarterly profit-and-loss sheet and the upcoming Christmas bonus. Or consider "family breakdown," that scourge of the impecunious, and reflect on the disordered patterns of family life represented by, say, the von Bulows or the J. Paul Gettys. (For "promiscuity," we need go no further than Rockefeller, Nelson, or the occasional Kennedy.)

But gluttony is probably the most disturbing feature of the culture of profligacy. We all know how the poor will mob any church that offers free bologna on white bread. But the rich routinely outdo them. A recent article on the new formal trend in dining depicted bevies of millionaires in gold lamé, eagerly licking the last traces of macadamia mousse from Ming dynasty bowls.

. . .

But please don't turn the page in disgust. Profligacy is *everybody's* problem—for two reasons. First, because ultimately it is *we* who pay for it. It takes 20,000 Americans working at $10 an hour—or 1,300 Mexicans at $3 a day—to generate enough profits to support one Leona Helmsley during the off-season alone. The rich, in short, are a terrible burden on all of us.

Second, there is strong evidence that the culture of profligacy is passed on from generation to generation, along with the trust funds and other collectibles. At the rate at which the rich are breeding, I predict that by the year 1995, the average American will have to either take a 50 percent pay cut or accept a 200 percent speedup to support the swelling ranks of the overclass. By then, few of us will feel like working at all, since those who haven't become part of the culture of profligacy will surely have been driven into the culture of poverty.

So far the government has approached the problem of profligacy with incredible forbearance. Recognizing the complex web of personal and community pathology that enmeshes the rich, the Republicans have chosen to treat them compassionately, with ever-larger tax breaks, corporate subsidies, and military contracts. The strategy, no doubt, is to educate through example, until finally that spirit of generosity spreads to the profligate themselves. "Here," they will say, "take our spare coins. Use them for some socially useful project of your choosing, perhaps a cozy tent city for the homeless." And we will all live together in peace.

You can wait around for that happy day if you want, but I say it's time for a kick in the pants. Nothing short of an all-out "War on Profligacy" will do. First we take away their money. No more Lear jets with chamois upholstery, no more stretch limos with Jacuzzis, no more evening wraps made from the skins of endangered species.

But you can't just throw money at problems, as they say—not even in reverse. We'll still have to deal with the *culture* of profligacy, and for this we'll need a vast slew of training and rehab programs. Let's start with courses on "Cash: How to Count It, Use It, and Store It," "The Supermarket: A Major Source of Food," and "The 'Job Concept': A Surprising New Way to Make Money."

[1987]

Fast Cars

•··•··•··•··•··•··•··•

OUT OF MY WAY, Tracy Chapman, I gotta get a fast car, one
of those new supercharged, turbo-charged, *high-performance* cars
that the automakers are coming out with. Maybe that Porsche
944 I've seen advertised on TV, the one that eats Ferraris for
lunch and scarfs down a couple of Corvettes over cocktails. Zero
to sixty in 5.7 seconds—wheee! Or maybe I'll go for Detroit's
new Corvette ZR1, with its 375-horsepower, 32-valve, V-8 engine—which is guaranteed, if I read the warranty right, to take
out a vanload of nuns at 180 mph, road conditions permitting.
Because I got places to go, man, things to *do*.

I wasn't always like this of course. You may remember, I was
the one tooling along in a four-cylinder slug with a bumper
sticker that read I'D RATHER BE PERFORMING ACTS OF KINDNESS.
I was so out of it I used to wear a seat belt in parking lots. Believe
it or not, I used to slow for *strollers*, which is just one of many
reasons the kids took to calling me "Road Worrier."

See, I didn't even grasp the principle of driving. I thought of
it as a necessary evil occasioned by the absence of effective mass
transportation and ecologically sound, human-scale communities. Why, I wouldn't even join MADD (Mothers Against Drunk
Driving) because they refused to drop the penultimate *D* and
start lobbying for the replacement of the interstates with bicycle
lanes.

I just didn't understand the whole principle of *deterrence*. You cut in front of me, sucker, and I'll tailgate you to hell or any other destination of your choice. You just *look* at me funny, I got a sweet little Magnum waiting in the glove compartment. And if you're armed with a two-ton Bronco, I'll get me a souped-up Silverado. Because you know me, pal, I DON'T GET MAD, I GET EVEN.

So driving is getting a little more dangerous than it used to be, so what? You could get blown to the hereafter for telling jokes about the Prophet Mohammed. Why, you could get blown to the same place even if you don't *get* the joke. Or you could be standing in a school playground, teaching little children the principles of sportsmanship, and be splattered all over the sandbox by a passing maniac with an AK-47. You could get cancer from an apple. Besides, I gotta get to the mall *somehow*.

As I see it now, speed is a requirement of the human psyche, ranking right up there with vengeance and the will to power. For countless centuries, most people were seriously deprived—just moseying around on foot or maybe going for an occasional joyride in an ox-drawn cart. The fastest anyone ever went was the terminal velocity of the human body (60 mph), but only under circumstances that prevented them from accurately communicating the *thrill* of it. Only a lucky few got to drive around on horses: Genghis Khan, that pioneer of vehicular homicide, comes to mind, and we are still talking a top speed of only 20 mph, horsepower 1.

Well, we're all in the cavalry now, thanks to Messrs. Ford, Ferrari, and Audi! And aggression, that's natural too. Back in the Dark Ages of the Pedestrian Era, people used to have to pussyfoot around saying things like, " 'Scuse me, ma'am," or "Oh, I'm so sorry, I surely didn't mean to step on your foot!" Well, we all know that happiness is never having to say you're sorry, either because you're already in the next county or because you're like me—BEYOND BITCH.

Besides, there's so much to *do* in a car these days! Like calling talk shows on the car phone or faxing memos to Congress protesting the (ha-ha) 55 mph speed limit. If you're like me, and you don't really have a taste for violence—say, you just want to get to the local penitentiary for an execution tailgate party as quickly and safely as possible—well, you don't have to get *involved*. Just turn on the stereo, plug in your electric shaver, get to work on that dictaphone, and remember, HE WHO DIES WITH THE MOST TOYS WINS.

So people get killed. So, for example, the death rate on rural interstates went up 22 percent in the year after the speed limit was restored to 65 mph. Well, believe me, more people die in *beds* every day than in cars. But is it anybody's business what we do in bed? Is anyone running around trying to regulate Sealy Posturepedic? So get off my *case*, man, and DON'T TELL ME WHAT KIND OF DAY TO HAVE.

You don't like my attitude, you say? Well, don't blame me, blame the big guys. Blame the pornographers of automotive violence: those Hollywood Jag owners whose idea of Driver's Ed is an hourly car-chase scene on the tube. Blame the boys in blue who would rather catch you for a month-old registration sticker on your windshield than a 375-horsepower killer engine under your hood. Blame the advertisers whose message is that safety sucks, and that real men drive to kill. Better yet, blame those CEOs in Detroit and Milan—blood brothers to the arms dealers and amphetamine pushers of the world—who've given up on plain old *transportation* because there's so much more money in murder and mayhem.

But don't let it ruin your whole day, because you know what the philosophers say: LIFE'S A BITCH AND THEN YOU DIE.

[1989]

The Gang in White Coats

●··●···●··●··●··●···●

ONCE AGAIN, we are being deafened by complaints that the American medical system "doesn't work." We spend $5.4 billion a year on medical care, the complainers allege, for no tangible benefits beyond what could easily be achieved through sorcery, environmental cleanup, or the free distribution of prescription drugs to all comers, regardless of ailment.

But let us look beyond the facile charges of the chronic malcontents. Who's doing the complaining, anyway? Is it the people who are in a position to *know* whether the medical system is working or not, i.e., the real experts—the doctors, hospital executives, and hardworking CEOs of the companies that make silicon breast inserts and lifelike hair transplants? No, from them comes only the profound silence of the recently and abundantly fed. The complaining comes almost entirely from—let us be honest—the *sick*.

And no wonder the sick are complaining! The medical system was not designed for people who have declined from the full bloom of health. Doctors don't like them, because they have figured out by now that sickness, along with injury and death, is a reliable source of malpractice suits. Hospitals don't like them, because sickness—and especially the more painful and flamboyant varieties—is deeply disruptive to the hospital routine and disorienting to the personnel. Insurance companies positively

hate them, which is why an exhaustive physical exam is required
for those seeking insurance—to rule out anyone who is now, has
ever been, or may someday, become sick.

And let us be really honest. *We* don't like them either. Consider their appearance: the hideous rashes, the open sores, the
feverish ravings, the ghastly neglect of personal grooming. We
don't let sick people be president. We don't want to see them
playing the romantic lead next to Kim Basinger. Why should we
let them tell us how to run our medical system?

Another thing about sick people: they'll complain about
anything. Put a tasty meal in front of them, attractively arranged
on a tray—say, mashed potatoes, army-green vegetables, color-
coordinated meat, and a savory lime Jell-o—and what do you
get? Complaints! Because that is almost the definition of sickness, the one universal symptom underlying the myriad varieties
of disease—kvetching.

The truth is, we have the finest medical technology in the
world. What other country offers in vitro fertilization, with its
fabulous success rate of over 5 percent, not only to the landed
aristocracy, but to the average possessor of fifty-thousand dollars?
What other nation can guarantee that no infant need fight its way
out of the birth canal as long as there are scalpels around, and
thousands of debt-ridden anesthesiologists?

I scarcely need mention our staggering diagnostic capabilities,
which leave those poor socialistic types—the English, the Ca-
nadians, the Swedes, and their ilk—gasping in envy. There's
the brand-new, multimillion-dollar infrasonic magneto detonator
for the detection of ear wax, for example. Or the temple-sized
ultraquark-powered graviton for the visualization of intestinal
gas. And so forth! Of course, the sick feel left out. The rigors of
our burgeoning diagnostic technology can be safely survived only
by the most robust and able-bodied.

Take the sick out of the system and, I tell you, the system
works just fine. So long, of course, as you understand what it's
trying to *do*.

Hospitals, for example, are best appreciated as an extractive industry, on a par with the more familiar forms of mining. In a hospital, human parts—blood, urine, kidneys, limbs, uteruses, etc.—are removed, thus leaving the general population lighter and sleeker. Some of these parts are recycled to people who are themselves in need of kidneys, blood, or, for that matter, urine. It is true, a few parts cannot be adequately accounted for. The fat removed in liposuction, for example, may have something to do with the texture of the french fries served at McDonald's, though that is only conjecture.

The rest of the human tissue removed is essential to the production of medical waste. Some analysts believe that the syringes washing up in our surf represent a unique laissez-faire approach to socialized medicine: load up the syringes and trust that each swimmer gets the medication appropriate to his or her condition! Who knows? But it cannot be denied that medical waste, inhaled as air pollution, contributes to the painless removal of the aged, infirm, and asthmatic.

Moving on to the medical profession: It is easily faulted, of course, if its mission is confused with mercy. Sociologists have long regarded the medical profession as a guild, but more recently they have decided it is more accurately described as a *gang*. Hence the characteristic white jackets, and the wearing of masks for undertakings of unusual violence or questionable legality.

The initiation rite—which clearly distinguishes medicine from rival gangs like the Crips or the Bloods—is organic chemistry, in which the competition for grades is so fierce that premeds are led to steal the reference books and smash the lab apparatus of their fellow students. Such rituals assure that our medical profession continues to select for the criminal element.

Like its aforementioned rivals, the medical profession has two main preoccupations: the protection of turf, especially from overeager upstarts in the nursing or midwifery professions, and, naturally, the distribution of drugs. Current laws put penicillin, for example, in much the same category as cocaine: It cannot be freely purchased over the counter, but obtained only through specialized salespersons, and then only by the wealthy, the wily, or the unusually desperate.

But the *sick*, you say! Where do they fit in amid all this grasping, grabbing, hustling, hacking, and feverishly rapid metabolism of money and body parts? Is there no place for them?

Yes, indeed, there's a place. It's called Canada, or Sweden, or even England. So get out and get better! And leave our medical system for those who really need it—the insurance company execs, the hospital directors, and, of course, the gang in white coats.

[1989]

The Right to Pollute

●··●··●··●··●··●··●

IT WAS THE YEAR that the Supreme Court set aside its black robes for white ones and began to cancel all rights as we had known them—civil rights, women's rights, minority rights, gay rights, constitutional rights. But just as the usual malcontents were gathering to build a papier maché Statue of Liberty and launch a democracy movement in the Washington mall, two brand-new and hitherto unsuspected rights were announced: the right to burn the American flag, and the right—made available through President Bush's new environmental program—to pollute. In fact, it was now possible and entirely legal to pollute a major patch of the countryside, if one was so inclined, with the thick, pungent smoke produced by thousands of flags on fire.

The business community was at first alarmed by the administration's plan to *sell* the right to pollute. Quite rightly, they complained that the right to pollute had always been free in the past. Quite understandably, they worried that a price tag would soon be slapped on those other inalienable rights enjoyed by the corporate community: the right to befuddle the American public with fork-tongued advertising, the right to move freely about the globe in search of the hungriest, most downtrodden employees, the right to sponsor TV programs so inane as to induce the widespread neurological damage on which the corporate order depends for its peaceful continuation, and so forth.

But not to worry! By thrusting the government into the pollution rights business, President Bush meant only to demonstrate, once again, the undying magic of the market. Many Americans, raised on Communist-inspired doggerel ("To market, to market, to buy a fat . . ." and "This little piggie goes to . . .") had come to associate the market with the more porcine side of human nature, or to think of it as something resembling a sty. With the sale of pollution rights, the administration hoped to establish, once and for all, that the Invisible Hand, which had up until now busied itself tossing filth into our streams and breezes, was in fact, soft, gentle, and admirably clean under the nails.

Of course, things didn't work out quite so nicely. First, once the EPA published its price list, an avid and seemingly unquenchable demand for pollution rights arose among the white overclass. We all know of the great real-estate mogul who was so pleased with his son's high grades in tennis and wine-tasting that he rewarded the boy with the right to pollute a medium-size midwestern city, by air and by water, with the toxins of his choice. Not to be outdone, Malcolm Forbes presented Liz Taylor with the right to pollute a well-populated mountain state with hair spray and shredded fanzines—which she accomplished by running about on foot, followed by hundreds of gaily shrieking celebutantes, spraying and shredding as they tore through the designated land mass.

Soon everyone was vying to participate in the conspicuous consumption of pollution rights. On sale days, long lines formed outside the EPA: yuppies seeking the right to hurl Evian bottles from their BMWs, suburbanites in the market for the right to toss doggie doo onto their neighbors' lawns, even schoolchildren who had saved their pennies for the right to affix chewed Trident to the undersides of their desks. It was said that you could judge a man by the trail he left: the size of his oil slick, the density of the chlorofluorocarbon vapor lingering after him.

But that wasn't the end of it. The magic of the market kept on unfolding! Soon smart young B-school grads, recognizing that pollution rights were now a commodity just like pork bellies and Third World debts, went into the business of trading pollution rights, and then into the business of trading pollution rights futures, and then into the sale of highly speculative "junk rights" involving untested carcinogens and uninformed populations. Honest polluters complained that the business was being overrun by callow speculators who had never in their lives produced an honest day's supply of carbon monoxide or PCBs. But who cared! Wall Street was jumping as bets were taken on the price of engorging Walla Walla with plutonium, on the future cost of shrinking the ozone layer to the size of Rhode Island, and on the probable date of the end of the world.

Then there was the inevitable pollution-rights-related crime wave. In Dallas, a well-heeled gent was mugged and relieved of the right to scatter Styrofoam peanuts over the state of Montana. On Wall Street, there was a wave of inside trading in pollution rights markets. Everywhere, crafty brokers sought to bribe the ecologically minded with tasty tofu dishes, hoping thereby to inflame the environmental movement and thus covertly raise the future price of soiling and desecration.

But the market had a solution for a crime, too, as one of the savants at the American Enterprise Institute was quick to point out. If the government could sell the right to pollute, why not also market the rights to embezzle, loot, and pillage? Soon corporate jets and personal helicopters buzzed thickly around the Justice Department, as representatives of the overclass bid for the rights to lie, cheat, and defraud the public. We all know of the brilliant career of that young Yale-educated investment banker who started out as a humble broker in pollution rights, moved on to inside trading in pollution rights futures, and then redeemed himself by buying the *right* to be an inside trader. From there it was an obvious leap to *trading* inside trading rights, and finally to *inside* trading in the inside trading rights futures market!

Unfortunately, the environment, which had been more or less forgotten in the frenzy of speculation, continued to head for hell in a handbasket. But what could I do? I could barely afford the right to throw thumbtacks in a sandbox. Then I realized: the market has a solution for everything! The right to riot and revolution is a bargain these days, and the Justice Department assures me I can pay with a credit card.

[1989]

LIFE, DEATH,
AND THE
UNIVERSE

•··•··•··•··•··•··•

Stand by Your Flag

●··●··●··●··●··●··●··●

IF YOU LIVE, as I do, near one of the great scenic spots of this great nation—say, the Grand Canyon, the Statue of Liberty, or the World's Largest Peanut in Ashburn, Georgia—then you've probably had some run-ins with foreign tourists. First they offer your kids a stick of gum for agreeing to be photographed in front of the scenic spot. Then they flash a few kroner or yen and ask if you know of a place to eat where the entrée is not served inside a biscuit, bun, or pita bread. Finally, when the conversation warms up, they offer to buy you a cup of coffee if you'll sit down with them for a few minutes and explain U.S. foreign policy.

Now I always figure that if you're old enough to be drinking coffee in the first place, you ought to be able to explain your country's foreign policy to any foreigner who comes along—particularly if they're from some two-bit place like England or West Germany that doesn't have a foreign policy of its own and is always having to borrow ours. So I say, sure, just throw in a cruller and I'll tell you anything you want to know, so long as it isn't about Vietnam, which is already available as a movie genre, a videocassette industry, a miniseries, and a sitcom for anybody willing to just sit back and enjoy it.

Sometimes they'll start way back in history and ask, why, other than to provide a plausible plot line for *Heartbreak Ridge*, did we ever invade Grenada. I am pretty sick of this question, but I just take a deep breath and tell them the truth: "Because they were building an airport, of course. And you know what that could have led to."

"Well, what," they ask, "a Holiday Inn?" "That's right," I tell them, lowering my voice. "Possibly an Avis dealership, a Marriott, who knows? We stopped them just in time."

That's probably the easiest question you'll get, though, because next they're likely to get into something more intricate, like the Persian Gulf. I must have had a half-dozen Norwegian backpackers and vacationing English nannies ask me that tiresome old question of why, if it was the Iraqis who hit the Stark, we decided to go after the Iranians. "Well," I say, just as patient as could be, "because the Iranians are fundamentalists, and we hate fundamentalists, except the kind that believe in nuclear war as the Second Coming and the eternal torture in hell of Jews, atheists, and unbaptized baby sinners. So we figured that while we were in the neighborhood . . ."

Yes, of course, they say, or *mais oui* or some such, but just a short time ago weren't you giving those same Iranians discount Hawks and day-old cakes? "Don't you read the papers?" I ask in exasperation. "We gave the cake to the moderates. They're the ones who, while everyone else is chanting 'Death to America,' are chanting sotto voce, as it were, 'A Wasting Disease to America,' or 'The Intolerable Itch of Hemorrhoids to America,' or something moderate like that."

Sooner or later, they always bring up that old canard about U.S. support for right-wing dictators, to which I just say, "Whoa there! That was then, this is now. Now we just let revolution, free elections, etc., take their course, then we move in to help the local right-wing malcontents mount a little low-intensity harassment. These days, we're proud to be on the side of the underdog—UNITA, the contras, Renamo, plus any other exotic fellows you may have seen modeling combat fatigues in *Soldier of Fortune.*"

Of course, this always leads us to Nicaragua. "Do you Americans really believe," I've had a bevy of Belgian schoolteachers ask me, "that the Sandinistas are planning a human wave assault on Fort Lauderdale?" "It's not that simple," I have to say. "There are three million Nicaraguans, which is more people than we have in the great cities of Altoona, Pennsylvania, and Bozeman, Montana, combined. They are all hard-core Marxist-Leninists except for the overwhelming majority who are eagerly awaiting liberation at the hands of William Webster and his band of Freedom Fighters. So, you see, it's the least we can do."

Some foreigners give up at this point, figuring that the language barrier is a little steeper than they'd realized, but the really hard-nosed ones just order another round of crullers and hit me with some trick question they must have been practicing all the way from Gander. Like this one: "Look, the Iranians support terrorists who actually torture and kill American hostages. But the Nicaraguans captured two Americans engaged in acts of war —Hasenfus and Hall—and released them unharmed, with a free psychiatric consultation thrown in in the case of Hall. So the United States sells arms to the Iranians and uses the profits to overthrow the Nicaraguans. I mean, maybe I missed something, but . . ."

At this point, you have several options. The first, which I call the "Ronald Reagan," is to duck your head down toward your right shoulder and say, "Jeez, just because I live here doesn't mean they tell me everything, you know." The second, known around town as the "George Shultz," consists of pounding the table and saying, "By God, you've got a point there. In fact, I've said the very same thing myself, in no uncertain terms and on numerous occasions, to that waitress right over there."

Then there's always the "Ollie North," by which I don't mean the well-known sandwich (bologna and shredded-lettuce hero, on a roll, ha-ha) but the equally famous speech: "All right, so maybe it doesn't sound like a foreign policy. Maybe it sounds like the deranged rumblings of a loose cannon rolling around on the gun decks of the ship of state. Well, it's the only foreign policy we have, and this All-American gal is here to tell you that she's proud of it. Darn proud!"

Or just tell these Eurotrash busybodies to cram their crullers and go back to Russia, where they obviously came from.

[1987]

Iranscam: Oliver North and the Warrior Caste

●‥●‥●‥●‥●‥●‥●‥●

WHEN I FIRST SAW Oliver North on television, testifying—or rather, declining to testify before the House Committee on Foreign Affairs—I was so taken by the expression on his face that I almost missed the main point. The expression was one of exaggerated attentiveness: eyebrows drawn up high into the center of his forehead, the corners of his mouth tucked down ceremoniously toward his chin. It was the kind of face you might wear for a solemn occasion where it would be tactless, if not incriminating, to break out into a grin.

The main point, however, is not that Oliver North may have enjoyed his role in Iranscam, or been amused by the feeble institution of Congress. The main point—the only real message of his silent testimony—was the uniform. This prince of Reagan's secret government had chosen to confront the public in a costume that proclaimed his license to kill—not just impersonally, as a president may by pressing a button—but, if necessary, messily and by hand. A civilian official in a civilian government, he had chosen to come as a warrior.

I think that this may be one of the more useful ways to think of North and his cabal of collaborators: as members of the oldest male elite there is, the Warrior Caste. Not that, in the crafting of Iranscam, ideology was unimportant—or profiteering, or personal neurosis, or sheer hell-raising adventurism. But the same mixed motives have inspired the warrior elite throughout history, from the sacking of Troy to the raids of Genghis Khan and the Crusades against the Muslim world. What defines the Warrior Caste, and sets it apart from the mass of average military men, is a love of war that knows no bounds, accepts no peace, and always seeks, in the ashes of the last battle, the sparks that might ignite the next. For North and many of his key collaborators, the sequence was Vietnam, then Nicaragua, with detours into wartorn Angola and prerevolutionary Iran. The end of one war demanded the creation of the next.

I have been thinking about the Warrior Caste ever since a remarkable book, Klaus Theweleit's *Male Fantasies*, introduced me to a group of men who might be considered the psychological prototype of the modern warrior elite, the German Freikorpsmen. These were officers who refused to disarm after World War I, but instead returned to Germany and organized private armies to battle the rebellious working class of their own nation. They went on, in the thirties, to become the core of Hitler's SA and, in some cases, key functionaries in the Third Reich. Thus for them, the period between 1914 and 1945 was continuous, almost uninterrupted war, in no small part because they made it so. Historian Robert Waite quotes a Freikorpsman who had enlisted in the German army at the age of sixteen: "People told us that the War [World War I] was over. That made us laugh. We ourselves are the War. Its flame burns strongly in us. It envelops our whole being and fascinates us with the enticing urge to destroy. We obeyed . . . and marched onto the battlefields of the postwar world just as we had gone into battle on the Western Front: singing, reckless and filled with the joy of adventure . . . silent, deadly, remorseless in battle."

We are a long way, of course, from the trenches of the Western Front and the street battles of postwar Berlin, but some of the same "joy" and "enticing urge" seem to have driven Oliver North. The son of an army colonel and brother of two officers, North had been in such a hurry to get to Vietnam in 1968 that he skipped a summer leave. According to the *Washington Post*, friends said he didn't want to miss the war. In Vietnam, he was a hero, or, depending on your point of view, a maniac. "He burned inside," a Marine Corps buddy has said, unconsciously echoing the Freikorpsman quoted above. "He was a zealot."

Back from Vietnam in 1969, North poured his energies into his job as a Marine instructor. Other instructors seem to have thought him a bit mad, coming to class in camouflage paint, bush hat, bandoliers across his chest, with four guns and three knives tucked about his person. "He was pumped up after Vietnam," a friend explained to the press, and dashed back to that unhappy country at his first chance—to testify in 1970 on behalf of a fellow Marine charged with murdering sixteen Vietnamese women and children at Son Thang. While the trial dragged on, he passed the time by volunteering for "killer teams" on night-time patrol. Even hardened Marines thought this was going a little far, "hiding behind trees and slitting throats on his own time."

North could take anything, except, apparently, the stress of peace. Assigned to a routine Marine Corps job in 1974, he experienced a psychotic episode. His superior officer reportedly found him in his quarters, "babbling incoherently and running around naked, waving a .45 pistol." He had nothing to live for, he explained, and he may have meant nothing to kill for.

That problem—the horror of peace—would be solved once he reached the dark inner core of Reagan's secret government. North had spent the rest of the 1970s in the Marines and then headed for the Naval War College, where he impressed enough higher-ups to get a White House appointment in 1981. From his post in the National Security Council he designed the invasion of Grenada, abetted the South Africa–supported guerrillas in Angola, engineered the hijacking of the *Achille Lauro* hijackers, and seems to have almost single-handedly managed the covert war against Nicaragua. He no longer had to wait for war or worry about getting to a war too late. He could make his own.

It matters, of course, that North has a specific ideology to defend. No doubt he sees himself as a steadfast crusader against communism, and not as a macho thrill-seeker. But the thrill is there, and even temporary warriors, soldiers who gladly return to the routines of peacetime, often describe combat as the peak event of their lives. "I had the most tremendous experiences of all of life: of fear, of jubilance, of misery, of hope, of comradeship, and of the endless excitement, the theatrics of it," a World War II veteran told Studs Terkel in his book *The Good War.* After an experience like that, "everything," to quote another of Terkel's vets, "is anticlimactic."

I will admit that this is alien territory to me, the psychology of the warrior. In part, this is because his anticlimactic "everything" is all that I, and probably you the reader, have ever known or experienced: work, love, children, family, friends, and the peaceful struggles we wage in the name of love and children. As feminists, we may honor myths and tales of women warriors, but, overwhelmingly and throughout history, women have inhabited a world that warriors happily leave behind, or arrive at— only to destroy.

There is another reason for our ignorance of the warrior mentality. In our generation of feminist scholars, the history of war and warriors has taken second place to "social history"—the attempt to reconstruct how ordinary people have gone about their lives, producing what they need and reproducing themselves. We rejected the conventional history of "kings and battles" for what Sheila Rowbotham has called the "hidden history" of everyday life, almost to the point of forgetting how much of everyday life has, for millennia, been shaped by battles and dominated by warrior elites.

But I do not think we will ever understand either history or women's place in it without a *feminist* understanding of the Warrior Caste: history, because so much of it is made by warriors; women, because our very absence from the warriors' ranks must be understood, finally, as a profound clue to the mystery of male power and gender itself. The absence of women, I would argue, is not a mere "result" of patriarchy or a "consequence" of sexism; it is intrinsic to the psychology of the warrior, just as war itself—and the endless preparations and celebrations it demands —may be intrinsic to the perpetuation of patriarchy.

In his brilliant psychoanalytical study of the Freikorpsmen, Theweleit offers one of the links between militarism and patriarchy: war, to those permanent warriors, was a condition of life *because* it was an escape from women and all things female. The Freikorpsmen, whose letters and diaries Theweleit analyzes, did not just hate women; in a way they did not even *see* women, including their own wives—except as intruders, threats, yawning "swamps" in which a man could be engulfed. Nor was this a matter of "repressed homosexuality" or sexuality of any kind. For these prototypical warriors, the only resolution of the horror of women was the murder of women (as well as men), an act they describe not only with relish, but with relief.

Now, quite aside from Theweleit's thesis, I would argue that any prestigious, socially pervasive, all-male institution serves to perpetuate patriarchy, whether it is the men's longhouse of a tribal society or the exclusive class of an industrial society. The reason is simple: as long as the male career trajectory is a movement from a world centered on women (mothers) to a world in which there are no women, "growing up" for men will always mean growing away from women. And for the men who "grow up," women will always be reminders of their own vulnerability and helpless infancy. Women will be feared, contemned, or perhaps merely patronized as incomplete and childish versions of men.

Some feminist theorists have suggested that the earliest such institution of patriarchy was the male hunting band. But for most of recorded history, and in most of the world, the premier institution of male power has probably been the military, and especially the warrior elite. Not all societies hunt, and not all societies organize their religions around male-only hierarchies, but almost all societies that can make any claim to being "civilized" have cultivated the Warrior Caste. I think, for example, of the remarkable parallels, even in their style of warfare and codes of honor, between the samurai of feudal Japan and the knights of feudal

Europe: as if their Warrior Caste had a kind of historical inevita-
bility, transcending physical distance, language, and everything
we know as "culture."

My guess is that the historical "success" of the Warrior Caste
rests on the fact that it is, in more than one sense, self-propagat-
ing. First, in a geographical sense: the existence of a warrior elite
in City-State 1 called forth its creation in City-State 2—otherwise, the latter was likely to be reduced to rubble and the mem-
ories of slaves. Natural selection, as it has operated in human
history, favors not only the clever but the murderous.

Second, and quite apart from ordinary biology, the Warrior
Caste has the ability to reproduce itself from one generation to
the next. Only women can produce children, of course; but—
more to the point—only wars can produce *warriors*. One war
leads to the next, in part because each war incubates the warriors
who will fight the next, or, I should say, *create*, the next. The
First World War engendered the warrior elite that ushered in the
Third Reich, and hence the Second World War. And Vietnam
created men like Oliver North, who, through subterfuge and
stealth, nourished the fledgling war in Central America.

But to return to North: the real point, it occurs to me, may
not have been the uniform, after all. For the key characteristic
of the Warrior Caste in its modern form is that it does not dress
up in battle costume or indulge in recreational throat slitting.
The men of the true warrior elite in the United States today (and
no doubt in the Soviet Union as well) wear tailored suits, kiss
their wives good-bye in the morning, and spend their days at
desks, plotting covert actions, megadeaths, and "low-intensity"
interventions. They are peaceable, even genial fellows, like
President Reagan himself. But still I would say, to the extent
that they hoard the resources of society for the purposes of destruction, they live for war.

The real lesson of Iranscam, with its winding trail of blood
and money, guns and drugs, may be to remind us that we have
not evolved so far at all from the most primitive barbarism of the
Warrior Caste. That caste has institutionalized itself in the bu-

reaucracy of the "national security state"—the CIA, the National Security Council, the Pentagon. But insofar as their business is still murder (and there can be no other name, I think, for the business of the contras and their American supporters), our modern, gray-flannel warriors are blood brothers to the mercenaries and thugs who made up North's "secret team"—and are spiritual descendants of that Freikorps officer who could say in exultation, "We are the war."

Our task—we who cherish "daily life" and life itself—is to end the millennia-old reign of the Warrior Caste. There are two parts to this task. One is to uproot the woman-hating, patriarchal consciousness that leads some men to find transcendence and even joy in war, and only war. That will take time, though we have made a decent start. The other part is to remember that war itself is the crucible in which new warriors are created. If we cannot stop the warriors' fevered obsessions, and bring these men back into the human fold, we can at least try to stop their wars.

[1987]

Phallic Science

●··●··●··●··●··●··●··●

SOMEWHERE, DEEP WITHIN the human genome, a tiny voice calls out, "Copy me! Copy me! Make more and better copies!" For millenia, this tiny voice exerted its influence solely on the gonads, forcing their owners into the curious positions and sticky relationships required for human reproduction. But now, thanks to the modern biotech industry, the imperative to replicate the genes has taken over the human brain: specifically, the very best, Nobel Prize–winning brains, which are determined to "map" the human genome right down to the last DNA subunit (A,G,C, or T). In laypersons' terms, this means that the genetic information now conveniently stored in, say, a sperm cell, will be translated into chemical sequences which will fill an estimated one thousand phone books. These can, in turn, be Xeroxed.

Spoilers and Luddites will no doubt protest that the $30 million or so it will take to put the genome down on paper might be better applied to figuring out a way to grow rain forests on the Bikini atoll, or move the ozone layer from Los Angeles back up to the stratosphere, or doing something truly mundane like finding a cure for AIDS. The spoilers forget that, from the point of view of the pharmaceutical industry, the AIDS problem has already been solved. After all, we already have a drug which can be sold at the incredible price of $8,000 an annual dose, and which has the added virtue of not diminishing the market by actually curing anyone.

Besides, there is an iron law of scientific development at work here. The law says that science will bumble along for decades, doing things like studying the thought processes of nematodes as a function of sunspot activity, and then—POW!—a new *paradigm* emerges: quantum theory, relativity, the genetic code! For a few months, the scientific community bubbles with creativity, as great minds jockey for the Nobel Prize and a hot write-up in *Scientific American*. Then, inevitably, comes the next phase, in which thousands of lesser minds pick over the paradigm, looking for bits and pieces which can be turned into grant applications, journal articles, and lectures tedious enough to dim the minds of the competition. This phase, known technically as "Nerd Science," is already well advanced in mathematics, where some person of genius just figured out how to divide a number 100 digits long—and there are reports that a 103-digit number is already in the works.

Then Nerd Science grinds along for a while, bringing us things like the amino acid sequence of egg albumin and the 300,000th digit of pi, until, by some chance, it comes into contact with Big Money, which activates a remarkable transformation: Nerd Science becomes Phallic Science! It puffs and swells, demanding particle accelerators as big as the Gobi Desert! Multibillion-dollar space stations which do nothing at all! (But, hey, no one will be able to get to them anyway.) And now the human genome project, which the layperson may usefully envision as a vast ejaculate consisting of over a billion telephone books.

What a leap, you must be thinking, beyond that other recent big-brain exploit: the fabled sperm bank offering the effluents of certified Nobel Prize–winning males. We can already see that as a primitive first step toward the genome project—an attempt, on the Nobel laureates' part, to respond to that tiny voice saying, "Copy me, copy me!" Now they understand that the tiny voice in our genes is actually saying, "Publish me, publish me!"

I'm not saying the genome project isn't important, or that it won't change our very way of life. Courtship, for example, will be transformed once it is possible for the betrothed to peruse each other's thousand-volume genomes, deciding which patches of DNA should be included in the offspring, and which would only give rise to unpleasant traits, such as a tendency to drop socks or overcook vegetables. Prenuptial agreements will be negotiated by molecular biologists, and divorces will be fought over as little as a guanine-cytosine base pair.

In fact, why have children at all? The tiny voice in our genes doesn't say "make human copies," it just says "copies." Many people, given the chance to have their own, unique, thousand-volume genome prepared by the biotech industry, will simply opt to publish it in quantity. "Would you like to see my genome?" will become a common invitation to intimacy—and a warning that you are about to be presented with one thousand telephone books saying "ACCCTGATTAAATC" and the like.

But surely we wouldn't be investing $30 million and the best minds of our nation just so that you and I may someday have a leather-bound edition of our genetic heritage! Of course not, dear layperson, so let me fill you in briefly on the secret goal of the genome project. Our bioscientists have indeed noticed the increasing uninhabitability of our planet (the ozone, the epidemics, and so forth). They also know that anything which can be written in a thousand volumes can be inscribed, in due time, on a thumbnail-size silicon chip. Hence the plan: put the top scientists' genomes onto chips, put the chips into special computers designed to build human beings from the genetic instructions encoded on the chips, put the computers into space ships, and blast off! For by this time, that tiny voice in our genes is no doubt screaming, "Let me out of here! Let me out of here!"

Thus will the fondest dream of Phallic Science be realized: a pristine new planet populated entirely by little boy clones of our great scientific entrepreneurs—thousands of James D. Watsons, perhaps, or Edward Tellers—free to smash atoms, accelerate particles, or, if they are so moved, build pyramids—without any social relevance or human responsibility at all. And why not? Unless, as luck would have it, one of those computer viruses gets into their genome program and, a few light-years after the launch, eats it, right down to the last A,G,C, and T. . . .

[1988]

The Peace Thing

●··●··●··●··●··●··●

No! I can't take it anymore. The shame! The humiliation! First they took their intermediate-range missiles out of Europe. Then they pulled out of Afghanistan (a cute trick if ever I saw one!). Then they threw out their uranium supplies and cut off military aid to Nicaragua, and now they want to talk about chucking their short-range missiles. So I got Dick Cheney on the phone. "Dick," I said, "do you realize they're pulling down the barbed wire on the Austro-Hungarian border and talking about turning Checkpoint Charlie into a duty-free boutique? I mean, when are we going to *retaliate?*"

There was a silence as of a man in pain. "Barb," he finally said at last, "I know how you feel. But we don't fight dirty. We're against germ warfare. We take a dim view of genocide. Our stand on public cannibalism is well known. But there's one thing we never thought they'd stoop to . . . one thing so cunning and evil we thought even a Commie wouldn't touch it . . ."

"You mean public relations, Dick?"

"And not only that," he said, his voice dropping to a hoarse whisper. "Charisma, Barb, leadership, intelligence . . . possibly brilliance—the whole shooting match!"

I replaced the receiver soundlessly, his dry sobs still echoing in my ear. If it came to warheads, we could beat them anytime. But with IQ points, well, we were clearly outnumbered. And then there was the charisma gap: they hadn't wasted any time moving in on that . . . but no time to brood! Like all the other really important national columnists, I'd gotten an invitation to dinner at the Bushes'. I had just enough time to slip into a nice little oufit from L. L. Bean, grab a pocketful of doggie treats, and rush over to the White House.

George and Barbara met us—can you believe it?—in their own bedroom. They were so down-to-earth, standing around and bantering about who left the cap off the toothpaste, and then pretty soon they were wrestling, just in a friendly way of course, and squirting each other with the Crest and generally whooping it up. Everyone was getting into the spirit of it. Some young fellow named Newt was going through the president's underwear drawer, pocketing loose change and cuff links. Dan was rolling on the floor with the puppies, and Marilyn was striding around with a tape measure, muttering about natural disasters, assassinations, and the like.

But just then the phone rang, and John Sununu listened gravely for a few minutes before reporting: "It's Mikhail, sir. Says he's planning to issue the entire Red Army frisbees and love beads. But I told him you were in the bathroom, sir." So we all filed down to dinner trying not to let our horror and outrage show, and pretty soon I was chatting away with Dan about all the preparation he'll be doing for his next diplomatic venture —actually learning a language, he told me, probably Swiss.

I was just refilling my plate with popcorn when the phone rang again. "Mikhail again," Jim Baker announced grimly. "He wants to know who he should talk to about making Moscow and Washington into—how'd he put it?—'sister cities.' " There were shrieks of righteous anger: "Commie bastards!" "Red devils!" "Drugstore cowboys!" and so forth. But the president, I am proud to report, never lost his grip. We'd go right on with dinner, he told us calmly, only dessert would be served down in the Situation Room. Just in case.

So we all crowded in there with our blueberry cobblers, Dan and the puppies included, and settled down to business. "Do

we press the button now?" squealed Marilyn, excited to be present at the genesis of a world-class disaster unrelated to herself by
blood or marriage. "Wait a minute!" shouted Roger Ailes. "This
is a job for . . ." There was a pause as everyone turned to look
at the odd-looking fellow in the corner, dressed as one of the
Blues Brothers, and bopping, as it were, to a distant drummer.

"Thank God you're here, Lee," said the president. "What've
we got on this, uh, general secretary guy? Any, like, trouble with
the woman thing? Failure to pay income tax? Acts of mercy
toward known felons, rapists, or members of minority groups?"
But Lee just went on snapping his fingers and engaging in
rhythmic chin-thrusting motions. "Well, then, what about this
world domination thing? Wasn't it Lenin's last wish to be buried
in Epcot Center? I mean, isn't that the whole point?"

A light came into Lee's eyes. "Yo, Prez," he started to say,
but it was the phone again. Marlin Fitzwater picked it up this
time, listened in silence for a moment, and then sank back down
into a chair, his face ashen. "It's Mikhail, sir. I don't know how
to tell you this, sir. He's offering unconditional surrender, sir.
Says they're no longer interested in the concept of the nation-
state. Says it was a dumb idea in the first place and should have
been abandoned in the nineteenth century. Invites you to send
over a proven administrator if you like, someone of the caliber of
Clint Eastwood. If he could be spared, that is . . ."

"That's it," said the president sagging. "It's all over. The
end." Dick and Lee and Rog and Newt were all crying softly
into their cobblers. Marilyn was frowning. The puppies were
howling. From the back of the room, I heard a commotion and
Dan's voice crying, too: "It is not bedtime. It is not!"

Then Barbara got up—God, how I love that woman's style—
and walked over to George, just as calm as could be, and began
stroking his head, cooing ever so softly: "It's not the end, Pop-
pie, not yet. Don't forget—you've still got Noriega."

[1989]

Blocking the Gates to Heaven

●‥●‥●‥●‥●‥●‥●

WHEN I WAS the age my children are now, that is, old enough to know everything but still young enough to be dissatisfied with the limited information available, the night sky meant a lot more than a connect-the-dots lesson in ancient Roman mythology. It was a threshold leading to better worlds, where, according to my monthly *Galaxy* magazine, humanoids of great strength and surpassing intelligence drove about purposefully from star to star. In sci-fi convention, life-forms that hadn't developed space travel were mere prehistory—the horseshoe crabs of the cosmic scene—and something of the humiliation of being stuck on a provincial planet in a galactic backwater has stayed with me ever since. But now, with the prospect of Star Wars, I am beginning to feel claustrophobic. It is bad enough that the heavens are still inaccessible, but they are about to become a "shield," which means, for all practical purposes, a lid.

This is no idle metaphor, for NASA is already so compromised by military priorities that we might never really get off the ground. What was the ill-fated shuttle for, if not to show the Russians that we're honing the capacity to pelt them with warheads from beyond the Van Allen belt? Unfortunately, all the shuttle demonstrated is that NASA (and hence, no doubt, the Pentagon) is still stuck at the balsa wood and airplane glue level of technology, in which the key engineering question is whether part A will stay attached to Part B, even in the cold and without a rubber band.

Perhaps, though, in some subtle and unacknowledged way, we've been losing interest in the universe. From an entertainment point of view, the solar system has been a bust. None of the planets turns out to have any real-estate potential, and most of them are probably even useless for filming *Dune* sequels. We may also be despairing of finding any friends out there, and America badly needs friends, since so many of the ones we have on earth are either bad-tempered tyrants or wealthy vagrants who have been forced to leave the tyrant business. A few years ago, Hollywood promised us a universe populated by short, sensitive fellows who would, at the very least, be ideal companions for single mothers. But the search for extraterrestrial intelligence (SETI, to us insiders) has so far only proved that no matter what you beam up—the Pythagorean theorem, pictures of attractive nude people, etc.—the big 800 number in the sky does not return calls. So, in the cinematic imagination, E.T. was replaced by a batch of gremlins and ghosts, all of unknown provenance and dubious morality.

It could be, though I hesitate to suggest it, that the universe is simply going out of style. It was big in the fifties, with the likes of Asimov and Clarke promoting it, and before we had fully realized that Einstein was serious about a cosmic speed limit that would put even the nearest star about three years away by express flight. Black holes, when they came along in the late 1960s, seemed to solve the problem. If you were willing to forgive them for their shrewlike capacity for guzzling whole nebulae and occasional solid matter like stars and planets, they looked as if they could have been put to use as secret passages through which a crew might burrow from galaxy to galaxy before Alzheimer's set in. Such luminaries of sci-fi and sci-fact as Joan D. Vinge and Carl Sagan have already employed black holes as cosmic mass transit systems; and if you don't mind being chewed down to your bosons and spat out on the other side of creation, I suppose it beats staying at home and watching *Star Trek* reruns.

Recent discoveries, though, may have made us wonder whether it's worth the effort. Just a few months ago there was the unsettling news that the universe has, as a result of explosions subsidiary to the big bang, a "bubble structure"—that is, the galaxies seem to be arrayed on the surface of massive bubbles, more or less like dust specks on beer foam.

Now, this is not the kind of thing we were brought up to expect from the universe. A great deal of human tradition and prejudice says that big things are automatically majestic and only small things can be silly. So how are we to comprehend such megascale frivolity? It was hard enough to adjust to a grim and indifferent universe that had some purpose other than giving tips to astrologers. But are we ready for a carbonated universe, potentially as "lite'" as a dinner from Lean Cuisine or a *USA Today* story on African starvation?

Another bit of bad PR for the universe was the discovery in 1986 of "bizarre structures"—described as threads, loops, and shells—within our own galaxy. We are not talking about some fuzz left on a telescope lens; the threads are one hundred light-years long by a light-year wide. There must be an explanation, of course, and astronomers are already blaming the big bang, which started the universe, but it is hard to be filled with reverence toward a firmament filled with objects that look so much like pasta.

Then there's the big bang itself. If that's how it all started, then we might as well face the fact that what's left out there is a great deal of shrapnel and a whole bunch of cinders (one of which is, fortunately, still hot enough and close enough to be good for tanning). Trying to find some sense and order in this mess may be as futile as trying to understand the culture of Japan from the wreckage of Hiroshima, or trying to reconstruct the economy of Iowa from a bowl of popcorn.

So I can well imagine the top scientists at NASA pouring a rare dollop of gin into their Tang and deciding that the universe no longer has the right stuff. Maybe that was when they decided to drop "manned" space travel in the classic sense and fill the available shuttle seats with women, blacks, Jews, Asians, and members of the traditionally Democratic teachers' union. Maybe, a few dollops later, these same famous scientists decided that the noblest course for "man" would be to emulate that great and witty Engineer who designed the universe (with some help, no doubt, from the likes of Morton Thiokol and Bechtel) and go out with the biggest little bang we can muster. Hence Star Wars, an ingenious, trillion-dollar technology devised to squelch all meaningful arms talks, subvert the space program, and generate the national arrogance required for that essential first strike.

There are still a few of us left, though, who don't feel we're too good for the universe, no matter how much it lets us down. Maybe it isn't a vast demonstration of eternal law and order put up there for our edification. Maybe it's more like a room after an all-night party, strewn with random debris by Someone whose idea of a good time we can never hope to fathom. I'd still like to meet whoever's out there, still like to think my descendants won't be stuck here forever, toiling away on a large rock near a small-size star. And for the time being, when I look up at night, I want to sense the huge untidy humor of infinity—not a gravestone of our own making pressing down on us.

[1986]

The Bright Side of
Nuclear War

●··●··●··●··●··●··●

THE ONE THING I envy certain religious groups for is their
ability to see the bright side of nuclear war. The Moral Majority,
for example, offers some pamphlets entitled *Nuclear War and the
Second Coming* and *Armageddon and the Coming War with Russia,* in
which it is explained that Armageddon (nuclear or otherwise)
will usher in the millennium. Some of their optimism may have
spread to President Reagan, who admitted in one of the campaign debates to being interested in Armageddon, much as you
or I might be interested in chess or the return of Halley's comet.
A sentence or two later he referred, even more cheefully, to
"Armageddon and so forth."

In the scenario of the Moral Majority leader, the Reverend
Jerry Falwell, true, born-again Christians will rise up to the sky
in a "rapture," leaving their clothes behind in neat piles on
kitchen chairs or the carpets of rec rooms or wherever they happen to be at the moment of apocalypse. As he tells it, this mass
ascension of rapturous Christians will cause terrible inconve-
nience for the unsaved, especially those who had put their lives
into the hands of a born-again airline pilot or car-pool driver.

Mr. Falwell did not mention that the electromagnetic pulse generated by the nuclear blast would stop the cars anyway and would
send the planes tumbling straight to the ground. (Which is why,

incidentally, it would be useless for safety-minded Hindus, animists, atheists, etc., to seek to confiscate the driver's licenses of born-again Christians.) What happens to the rest of us after the megatonnage goes off will be of no further consequence to the saved, who will be preoccupied, by that time, with the various festivities associated with the Second Coming.

I guess that, nattering away in everybody's subconscious mind, there is a childish impulse to find a bright side to nuclear war. For example, my father, who would qualify as a secular humanist if he were inclined to anything as species-chauvinistic as humanism, always reassured me that the radiation would produce some mutants who would be smarter than people. These superior beings, who would not necessarily resemble us at all, would then get on with the true mission of any creature that happened to be stuck on a hick planet on the outer rim of an undistinguished galaxy within a run-of-the-mill galactic cluster —that is, space travel.

I derived some comfort from this scenario until I was old enough to read Isaac Asimov, who explained that the likelihood of a mutation leading to anything better was about the same as the likelihood of a fine watch's being repaired by smashing it repeatedly on the ground. DNA is a fragile, fussy kind of molecule, and if it is sufficiently abused, we may get some cleverer cockroaches or a more ambitious strain of lichen—but I wouldn't count on it.

Another bright-side fantasy comes to me from an eccentric old scientist who is spending his retirement trying to calculate how much megatonnage will have to go off in order for the blowup to be visible from outer space. He figures that the blaze may be just what it takes to attract the attention of those extraterrestrials who have so far disdained to answer the coded radio emissions we keep beaming out to space, most of which deal with something dull and obvious, like the Pythagorean theorem. I can't vouch for his calculations, but he thinks we need another six years of the arms race to achieve sufficient candlepower to interest astronomers in the neighborhood of Alpha Centauri—and possibly only three years if Congress goes along with the Star Wars buildup.

Gluttons as we are for the attention of superior beings, this is not the most comforting scenario. What would you think of a fellow whose car gets stuck on a lonely road and who, lacking a flare, attracts the highway patrol by siphoning out some gas and immolating himself? The astronomers on Alpha Centauri, noting our brief flicker, will shrug to themselves: "There goes man" (or whatever their name for us might be). "Never did think he'd amount to much."

I should explain, lest you think I am as addled as my old scientist friend, that bright-siding nuclear war is not something I devote conscious mental energy to. Rather, it's the kind of thing that goes on at some subcortical level at odd moments—like, for example, when I'm going down the canned-goods aisle of the supermarket and catch myself wondering whether to stock up on baked beans just in case we still have any appetite after the firestorm. Not a pretty thought, nor exactly a sane one, so the mind grasps feebly for the delusion of some redeeming outcome.

So far, the only bright side I can come up with—at least the only one I can sanely recommend—is the certainty that, in a nuclear war, the perpetrators will also die. In fact, since they are no doubt somewhat better prepared for it than we are, the likelihood is that they will die more slowly, and with a more agonizingly clear awareness of what's happened, than the rest of us. But even this prospect gives me only cold comfort. I have never understood those bereaved parents who, as is occasionally reported to us, find it in their hearts to rejoice at the execution of their child's killer. The thought of the Pentagon brass stumbling in terror through a darkened bunker or the Kremlin leadership preparing to wash down their cyanide pills with shots of Stolichnaya, does not, I am afraid, begin to compensate.

I am beginning to realize that revenge may have been a fine and nobile impulse in the days of short bows and lances, but it is a deadly luxury for those who live in the shadow of cruise missiles and SS20s. Without revenge as a motive, the demented logic of deterrence and mutual assured destruction would unravel at once, and I happen to think that would be a good thing. Why do we assume that the leaders of the superpowers are such thoroughly vicious men that they will insist on taking the whole world—down unto the last unregistered voter and Third World bystander—with them? The greatest possible act of humanity, and the only one deserving of an interstellar audience, would be for the victims of a first strike to forgo their technologically guaranteed revenge and—as most Christians would surely advocate —turn the other cheek. As a tiny step in that direction, I promise to seek no further satisfaction from the fact that those who have lived by the sword will die just like the rest of us.

But I might not be able to keep this promise if I hear too much more idle chatter about Armageddon "and so forth." I am no saint, and in this case I might just revise my bright-side fantasy to include myself, crouching outside the bunker where the men in charge have taken refuge, waiting for the heavy door to come creaking open, with a rock in my hand.

[1985]

Acknowledgments

•··•··•··•··•··•··•··•

Grateful acknowledgment is made to the *New York Post* for permission to reprint "The Lesson of Mary Beth" by Barbara Ehrenreich. The other essays in this book were originally published in the *Atlantic, Mother Jones, Ms.*, the *Nation*, the *New Republic*, the *New York Times*, and *New York Woman*, as noted below.

LURCHING TOWARD BABYLON
"Spudding Out" (*Mother Jones*, 1988)
"Food Worship" (*New York Times*, 1985)
"The Cult of Busyness" (*New York Times*, 1985)
"Star Dreck" (*Mother Jones*, 1988)
"Premature Pragmatism" (*Ms.*, 1986)
"Good-bye to the Work Ethic" (*Mother Jones*, 1988)

FRAUD AND LOATHING
"The Unbearable Being of Whiteness" (*Mother Jones*, 1988)
"Language Barrier" (*Mother Jones*, 1989)
"Give Me That New-Time Religion" (*Mother Jones*, 1987)
"The Great Syringe Tide" (*Mother Jones*, 1988)
"Our Neighborhood Porn Committee" (*Mother Jones*, 1986)
"Drug Frenzy" (*Ms.*, 1988)
"Someone You Know?" (*Ms.*, 1989)

DEMOCRACY IN DECAY
"Automating Politics" (*Mother Jones*, 1988)
"The Liberals' Disappearing Act" (*Mother Jones*, 1986)

"The Unfastened Head of State" (*Mother Jones*, 1987)
"The Bathtub Tapes" (*New Republic*, 1989)
"My Reply to George" (*Mother Jones*, 1989)
"Put on a Happy Face" (*Mother Jones*, 1987)
"The Moral Bypass" (*The Nation*, 1985)

THE MAN EXCESS
"Tales of the Man Shortage" (*Mother Jones*, 1986)
"Talking in Couples" (*Ms.*, 1981)
"At Last, a New Man" (*New York Times*, 1984)
"Wimps" (*New York Times*, 1985)

STRIDENT WOMEN
"Stop Ironing the Diapers" (*Ms.*, 1989)
"Why We Lost the ERA" (*Atlantic Monthly*, 1986)
"Their Dilemma and Mine" (*New York Times*, 1985)
"The Lesson of Mary Beth" (*New York Post*, 1989)
"Strategies of Corporate Women" (*New Republic*, 1986)
"The Mommy Test" (*Mother Jones*, 1989)

ACROSS THE CLASS DIVIDE
"Small Talk" (*New York Times*, 1985)
"Two, Three, Many Husbands" (*Mother Jones*, 1986)
"On the Street Where You Live" (*Mother Jones*, 1987)
"Profile of a Welfare Cheat" (*New York Times*, 1985)
"Is the Middle Class Doomed?" (*New York Times*, 1986)
"Marginal Men" (*New York Woman*, 1989)

MONEY AND MAYHEM
"Welcome to Fleece U." (*Mother Jones*, 1987)
"How You Can Save Wall Street" (*Mother Jones*, 1988)
"Sanity Clause" (*Mother Jones*, 1989)
"Socialism in One Household" (*Mother Jones*, 1987)
"How to Help the Uptrodden" (*Mother Jones*, 1987)
"Fast Cars" (*Mother Jones*, 1989)
"The Gang in White Coats" (*Mother Jones*, 1989)
"The Right to Pollute" (*Mother Jones*, 1989)

LIFE, DEATH, AND THE UNIVERSE
"Stand by Your Flag" (*Mother Jones*, 1987)
"Iranscam: Oliver North and the Warrior Caste" (*Ms.*, 1987)

"Phallic Science" (*Mother Jones*, 1988)
"The Peace Thing" (*Mother Jones*, 1989)
"Blocking the Gates to Heaven" (*Mother Jones*, 1986)
"The Bright Side of Nuclear War" (*New York Times*, 1985)

About the Author

Barbara Ehrenreich is the author of seven books, including *Fear of Falling* ("a major accomplishment" —*Los Angeles Times*) and *The Hearts of Men* ("brilliant" —*New York Times*). Her much-discussed essays and articles have appeared in the *New York Times*, *Mother Jones*, the *Atlantic*, *Ms.*, the *New Republic*, and other newspapers and magazines around the country.